# Pick of Punch

# PICK OF

# PUNCH

PUNCH and HUTCHINSON of London

A Punch book, published by Punch Publications Limited
in association with
Hutchinson & Co (*Publishers*) Limited
178-202 *Great Portland Street, London, W.1.*
London Melbourne Sydney
Auckland Johannesburg Cape Town
and agencies throughout the world

© 1970 by Punch Publications Limited

Printed in Great Britain by The Bradbury Agnew Press Limited

ISBN 0 09 104900 8

# Contents

# Introduction

Some forms of humour are universal. Slapstick is understood—and appreciated—everywhere. And many jokes travel around the world at supersonic speed. Cartoon clichés like the desert island, the ark, and "son, some day all this will be yours" appear in newspapers and magazines all over the globe. But, of course, there are other forms of humour. The best, for me, are those based on skilful observation—the cartoons, the articles, and the sketches which draw their inspiration from the comedy of our surroundings.

The main purpose of all humour must be to make people laugh. But there is no reason why there should not be other objectives too. "The goal of satire," W. H. Auden once wrote in an essay on the subject, "is to reform." And why not? Ridicule is a powerful weapon; one good political cartoon can often be more effective than a long, pompous leading article.

English humour has changed over the years—and, I think, for the better. We used to get our laughs at the expense of stupid servants, cockneys who dropped their aitches, and foreigners who couldn't cope with our customs. In short, we laughed at others, and not at ourselves. Today we are much more inclined to do the latter. I, for one, find this healthier.

We have also become more outward looking. We appreciate other people's humour as well as our own. Television has had much to do with this: it is easier to understand what makes another man laugh if you know how he lives.

There are still some people, of course, who regard humour as a luxury. They are wrong: it's a necessity, and never more so than today.

WILLIAM DAVIS

HARGREAVES

# The Golden Age of Gastronomy

## By ALAN BRIEN

When we regret the way we used to eat in the old days, we are usually envying our lost appetite rather than our vanished meals. In middle age, food tends to become a household chore, something to be cleared off, cleaned up and stacked away, like the pots and pans and dishes. It is a turnpike we must get through to arrive at television, or the evening paper, or bed. Food is the enemy which infiltrates, undermines and sabotages the precarious balance of our metabolic economy. It clogs the arteries, inflates the waistline, thickens the jowls, yellows the eye-balls, explodes blood vessels, like purple nova in the Milky Way, across the cheeks. After the age of forty, eating is a dangerous occupation, like walking through a mine-field. You expect to pay for your pleasures by later pains. Describing what a marvellous dinner he had enjoyed the night before, a friend of mine boasted: "I had such a heartburn, if you could have tapped it, you would have fuelled the 'Flying Scotsman' from London to Edinburgh."

No wonder we push the golden age of gastronomy back to our childhood and beyond. We remember how we were cajoled and bullied and wheedled into emptying the plate—just another great hillock of buttery turnips, sweet and earthy carbohydrate dunes; just another layer of white mashed potato, fluffy paddy-fields flooded by dark thick gravy; just another suet dumpling, a cannon-ball wrapped in molten goo; just another cannibal slice of pinkly oozing meat, carved from the new-cooked corpse. Eat up, eat up. To be fat is to be lovable, and loving. Hunger is the greatest compliment you can pay to your parents.

You are the zeal of the house, the performing zeal, and each trick is rewarded with a titbit. In every other house you enter, grownups unlock the hoards of goodies, push the fruit bowl at you, smuggle you sweets, order up in advance spreads of cakes, garish and glittering, like edible Christmas decorations.

They take a voyeur's delight in watching you at it, and you are not ashamed at having an audience for your exhibitions.

No wonder that, until the age of fifteen or so, you are conditioned to believe that conspicuous consumption is the first duty of mankind. Adults would rather feed you than talk to you. You imagine it will go on like this for ever, only with more courses, bigger helpings, later meals, increasingly varied dishes. Wine will be like lemonade, but with bigger bubbles, so sweet it makes your teeth ache, and corks which hit the ceiling. There will be chips with everything, and ice cream for ever on the side. Chocolates will come in padded boxes, like jewel cases, instead of

THE PUNCH TABLE IN 1891

squashed in paper bags. There will always be one more layer underneath the litter of empty, crisp wrappings which smell almost better than the chocolates themselves. What else could there be to spend your money on? This is what you have been trained for—taking your O levels in simple nursery Mastication, your A levels in advanced adolescent Omnivorousness, looking forward to the day when you graduate in Gluttony, silver knife and fork in hand, silk napkin tucked in your collar.

You are almost as eager to eat your first wild rice as to sow your wild oats. You wonder whether you are a breast or a leg man as the chicken is plucked from the harem for your inspection. Is it really true (as some of the lads have been whispering in the playground) that there are fifty-seven different ways to cook eggs—including one known only to the Emperor of China? Are there techniques for prolonging the pleasures of the table, sent under a plain wrapper to Adults Only or Bona Fide Students? You cannot wait to be given the key to actual dining *clubs*, *private* dinners in upstairs rooms, where dedicated voluptuaries gather with their minds on *just one thing*. In this permissive age, you learn, there are even public establishments where the customer can carve for himself as much as he likes.

Alas, disillusion sets in all too soon after those early wild sprees of oral debauchery. Older men take you aside and warn you of the dangers of promiscuous eating. There are such things as gastric diseases, about which it is better to be safe than sorry. Some notorious restaurants in London have killed more unwary gourmets than the Blitz. Those frothy, exciting dishes are all right for an occasional night out on the town—a man would be a fool to turn them down on a week-end in Paris—but for a permanent diet you would be wiser to stick to a rare steak and a green salad.

An eye for a pretty gateau, a taste for sweet young things, you discover, is rather ludicrous in a man over thirty. Leave those brown sherries and pink champagnes to the ladies, young fellah. You'll be more respected in the executive suite or on high table if you insist on your drinks being "dry, very dry." You can't go wrong if you ask for everything to be underdone. Professor Leslie Fiedler says all American literature betrays "a fear of the failed erection." The fear of the failed digestion is equally omnipresent in our Western culture. After all, you'll want to eat as long as you live.

Whatever orgies were staged by the Victorians and Edwardians in their dining rooms, heroically wooing a pair of chops at breakfast, lasciviously toying with a baby pigeon between the fish and the meat, indecently assaulting a cheese at midnight, they are only folk memories to most of us today. Nostalgia, strictly speaking, means home-sickness. What we are bemoaning when we say "they don't eat like that any more" is that we cannot eat the way we did in our youth. Food has become the province of doctors rather than chefs. Cookery books are outsold by anthologies of diets. The innocence has gone out of eating. It has become yet another kind of addiction and grown men pay large sums to be locked up in health farms, with a glass of warm water and a lemon, in order to kick the disgusting habit. If I am nostalgic, it is for the only past I ever had—when eating was a virtue and the future was all cakes and ale.

*"But I don't want to see a truthful little film shot with a hand-held camera. I want to see a big lying movie made with the latest sophisticated equipment."*

"Basically you're not bad, it's just that everybody expects you to be bad, and that makes you bad."

"We'll still see each other. It's just that as a group we feel washed up."

# What Shall We Tell the Children?

**by HEATH**

"Don't worry, pig baby, we won't let any capitalist wolf throw you out on the street."

"Listen boy! I'm the best agent in the game and I'm not taking you on until you change your act. People expect more nowadays than falling off a wall."

# Grindstone, Here I Come

## By BASIL BOOTHROYD

After the weekend, the week. Not too bad, I daresay, if you live over the shop, like grocers or Chancellors of the Exchequer; just a matter of remembering it's time for a collar and tie again after two days of informality. But these happily placed breadwinners are considerably outnumbered by you and me, for whom Monday means saddling up once more for the hard trail from Chipping Ongar, Aylesbury, Haywards Heath. We don't mind the work. No, honestly. It's getting to it that kills. It may be just as tough for the toil-bound of Liverpool, Glasgow, Birmingham, but I can only speak as I find, and what I find is travel sickness. Also no bus shelters at London Bridge.

I've been meaning to mention this for some time.

It's a thing that worries me less as the week wears on. Even as early as Wednesday the end is in sight: two days, faintly showing at the end of the tunnel, when you won't have to be at London Bridge. But Monday, as the east wind scythes in, or the soft, refreshing rain cascades out of my hat, I feel the deprivation keenly. They tell me it's the same at Victoria, which means it also goes, very probably, for Liverpool Street, Marylebone and Waterloo. I don't know. My working glide-path is restricted. I don't see these outposts in the ordinary course of business.

If it's true, where are the responsible authorities? Not waiting for a bus, with the next man's umbrella in their eye, that's for sure. If they're whispering in from Chequers in their weatherproof limousine, agonising over the productivity shortfall, it might pay them to make a detour and have a look at us, stooped and disconsolate, waiting to be splashed up to the ears by a No. 13 (marked Very Rare in the timetables). I'm not arguing for the soft life—just the state of the nation. Any rural bus stop, with a daily turnover of eight customers and an inspector, has its stout cabin against the elements. You and me and the rest of the commuting millions, no. Let the responsible authorities ask themselves, "What sort of a day's work do you get out of workers who start the day—and more particularly the week—like this?" By the time they've steamed for an hour on the office radiators, and collapsed into the old tilt-and-swivel for another half-hour's scarifying exchange of journey stories, all they're good for is—I was going to say the journey back . . . but they'll need a couple of gins and a long restoring lunch before they begin to feel equal to that. (In the case of the typing pool, a paper cup of anonymous fluid from the drinks machine and flake out in the ladies' rest room.)

There's nothing to be done about the railways, of course. We bow to the official view. Oh, the ads speak well enough of the Inter-City lark, and if we

*"I'm sorry, Tchaikovsky, but I don't think the public are ready for swans."*

ever presumed to address the class of worker who spins up and down on the King's Cross-Edinburgh run he might well confirm. But we Chorleywood-Liverpool Street lot wouldn't aspire. We've grown up with the points breakdown, broken rail, power failure, signal collapse, defective stock, missing guard and the rest of the familiar apology-fodder. It's our own fault, for being so many, and having to get to work. We see that. If we don't like it we should move the office to Budleigh Salterton. Just a matter of fixing it with the boss, who unfortunately hasn't stood in a corridor for years, though he may sometimes get a bit testy at the way we block the view from his first-class window on that side.

It's equally a fact of life that we can't look for better times on the dear old tube. I don't know who's decided this, but as long as it's accepted, right up the scale from the traveller who never has his coat pressed because he knows it'll get pressed for him by his fellow sardines, to the official defeatists at the top,

where's the point in beefing? You can't expect Barbara to waste good Employment and Productivity men down there, taking a rush-hour survey of crushed feet and claustrophobia. Even if she did, they couldn't get a hand free to take notes. To be fair, I fancy the Rt. Hon. Richard Marsh did get himself photographed on the new Victoria Line, but then there wasn't much cramming on opening day, unless the Queen jostled him at all. The last survey I was taking in those parts, two girls fighting their way out of the train took a small man with them who didn't want to go, but they'd got him trapped between their handbags.

All right, we're stuck with the trains, above ground or below. The price of progress. But I still don't see that we have to be wet. Can't someone hook a few hundred thousand back from Concorde, and prop a bit of roof on a few tin poles outside London Bridge? It's not much to ask in return for a zestful grin over a million Monday morning white collars.

Well. I said I'd been meaning to mention it.

"It's Mr. Harmsworth, ma'am. I think they've eaten him."

But at least the morning struggle between home and office—and perhaps the Whitehall psychologists are on to this after all—has brightened the concept of the work place. It's not only a small recurring victory just to arrive, but here is an ordered clearing in the chaos: the pens, the pin bowls, the stapler, the trays, the mail . . . the blotter, sweetly symmetrical by an earlier, vanished hand . . . the same old hat-peg, telephone, hole in the carpet. At times, when domestic farewells have been curt or tearful, the office seems a good deal more womb-like than the home. We see more of it, and more of its faces. Some statistician with an idle hour might like to go into this. Or hadn't it struck you that you see more of the boss, and old Fred at the next desk, over a working lifetime, than you do of your wife and associated loved ones? You probably have to wait for retirement until it really comes home to you. It's a big shake-up, reversing the social proportions. When we see those mystifying reports of divorces between sexagenarians, and say to ourself, "Married thirty-five years, and only just spotted the error?", we only have to think on a bit to see how it could happen.

There's a line in my long-dormant subconscious. "When I see that suit, I always know it's spring." Spoken in my first office, by one wage slave of some seniority when another one, in a napless but neat light grey suit, looked in from the room next door. It would be summer when the biscuit-coloured flannels came

round: autumn, the navy chalk-stripe. Winter rang the changes on chokers: one green, one check, one club. It had a sadness, parcelling out the seasons by the wardrobe of the man next door. But something comfortable too. Rhythm is the thing. And the working pattern has the edge over the domestic sprawl any time. You certainly know it's Monday, when old Fosdyke reports his weekend triumphs over greenfly, with a rose in his coat to prove it. Or young Bert, proud of his hangover as only youth can be, unloads his beer-consumption figures, and the blow-by-blow account of girls. It appears that Harry's car blew up last night on the A24. He was coming back late from Worthing, when there was . . . This one's going to take time, and you ought to be giving Miss Wills some letters, and hearing how she got on redecorating her little lonely bathroom. Still, hang on a bit—might be able to get yours in, about the oil leak dripping on the manifold and stinking like a—"Oh, good morning, sir. How was the golf?" Even the boss, on the extraordinary thing that happened on the eighth green, is a part of the grand design.

But what's this we've stumbled on? That the Monday morning feeling is a myth? That on the whole, and given an average slice of vocational luck, the office isn't all it's cracked down to be? Looks a bit like it. Anyway, once you've got there.

And if you can forget, for a few carefree hours, that you've got to get back.

*"See, Councillor, that's gypsies for you!"*

14

*"No Madam, I'm afraid it won't be ready by the time your husband comes home tonight."*

# Smile, Tovarich!

## By WILLIAM DAVIS

There's a popular Russian joke about the traveller from Moscow who arrives in a small town and asks whether there is any night life. "Yes there is," the hotel receptionist informs him. "But she's ill today."

Another well-loved joke stars a peasant who for years has let his horse do all the thinking for him. On a rare visit to the Big City, a friend shows him a car and carefully explains the various components—engine, steering wheel, clutch, gear-lever, brakes and so on. "Do you understand?" he asks after an hour of this. "Yes," says the peasant. "Any questions?" the friend demands. "Yes," says the peasant. "*How can it go without a horse?*"

Yet another joke which, it seems, never fails to tickle Soviet ribs, has a 102-year-old Georgian meeting someone from Leningrad. "Leningrad?" he says, "where is that?" The visitor explains that it used to be called St. Petersburg. "Ah yes," says the old man, "there was a little fighting there some years ago. Who *won*?"

Moscow Radio has a "humour and satire department" which dispenses chestnuts like these, and there are a large number of publications in different parts of the vast Soviet Union which try to keep the comrades happy with a similar diet. Russians like to laugh, but much of their published humour is old-fashioned and heavy-handed. And, of course, there are definite limits. Officialdom frowns on what it calls "indelicate" jokes (though Russians are as fond of them as anyone else) and the Kremlin is taboo. People make cracks about their leaders, of course, but they're never repeated on radio and in the press. Nor would any writer mock the Government's absurd passion for plastering ideological slogans all over the place ("Comrades! Fulfil the five-year plan before 1970!") Privately, Russians swap all kinds of anecdotes. There is, for example, the story of the two peasants

*"No, we don't make human sacrifices any more, we just bung a credit card down once a year."*

15

who've been to see Lenin's embalmed body in the Red Square mausoleum. "Just like us," says one to the other. "Dead but not yet buried."

The stock answer to a foreigner who asks a Russian journalist whether humorous magazines are allowed to attack the leadership is that "it is not necessary." Any Soviet editor who tried to suggest, in articles or cartoons, that the top brass occasionally makes mistakes would soon find himself out of a job. And, of course, every magazine sticks rigidly to whatever line the Government may take on foreign policy at any given moment. The fact that past leaders, like Stalin and Khrushchev, are officially acknowledged to have committed every crime in the Communist book is not considered to provide an excuse for criticising the men currently in the Kremlin. Nor would anyone think of arguing, publicly, that satirical comment on, say, the Kremlin's attitude to China is justified by past shifts in policy. Soviet humour magazines have stuck to much the same foreign targets over the years. The Americans still top the list, followed by German militarism and British imperialism. The *Krokodil* cartoons are often well drawn (the cover reproduced by us this week is a fair example) but they are boringly repetitive. Americans are invariably portrayed as top-hatted capitalists, and warmongers. The fact that no one on Wall Street wears a top hat these days, and that the American public has grown heartily sick of war in Vietnam or anywhere else is brushed aside. West Germans are invariably shown as steel-helmeted, goose-stepping Nazis, wearing huge swastikas, and parading under the benevolent eye of US commanders. The fact that Germany has now had twenty-four years of democratic Government, that its young people are bitterly opposed to militarism, and that the neo-Nazis are getting nowhere, gets no more acknowledgement than the fact that Britain no longer tries to be a great imperial power.

*Krokodil* played down the invasion of Czechoslovakia on the feeble excuse that most of its five million readers are not interested in events abroad. Why they should be any more interested in repetitive propaganda about the US is hard to understand, but it doesn't do to ask too many questions. One curious thing is that, although Peking and Moscow may be on the brink of war, magazines like *Krokodil* seem to go out of their way to avoid giving offence to the Chinese. This, unquestionably, reflects the official line, but it also owes something to the reluctance of its editors to upset the magazine's large number of Asian readers by portraying slit-eyed villains. The Editor-in-Chief, Manuil Semenov, told me that, with a circulation of five million, *Krokodil* had to be careful not to make fun of people's national characteristics. "We don't," he said, "laugh about a man's nationality, or his traditions." *Krokodil* even tries to avoid showing Georgians with the familiar black moustache "because it would annoy them." (Semenov, a jolly little man who spent many years on various newspapers before becoming *Krokodil's* thirteenth editor-in-chief, also applies a rigorous ban on sex and sick humour.)

If writers and cartoonists find the political limitations frustrating—and they do—they console themselves with three basic arguments. One, only a minority of readers is interested in high-level politics anyway. Two, unlike newspapers, humorous magazines are not forced to print the reams of statistics, speeches, and turgid ideological prose which is such a prominent feature of the Soviet scene. They may not be allowed to knock the leaders, but they don't have to praise them either. Three, *Krokodil* staff is actively encouraged to attack bureaucracy and inefficiency, two of the Soviet Union's biggest sins, with remarkable freedom and vehemence. Readers' complaints about pompous officials, corrupt shop-

*"The tourist trade means a lot to the town's economy, sir."*

keepers, leaking roofs, and countless other irritations are followed up, and if they prove to be justified, *Krokodil* uses its own brand of attacking satire to cut the offenders down to size. Any small-time official picked on for backsliding is always named and usually denounced. Punishment in the form of demotion frequently follows. The magazine can be taken to court, but the Soviet libel laws are more generous than ours. There is no financial compensation for injury to one's reputation; the most one can hope for is a printed apology.

Semenov sees his role as the small man's champion as the most satisfying part of his work, and maintains that, as the bureaucratic set-up *is* the Government, *Krokodil* can be regarded as a vigorous opponent of the State machine. Since the attacks stop at a certain level this is debatable, but one only has to spend a few days in the Soviet Union to see why Semenov likes this side of his job. If you think we in Britain are swamped by bureaucracy, you should see the workers' paradise. This is, in every sense, the land of red tape. The endless form-filling, the arrogance of petty officials and their unwillingness to take even minor decisions are one of the most depressing features of every-day life behind the Iron Curtain. For most Russians the real oppressor is not some shadowy figure in the Kremlin, but the little dictator strutting about in a scruffy office down the road. The inefficiency of central buying and selling organisations, and of anything remotely connected with the service industries, is equally notorious. If you eat in a Moscow hotel, you must be prepared to wait up to thirty minutes before you're handed the menu, and even a simple lunch takes at least two hours.

It's a formidable challenge to one's sense of humour, but *Krokodil* does its best to raise a laugh. It makes fun of Moscow's interminable queues ("you even have to queue to get into a queue," one of its editors said to me), of the muddle which is

HARGREAVES

*"He's terribly possessive."*

invariably produced by the onset of winter, of the annual confusion over the marketing of apples, and of the difficulty of getting spares for state-produced goods like tractors and TV sets. One regular gag shows hardware coming off the assembly line and being carried straight over the road to a shop labelled "repairs."

*Krokodil's* cartoonists meet once a week, in the magazine's rather austere offices, and I was invited to take an active part in one of their sessions. Semenov explained to me beforehand that "if you hear loud laughter, it's a sign that the cartoon is very stupid or indecent. If a cartoon is witty, there is absolute silence." We went into a large room, and about thirty artists filed in after us. Only one was a woman. The editorial board of eight sat at a table, and each "rough" drawing was held up for all to see. There was the usual crop of cartoons on American warmongers and German militarists, and one on the Greek colonels. It showed a tourist guide on the Acropolis, telling his flock to "look neither to the right nor to the left." In the cartoon, the Acropolis was flanked on the right by a concentration camp, and on the left by a gallows.

There were a number of cartoons about drunkenness—a major problem in the Soviet Union—and about Moscow's chronic housing shortage. But only two gags won universal approval. The first showed a small man walking into a works canteen, accompanied by two huge companions. "They've come," he explained to the manager, "to chew my meat for me." The second had a girl sitting on a bar stool, sipping a cocktail. Caption: "Through this straw she sucks in my whole salary."

*Krokodil* prints eight or nine anecdotes in each issue, and frankly admits that a lot of them are taken from Polish, Hungarian and even Western magazines. To make it clear that the story is set in, say, Britain, the editors usually change the names of the characters from Tom to Vanya, and add the word "Sir."

*"What really hurts, right here, our Vera—is that you had to go down South to get bloody well pregnant!"*

One of the many odd things one comes across in Moscow is the immense regard everyone has for the dollar (so vigorously attacked in the cartoons) and even the dear old British pound. The big hotels all have shops in which one can buy goods not available in Russian stores, providing one has foreign currency. Prices are given in dollars, and the story is told of a Soviet couple who walked into one of these shops, delighted with the unexpected array of goodies, and produced their Russian roubles. "Roubles," they were curtly told, "are no good. You must have dollars." The husband looked puzzled, and then asked: "And where can I get these dollars?" Inevitably, there is a black market in foreign currency. In Leningrad, I was twice stopped in the street by young men who asked if I could sell them pounds or dollars. They offered five roubles for each pound—more than double the rate available in the hotels. Another discovery one quickly makes is that tipping, though officially frowned upon, is universally expected. When the the Soviet press ran a Kremlin-inspired campaign, not long ago, suggesting that tips were an insult to the workers' dignity, it was laughed out of court. People went around asking each other "Can I insult you?" and foreign tourists were politely informed that "all kinds of monetary humiliations are welcome."

Government propaganda becomes much less obtrusive once you leave Moscow. This is one of the reasons why I found Leningrad a lot more pleasant. And there is even less sign of it in Tiflis, the Georgian capital. I flew there, via Kiev, to talk to the editors of the local humour magazine. Georgians are highly sensitive people, proud of their country and not particularly renowned for their sense of humour. They are the butt of many unpublished Russian jokes, but my companion from *Krokodil* took care not to pass on a single one of them. (Sample: a slow-witted, slow-moving Georgian finds himself in Berlin as part of a delegation. He disappears on the first day and doesn't return until the evening. "Where have you been?" the others ask. "Well," he says, "when I was here in 1945 our major ordered me to blow up a bridge . . .")

It was in Gori, Stalin's birthplace, that I had what will probably be my most unforgettable experience. We were inspecting the tiny house where Stalin saw his first red sunset, when the local police chief appeared, accompanied by several henchmen. He bared his gold teeth in a snarl, thumped his plain-clothed chest, and spat out a torrent of angry Georgian prose. I remembered the good advice I had collected back home. "Don't tell Western jokes," the *Director* magazine had said. "Don't be as foolish as I was," Gerald Brooke had told me. Now there I stood, far from home, faced with the moment of truth. And I'd forgotten to bring my overcoat. It would be cold in Siberia.

The chief was trembling with rage, and I could see myself eating dandelion soup and carving chessmen. Funny how important little things become when you are about to be deprived of them. No more Gillette blades, Alka Seltzer, spaghetti Bolognese, and going to work on an egg. No more mini-skirted dollies, *Times* leaders, special fried rice, bank holidays, and Ulster punch-ups. What had I done? And who on earth was left in our jails with any trade-in value?

One of the henchmen took a step towards me. "Gamlet," he said in Russian. "Gamlet?"

"Da, da, Gamlet," he said, nodding vigorously. "Shakespeare. Very good."

My Moscow companion, who had been as puzzled as I was, looked relieved. The chief, he explained, was terribly fond of Shakespeare. He knew the whole of *Hamlet* off by heart, and I was the first Englishman he had ever met. So I had been treated to an extract. Now, the chief would do Mark Antony's funeral speech from *Julius Caesar*.

I offered the chief my hand and fulsome praise, and we went off to his house to continue the performance over a highly liquid lunch. I managed to chip in with "To be **or not** to be," and the chief collapsed with laughter.

Don't ever let anyone tell you that Soviet coppers don't have a sense of humour.

*"Were you plate glass, red brick or crumbling masonry?"*

"That was very naughty, Sir Pincus.
You're not supposed to **use** gunpowder—it's
only a deterrent."

# ARMS
# AND THE
# CASH REGISTER I SING by Handelsman

What would you think of a man who sold guns to children? All right then, what would you
think of a man who sold guns to grown-ups? Is there a moral or a practical difference?
If so, write the difference on a large sheet of paper, fashion the paper into a hat, and wear it.

"Which of you is the British gentleman? His Excellency has decided
to purchase his bombs from you. He feels great concern about your
balance of payments."

"To Mrs. Gandhi: Dear Madam, If,
as you say, the equipment we sent you
is faulty, you may take comfort from
the fact that the Pakistanis are stuck
with it too."

"This tear-gas spray-gun is just what you need, madam, to protect you against arms dealers who accost you in the street."

"I hope you enjoy these planes, Monsieur, and I hope the Israelis, who also paid for them, enjoy them too."

"What's holding up deliveries? Both the police and the Mafia are running out of ammunition."

"I must say the Nigerians don't seem very grateful. Next time around let's arm the Ibos, if any."

"This is all very unfair! I have never killed anyone **personally**."

# Weekend at the TOP

## By LORD ARRAN

I suppose I have been to nearly a thousand weekend parties during my life. Nowadays, alas, the invitations are tending to drop off. One becomes less of a social asset as one grows older. "Boofy," I can hear my friends say, "is too slow and too deaf. And he's become rather messy with his food."

I should explain incidentally that I was brought up never to use the word "weekend" and I do so now with some distaste. My parents regarded it as very vulgar; and indeed I still avoid it when I remember

*"As an actor he was a great success in the early sixties, but he didn't seem to move with the times."*

to. The phrase was "Saturday to Monday" or "Friday to Monday" if one was shooting on Saturday.

But then the shibboleths are dying out. My aunts never asked for one's address. What is your "direction," they would say. This to the uniniated was misleading. "North-east by east," they would reply, or "I am a director of several companies." *I* say—God help me—"address."

Yes, I bow to the times and accept that the word "weekend" is now widely used, even by the French among whom it is apparently the smart thing to talk English among themselves—" 'Ow you getting along, Baby?"

"Top class, and you?"

To me the weekend party is the most marvellous thing in the world. If I am good, God will reward me with an unending series of them.

The excitement of arrival, the same excitement of forty years back. The question of who else will be there. Some hostesses tell you in advance, some don't. On three occasions I have had to leave at once because I found myself confronted by my worst enemy; why do one's friends so often like one's enemies—such bad taste. The whispered conversation with one's wife "Oh God, those boring Brigstocks again!" Or perhaps, usually in fact, the people one loves most. The kiss of affectionate salutation; then the large cold gin-and-tonic to take to one's bedroom and drink in one's hot bath. Tomorrow we shall do nothing, just talk and eat, particularly talk—often brilliant talk—with perhaps a little walk round the garden. This surely is what life is all about.

But, of course, though still much the same in many ways, the weekend has changed like everything else. Today most people arrive by motor-car. In 1930 one was told which train to catch. From Wilton one received a printed card with the time of one's own train, 4.30 ("Servants and luggage by the 3.30" to enable them of course to have unpacked for one in advance). Today quite often we pack and unpack for

22

*"It's the way he would have liked it."*

ourselves. Imagine! And tipping; before the war thirty bob was overtipping; double it now and you're never asked again because it gets back from the housemaid to the hostess that you're an old meanie.

## Weekend Investment

And if there's a big shoot on the Saturday, it costs about £30 all in, what with tips to loaders and keepers and cartridges at sevenpence a bang. True, you save the cost of the gas and the booze and the roast beef you would have had at home. But gracious living even at other people's expense sets one back quite a bit. And what it costs one's hosts! To be vulgar and talk about money, I reckon we have cost them more than £20,000 in all since we married. May I—and this is quite serious—thank them from a full heart for their kindness and generosity, more especially as we don't entertain them, or very rarely, in our own suburban villa chiefly because we can't hope to keep up with their standards.

And these standards are immensely high; higher by far than before the war. The comfort and luxury are greater—it is rare for each bedroom not to have its own bathroom; the food, always the best in the world and better than any Parisian restaurant, has now reached new heights, though of course there is less of it. Gone, thank God, those six-course dinners; in their place two or three.

## Wine, Women and Naked Butlers

The drink flows: in most houses there is a grog tray in the drawing room all day and all night so that one can give oneself a drink whenever one wants to. Personally I would never help myself without asking my host or hostess first, but many people do. Bad manners, I would say. Champagne before or after dinner or both. Claret or white Burgundy over the nosh. No one ever gets drunk though sometimes someone becomes a little argumentative.

Only in the matter of domestic servants has there been a change downwards. Three or four now do the work of thirteen or fourteen plus the hostess herself active behind the scenes. What the other ten used to do heaven only knows. To me they are epitomised by Hilaire Belloc's "the man who cleans the Billiard-room."

The women's clothes too are much simpler, though probably just as expensive if not more so. Short pretty frocks in the evenings, and gosh they look nice! No one ever wears what I believe is called a *robe de style*. True, I once stayed in the same house as a Countess—and being an Earl I am in favour of Countesses on principle—who changed five times in one day. But perhaps she just liked to feel nice and fresh.

I must admit the young men's clothes are a bit way out, though even I wear a frilly shirt and a blue velvet bow tie in the evenings, and very nice I look too. And after all it is only twenty years since the door was opened to a twenty-year-old girl relation of mine by a stark naked butler and received by an equally stark naked host, a defunct press lord. Being well brought up and capable of dealing with any situation, however unconventional, she remained as cool as a cucumber though not to the extent of taking off her own clothes. I think his Lordship was a little surprised and put out by her sangfroid, though it was almost certainly the first naked man she had ever seen in her life.

What next? Love. Sometimes it plays its part in the weekends we go to, but never noticeably, although my wife says I never notice *anything*. And I suppose it does go under my nose, licit and illicit: but I prefer not to know. Engaged or newly married couples seldom get asked because they are tiresome and embarrassing. Of course when I was young the first thing I did on arriving was to look for the prettiest bird in the party and try to have—again— what one of my aunts would call a "spangle." And as many of the parties of those days consisted of twenty or even thirty people, there was plenty of choice.

In my father's day, there was widespread, illicit romance at country-house parties, or so he told me. This was indeed connived at and even contrived by the most respectable hostesses in the greatest country-houses who would say to the housekeeper when arranging where the visitors were to sleep, "I think we will put Lord X in the Chinese room and let me see now—yes, and Mrs. Y in the Chippendale room" (the two rooms happened of course to be next door to one another). And on Sunday morning the whole party would go to church, including of course the

couple who had spent the night naked in each other's arms (I seem to have nakedness on the brain). But I do not propose to start writing about Edwardian hypocrisy, though there was much to be said for it.

So much for indoor games, now for sport. Hunting weekends are rare: but then I don't hunt, though my wife does. Most people hunt from home. Shooting is the biggest "occasion" if not the cause for weekend parties nowadays, and if you don't shoot, you miss a lot of parties. I am thinking of giving it up because having been a decent second-class shot, I can't hit a thing. But my wife begs me not to—"If you do, we shan't be asked anywhere," she says—and correctly. "But shooting as I am, we probably won't be asked anyway," I say, though I am not sure. People nowadays, with some notable exceptions, ask you for your company and not your skill.

Sometimes shooting does not follow the conventional pattern. One of my most loyal hosts has the habit of bringing out with him some of the larger carnivores. First it was a leopard, which used to retrieve or alternatively eat the dead birds. It used also to scare poachers into fits. Next it was a lion, which eventually savaged its trainer. Last an even more ferocious animal. This was the cause of some embarrassment to me. While enjoying a quiet kip in bed after shooting, I heard a scuffling outside and the door noiselessly opened to be shut immediately. I switched on the light. Facing me was a large Bengal tiger. It was growling. I kept my head, I said "Nice tigey, good tigey! Tigey, tigey, tigey!" More growls, and gales of giggles from outside. I drew all the sheets over me and waited for death. The tiger started scratching itself. After a while its owner opened the door. This year, if I am invited, I confidently expect a boa-constrictor.

But this is summer; what can we expect? Tennis and golf, of course, and almost invariably a big swimming-pool—occasionally an indoor pool, where the weather doesn't count. People coming over for drinks or luncheon, and "I really must see Hidcote this afternoon," or "Fairford is only twenty miles away. I want to see the glass."—"No. Let's do bloody nothing." And so we do bloody nothing, and we sleep and talk a bit and read the Sunday papers. And soon it is drinky time again. And after dinner most of us go home. Tomorrow we must work.

As we grow older and tend to spit and rumble internally, I deeply hope we may still receive the occasional letter beginning "Dear Fiona and Boofy, We wondered whether you could come to us for the weekend of September 28. Do try." And we shall feel wanted and know that two days at least of sheer joy lie ahead.

# LITTLE BROTHERS ARE WATCHING YOU

### Increased powers for Traffic Wardens, designed to relieve pressure on the police, may be only the beginning.

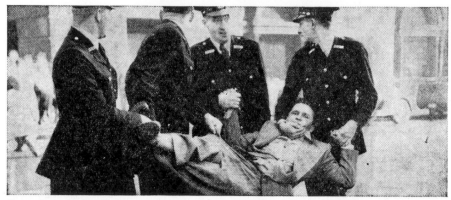

One of the first offenders under the Public Opinion Polls legislation, which makes it obligatory for anyone to answer questions put in the street "by persons producing a clipboard not exceeding the maximum dimensions laid down" was Mr. Ralph Westinghouse, of Dulwich. He was taken into custody after failing to answer the question, "Do you tie your laces in a single or a double knot?" put to him by members of a BBC documentary team. His case will be heard by Lord Hill, Mr. Charles Curran and Mr. Huw Wheldon.

Recipients of poorly-wrapped parcels are being taken into custody by Wiltshire postmen, as empowered by the Royal Mails Misdemeanour Order. (Pleas of non-responsibility for the actions of distant correspondents are no defence, says the Postmaster-General's legal department: the principle is the same as that under which unstamped items are charged double on delivery.) These offenders, found guilty by a Sorters' Tribunal, were sentenced to twenty-one days' forced labour at the Devizes GPO.

The home of Mr. and Mrs. Esau Dottle, 36 Ebury Close, Worcester, after dustmen had burned it down under the new Waste Disposal Operatives (Rights and Powers) Act. The Dottles, charged with insufficiently wrapped perishables and the wilful externalisation of bottles, were tried and sentenced during last Thursday's collection.

For displaying outstanding initiative under the Extended Functions of Nightwatchmen and Kindred Trades Order, Mr. Les Foljambe, West End store detective, has been promoted from Kitchen Accessories to Soft Furnishings. During the month of July he charged and sentenced more than forty customers for making frivolous complaints, cheeking salesgirls and leaning wet umbrellas on goods. All are now serving periods of detention in the store's boiler room.

Mr. Arnold Wavering, of Perry Barr, Birmingham, after being dragged behind a bus as punishment for not tendering the correct change. He plans to appeal against the judgment, on the grounds that the conductor, Mr. Eben Sayhaddin, (a) failed to consult with the driver before carrying out the sentence, (b) used the offending passenger's own belt to lash him to the rear of the vehicle, and, (c) failed to administer the Caution.

# Lady from Hell

## By ALAN COREN

There's nothing like a change of identity for taking you out of yourself, that's what I always say. Here today and Norman Jenkinson, QC, tomorrow, and if you can arrange for another wife and three kids on the other side of the Chilterns, so much the better.

Man is bound hand and psyche to the idea of his own perfectibility; and for most of us, the striving to realise our full potential is normally concerned with *doing* as much as we can. But for the enlightened fistful, the search is concerned with *being* as much as we can. As Wilfred Pickles used so succinctly to put it: "If you weren't you, who would you like to be?" and it was a query which left not a listening wither unwrung. Most of his questionees, in those far-off, happier times, answered "Sir Winston Churchill." It was a reply typical of the average human being's preference to deal with dreams rather than with achievable practicalities; especially since it frequently came from elderly ladies, who weren't really prepared, I'm sure, to go to all the bother of changing sex, smoking Havanas, and travelling to Yalta at all hours of the day or night. What they failed to realise was how simple it is, in fact, to become someone else, and in that metamorphosis discover whole new landscapes of personality; and not only of your own, either. I do not theorise, friends, I promise. Because, for the past sweet week, I have been a Scot.

No ordinary Scot, of course. There's little point in merely flattening your vowels and reading *Ivanhoe* on the Tube, if you're going to do it in a Burton's pinstripe serge; the essence of identity-change is that it requires total commitment, and is instantly appreciable by passing eyes, else it is nothing. Now, had you glimpsed me in a London street during the time in question, you would have had no difficulty at all in recognising me for what I wasn't: the honest giant brogues, clearly handed down from father to bairn, the long beige socks hugging calves that had obviously thickened from the rugged trials of ford and heather, the bright, hairy knees, virgin to the trouser's kiss, rimmed by the swinging kilt, the battered sporran worn by a lifetime's fingering at livestock sales, the nubbly tweed waistcoat and jacket, the smoky rustic tie—all testified to the presence in your urban midst of a man who'd smelt the tangle of the isles, whatever that is.

I, for my part, was required to do very little to ginger up the deception; it was all done for me by the willing watchers. I merely stood there, a total Gaelic statement, while the rest of the world made its automatic assumptions. Of course, to flesh out the stereotype, I had to go through one or two expected motions, if only to endorse what everyone thought they knew. I was, for example, uncharacteristically dour. And very pleasant it was, too: none of your superfluous chattings-up of barmaids or sales-assistants or cab-drivers, none of your tatty London wit, all those pointless words one spills out wearily in a dozen daily casual human contacts, the incessant "Looks like rain again" and "What about Harold, then?" and "Don't do anything I wouldn't do, yuk-yuk-yuk!" All I felt bound to offer was the raising of an eyebrow, or the curtest of Highland nods. No one expected me to be anything except A Man Of Few Words. I even found myself

*"It may sound a stupid question, but where, exactly, is the food . . .?"*

*"Say what you like about Jehovah's Witnesses—they're like lightning on burst water mains!"*

grunting, a pastime entirely novel to me, and extremely valuable, obviating as it did the need to take a chance with items like "braw" and "noo." I also goggled at neon signs and tower blocks, frowned in a terrible Presbyterian manner at miniskirts and long-haired youths, and, for the first time in my life, ordered whisky by name.

The returns for this tiny thespian outlay were immeasurable, confirming as they did my particular identity and enabling me to bask (albeit sternly, ye ken) in the world's instant admiration. Because a Scot, a fully recognisable *cap-à-pie* Scot, enjoys a staggering respect among Sassenachs which I was suddenly able to share: contrary to what you might guess from the disloyal easel of Donald McGill and the weird sub-literature of the music hall and its treasury of underwear jokes, a kilted man is not a comic figure, nor a butt for fools. What I gleaned from the conversations punctuated by my grunts and short, tough chuckles, was that the average Englishman sees in the mere defiance of the Scotsman's dress a whole range of remarkable qualities, like honesty, strength of character, moral rectitude (whoever heard of an adulterer in a kilt?), and an austere, yet genuine pride. I clearly, to the outsider, Stood For Something. Grafted on to this was a whole romantic transplant compounded of centuries of lumps rising in throats, from Flodden to Tobruk and Aden, and the pervading glamour of B. Prince Charlie, Tam o'Shanter, and the Queen Mother. It is no understatement to say that wherever an identifiable, that is to say kilted, Scotsman treads, there emanates from his homely tweeds a charisma which leaves the Kennedys and the Burtons in the starting-gate.

There are, of course, some delightful benefits ancillary to the primary one of looking, for once, like a decent human being: principal among these, inevitably, is the pleasure of being an instant focus of attention, no matter how competitive the circumstances. On the Sunday morning of the week under review, for instance,

I strode (what else can you do in shoes that look as though they were built on Clydeside?) into a trendy SW1 booze boutique called The Grenadier, which rises above a mewsful of Rolls-Royces and is always packed to the gunwales with stars of stage, screen and divorce court. Usually, I pass less than unnoticed there between the alabaster thighs of seven-foot model-dollies and squat Cockney bit-parters but on this occasion fifty overhung orbs swivelled and goggled as I clunked towards the bar, among them a pair belonging to David Hemmings, a man not normally upstaged by humorists. The barman, too, who usually spends his time attempting to overhear intimacies whispered by Vanessa Redgrave and studiously ignoring anyone with less than a seven-year MGM contract tucked into his hat-band, positively fawned. He may, of course, have thought I was Rod Steiger in drag, or something, but I prefer to believe that his attention was due to my rather bonny build and the accumulated associations of my clothes, a combination which has the reputation of reducing public houses to smouldering splinters if the service or liquor falls one iota short of impeccability.

A further delight is that one is a flint for conversation; my impression is that anyone who mopes around bedsitterland trotting out clichés about nowhere being as lonely as London needs only to slip into a kilt to have the world at his feet. Not looking up, preferably. Girls smile at you on the boulevard, while their eyes and yours exchange tacit notes on legs, men buttonhole you in pubs and buses with anecdotes of golf and battle, and everyone seems fraught with anxiety as to your welfare: I had only to stop at a street corner and look up at the name-plate, to have a couple of Londoners rushing over to ask me where I wanted to get to. London, in fact, came remarkably well out of the experiment. I had always believed that the wickedest city in the world was permanently waiting for foreigners to get off the train in order to relieve them of their last sou and stroll away cackling, but the opposite proved to be the case. To test my preconception, I drifted around Soho on Saturday night, hoping to get drawn into some seedy basement where the resident shysters would attempt to take me to the cleaners. But the come-ons were no more teasingly or dishonestly angled than usual, and one incident occurred which left me reeling. I was standing outside a strip-joint in Greek Street, listening to the spiel, when I felt a hand on my arm; I looked round to find a man beckoning me away with a nodding head. Assuming he was about to offer me something nefarious and exorbitant, I followed. And what he said was: "You don't want to go in there, Jock, they'll only make you pay through the nose for fruit juice and get some bird to promise you everything, until your money runs out." Then he walked away. Which was just as well, since his concern called for more than my slim repertoire of grunts, and I could not have borne to have had him disillusioned. Even a Sassenach has his pride.

"*Would you come down to the station, sir. It's your wife . . .*

*. . . we picked her up in the High Street, wearing a large hat and nothing else.*"

"*Good grief! Okay, I'll be along right away.*"

"*All right—how much?*"

# They are Curious-Yellow

## By PATRICK RYAN

In the roseate glim of the twenty-five watt paper lanterns, the walls of the restaurant were splendid with convulsive dragons, enamelled pagodas and slant-eyed maidens fleeing past arthritic trees. Though the buses of Barnsley swished by in the rain outside, from behind the bead curtains, ostensibly protecting the Ladies, could be sensed the ineffable tang of opium and the frou-frou of fan-tannery. I was the only customer thus early in the place and, as I studied the menu of lotus-blooming plastic, the inscrutable Chinese waiter stood by with pencil poised for ideography.

"Number 98," I selected, after due consideration of all runners. "Sausages, chips and garden-fresh peas."

"The Chef's Special," he grated in tether-ended tones. "Is very nice. Yoko Ono Pork Meat Balls with Water Chestnuts and Chop Suey Surprise."

"No, thank you. Just Number 98."

"What's wrong with Chinese dishes Numbers 1 to 97?" he demanded. "Never mind special banquets A to H. What have you got against Chinese food?"

"Nothing. I just feel like sausages, peas and chips."

"Chips!" If his tong had been handy, he'd have got it on to me. "The British. All the time, chips! This country is alive with yellow prejudice."

As an experienced explorer in darkest Yorkshire, I could see that the conservative eating habits of the natives had finally broken him down.

"Now, don't take on," I said soothingly. "Remember you're supposed to be inscrutable."

"Which is just another example of cunning, anti-Chinese discrimination. Why do the British press keep putting it around that we're inscrutable? Why can't honest oriental working men be allowed to let off steam whenever they feel the need, just like their white brothers?"

"Well, I suppose you can if you want too . . ."

"No, we can't. We've got to live up to this enforced reputation of inscrutability. We have to bottle up all our emotions and the frustration plays bloody hell with our digestions."

"I've heard that bicarbonate of soda in a little soy sauce is . . ."

"And your writers are forever trying to load us with guilt complexes and undermine our international moral reputation. Why, from Chu Chin Chow and Dr. Fu Man Chu downwards, do they always cast Chinese characters as villains? Why is a Chinaman never a hero?"

"There is Aladdin . . ."

"And with Widow Twankey beside him as a hideous caricature of all that is best in Chinese motherhood. Do we ever deliberately go out of our way to knock your Queen Victoria in our eight-hour plays?"

"I've never actually seen one . . ."

"Of course, you haven't. Yellow prejudice against Chinese actors and intent to discourage the advance of our national culture. Assisted by your ceaseless attempts to reduce our illustrious ancestors to figures of ridicule."

"I've never taken any ancestral micky . . ."

"No? What about the great Confucius? If I get one more local wag come in here and ask me have I heard that Confucius he say rape impossible because woman with skirts up run faster than man with trousers down, I'll be taking my noodle-chopper to his ears. Have you ever heard any Chinaman sinking so low as to make knock, knock, who's there, jokes about your Venerable Bede?"

"There is that limerick about the Venerable Dean of St. Paul's . . ."

"Sound like religious prejudice. It's the yellow brand that we're on about. And all the rotten anti-Chinese implications you've worked into your idioms.

Why is it always the Yellow Peril? What about the white peril or the black peril for a change? Why are your lousiest papers called the Yellow Press? And how do you think we feel about all your cowards having a Yellow Streak?"

"We do call them white-livered curs, as well . . ."

"But not often enough. Not as often as you spread your wicked calumnies about the flower of Chinese womanhood being horizontally deformed."

"Well, as a matter of fact, I'd always wondered if . . ."

"And while we're on women, it's high time the Race Relations Board checked up on the lyric of 'Limehouse Blues.' Standard vocalists down the coming ages have no right to infect young minds with the canard that the white slave trade is a Chinese monopoly. Let South American Joe have his share of the market. And now they've let the Sikhs wear their turbans on the buses, the Board might also inquire into why you never see a conductor wearing a pig-tail."

"I've never even seen a Chinese bus conductor."

"Which just goes to show how far yellow prejudice is entrenched in public transport. I'll have to have a word with Big Frank about it."

"Enoch might turn out to be more on your side. Might have a bit of the Mongol in him.

He looks like a primitive Chinese war lord when he's deeply pondering."

"Not so much of the *primitive* Chinese, if you don't mind. Don't forget that we were an ancient civilisation writing odes to nightingales when the highest expression of British culture was to paint either buttock in different shades of woad. You're still not civilised enough to eat with chopsticks and so we have to lay you spoons to scoop up your fried rice. We only give spoons to babies where I come from."

"And which part of China do you come from?"

"China?" he exclaimed witheringly. "I beg your pardon. I'm not one of your new-laid immigrants. I was born and bred in Tiger Bay, like my father and granddad before him. Third generation Welsh, man, and got the vote and everything. Scrum-half, I was, for Tongwyndowlais Wanderers before I done in that cartilage."

He came over all inscrutable again as the windbells tinkled at the arrival of another customer, and departed for the kitchen. He came back bearing his loaded tray and with, all the mystery of the East smouldering behind his impassive eyes, placed my meal before me. It was Yoko Ono Pork Meat Balls with Water Chestnuts and Chop Suey Surprise. With chips. And chopsticks.

*"Would you mind repeating the question?"*

# ONE OUT, THE LOT OUT!

Teachers, nurses, firemen, the traditional pillars of respectability and reliability,
are at last turning to strikes to dramatise their legitimate grievances.
Will they be the only social bulwarks to go? Or merely the first?

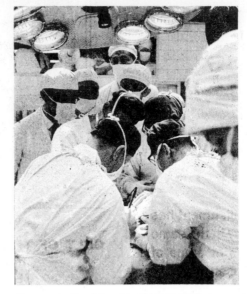

...ourse, we 'ung on as long as possible,'' the Suffragan
...op of Axminster told industrial correspondents today,
... the utter refusal of the authorities to comply with any
...r demands finally got on our wicks. Public apathy to the
...uct, crumbling places of employment, rotten hours, worse
...—I tell you, brothers, the industry's dying on its feet and
...agerial incompetence is to blame. We've been pressing
...ns for miracles since well before the last war, a pillar of
...a plague of boils, sunnink like that, just to keep up interest
...ne consumers, and what do we get? John Robinson,
...sname Muggeridge, David Kossoff! It's diabolical—
...'s the use of a lunchtime perishing sermon from George
...n at trendy St. Martin-In-The-Fields when what we're
... after is someone to do a bit of the old walking on the
...r.''

Surgeons flock to sign their final statement of grievance before
walking out: "The wind gets up you shocking in some of
these operating theatres, many hospitals refuse to allow tea-
breaks during operations, smoking is forbidden in three
intensive care units out of ten, and, despite vigorous union
protests, surgeons are still called out at night, even in rain, to
stop patients kicking the bucket.'' One particular grievance over
which surgeons were unanimously infuriated was the refusal
of patients to allow experimentation: Sir Edgar Struthe-Furbley
put the issue succinctly to William Hickey. "I'm currently
working on the theory that it ought to be possible to graft a
rat's head on to a human body. I had a bloke in with appen-
dicitis last week who had nice narrow shoulders, just right for
a rat's neck, but when I suggested he might care to advance
medical science, he started laying about him with a bedpan.''

...GE FOR YOURSELF is the slogan of these High Court
...es who have recently struck in protest against Press
...ism of court procedures and sentences. "And we mean
...ried strike leader, the Hon. Sir Gawayne ("Thumbscrew
...) McWhor, in Trafalgar Square this afternoon. "Let them
...a go! There's more to judging than sticking a dead ferret
...our bonce and waving a wooden hammer about. You
...dn't credit some of the books we have to study, in a
...ty of dead languages, not to mention dragging fag-ends
... inside your gown. You can't even send 'em down for
... years without some hack scribbler putting in his two
...'orth; we're not standing for it, and if they don't meet our
...nds to bring back quartering, flaying, transportation, and
...ng heads up on London Bridge, we'll turn it in for good.''

"Give us something to kill, or take the consequences. We
didn't join up for the bleeding water-skiing and running about
Salisbury Plain firing blanks, whatever the posters say.
Skilled operatives, and nothing to fill full of holes, it's disgusting! Redundancy staring us in the face, and no prospect of a
war for God knows how long, and what's the Government doing
about it, that's what we'd like to know: less than one per cent
of our labour force has ever seen a foreign corpse. If the
public knew how trained professionals spent their day, digging
latrines, walking goats up and down, cooking and sewing and
making bloody beds, there'd be hell to pay! And the RAF
say if we haven't invaded something by Thursday, they'll
come out in sympathy!" (*It is understood that if the soldiers'
strike continues, dockers may be called in to run the Army.*)

# POP TODAY, OP TOMORROW

In the art world Establishment has to keep running to stay in the same place. **Mahood** looks at some of its current obsessions.

## WORSHIP OF FASHION

## CULT OF THE MINIMAL

## INFATUATION WITH ELECTRICITY

*"Do I detect the influence of Thomas Edison?"*

## CONTEMPT FOR THE PAST

## OCCUPATION WITH THE
## [ES]OTERIC

## INSISTENCE ON PARTICIPATION

## [BEL]IEF IN EXPLANATION

"[I]n this piece the integral relation of the [tu]be activating the gaseous globes into a [spa]cial concept is eschewed as inimical [to] the formation of a single perceptual gestalt."

## TYRANNY OF SIZE

# It was fun while it lasted

## By HENRY CECIL

Some seventeen years ago I was sitting in my flat when the telephone rang. I was just over fifty and a widower, and I had been a County Court judge for several years. I picked up the receiver.

"Hello, *va bene*?" said a most attractive feminine voice, which I felt sure that I did not know.

"I beg your pardon?" I said.

"It is Angela, the little Italian girl."

"Who did you say?"

"Just Angela, the little Italian girl."

I knew no little Italian girl. No big one either for that matter. And I could not think of any girl with such an attractive voice. I thought hard to see if I could remember an Angela. I could think only of a maiden aunt long since dead and I soon knew for certain that the caller must have the wrong number.

I was about to say so and end the conversation when many thoughts began to race through my mind at an alarming rate. In their order of priority they went something like this. I should like to meet this Italian girl. If her face and figure were anything up to her voice she must be something quite exceptional. But County Court judges, even widowers, should not pick up little Italian girls, even if quite exceptional in voice, face and figure. And taking advantage of a wrong number would certainly be equivalent to picking up. On the other hand, there are not so many adventures round the corner for men over fifty. And, while pain is ready enough to strike, you must take your pleasures when they appear, or you must forgo them.

The mind works with incredible rapidity and these first thoughts only took a split second to materialise. Soon I was beginning to visualise Angela with dark hair and glowing, inviting eyes. Next I thought of a retired County Court judge who would be only too pleased to do my day's work for me.

"If I can get the day off, will you have lunch with me?"

"That will be lovely."

"*I think St. Gilbert's would be a wise choice for your son, Mrs. Simpson . . .*

*In the past we have produced two Prime Ministers, three Presidents and a Chancellor of the Exchequer.*"

"It's silly of me, but I've forgotten your address. Oh yes, of course. I'll be with you at half past twelve. Could you be looking out for me because parking is a little difficult around there and I shall be in my car. Bye-bye for the present."

I had begun the adventure. The next step was easy.

"Hullo, can I speak to Judge Dean, please? Oh, it's you, George. I wonder if you'd do me a favour? Are you doing anything special today? Good. Could you take my Court for me? Thanks ever so much. It is good of you. No, I'm perfectly well. It's just that I'm—I'm—I've just had rather an attractive invitation which I don't want to miss. Thanks ever so much. Bye."

This was very wrong, but at any rate I should have to pay the deputy judge's fee myself. And was there any real harm in it? After all, if a judge is supposed to understand the permissive way of life shouldn't he indulge in a little bit of it himself? People were always complaining that judges were too remote. Perhaps after an outing with Angela I should be a little less remote.

She was waiting on the doorstep and was everything which I imagined her to be. I got out of the car and went up to her.

"Good morning," I said.

"Good morning," she replied in a not unfriendly voice, though with the right amount of surprise in it.

"Angela," I said, "please forgive me but I couldn't resist your voice. You rang me this morning."

"But..." she began. Then she laughed. "Oh I see," she said, "but you don't know me."

"I'd like to," I said. "Will you come to lunch?"

"I've never done such a thing before," she said.

"Nor have I," I said. "Where would you like to go?"

To my surprise and pleasure I found that she knew something about food. She chose the only restaurant in London which is worth a visit if you're interested in food. We had a really splendid lunch and, when we weren't actually eating or drinking, we talked very happily. I learned that she was twenty-seven, unmarried and on holiday in England. She was having a gay time. After all one can only be young once.

"But, with men it is different," she said. "*Young* men are always young."

I'm afraid she learned nothing about me. I told her that my name was George Meadows and that I was a stockbroker. I added that I was a widower and that I thought she was one of the most gorgeous girls I had ever seen.

"But," she said, "how could you be sure? The telephone is an awful liar."

"Not on this occasion," I said.

Eventually we finished lunch and went for a stroll in Hyde Park. It was a lovely day and I certainly felt young. We talked of many things, music, pictures, mountains, and, finally, of love.

"I am in love," she said.

"Lucky man."

"Oh, it's no one in particular. I am in love with life, with everything in life. That includes you."

I took her hand. I did not care to imagine what the Registrar of my Court or the clerks or the usher would

"Well I'm not sure . . .

*Our Willie wants to be an engine driver.*"

think of me, wandering hand in hand along the Serpentine with a girl whom I had never met before. But I had better things to consider.

"Will you have dinner with me this evening?"

"I should love it," she said.

I called for her at eight o'clock, and we went to a big hotel. Her conversation over dinner sparkled. But it was her eyes that really did it. I wondered for a moment what a judge would do if a witness looked at him with those eyes. How could he disbelieve her?

It was over a glass of brandy that I made my approach shot.

"I've brought a suitcase," I said.

"Good," she replied. "They like one to have some luggage."

I was glad she required no persuasion. This could hardly be called seduction. After all she was twenty-seven and obviously capable of looking after herself.

After dinner I went to the reception desk to book a room. Just as I was about to give my name I heard a voice behind me.

"Hullo, sir. It is the judge, isn't it?"

I turned round. I haven't a good memory for faces and could not recognise the man who had spoken. But obviously he knew me.

"Good evening," I said. "I'm terribly sorry but for the moment I can't remember your name."

"I don't see why you should," said the man. "You appeared for me once when you were at the Bar, and

I've never forgotten it. An enticement case. You got me off. I nearly wrote to you on your appointment but then I thought that you'd have forgotten me, as of course you have."

"How d'you do?" I said. "No, I do remember the case, but I've a shocking memory for names." At that moment Angela arrived. She came right up to me and I had to do something about it. One of the few things I had learned as a County Court judge was to be able to make a noise that sounded like a name but which couldn't be recognised as any particular name.

"This is Mr...." I looked at him.

"Crowthorne," he said.

"This is Mr. Crowthorne," I said. "Miss—" and then I made my sound. Two or three consonants and a couple of vowels, part of it in the nose and part in the throat. If Angela hadn't come up at the time she did, I think I should have fled, but, when I saw her, she looked so radiant that I felt I would risk anything rather than forgo my adventure. So somehow I got rid of Mr. Crowthorne.

I then booked a room and we went up to it. As we shut the door behind us, with the thought of a glorious night in front of us, I realised that I did not even know her name. I asked her.

"Just Angela, the little Italian girl," she said.

"I'm sorry," I said. "I'm afraid you've got the wrong number," and I replaced the receiver.

But it was fun while it lasted.

*"Not good news, I hope?"*

*"They certainly built them to last in those days."*

# Van Dycks to the Right of Them

## By R. G. G. PRICE

Good afternoon. Can you close up a bit there? Splendid! This is the Great Entrance Hall. You are now on the site of the Norman cloisters. They were pulled down when the monks were turned out and the Family moved in. This part of the building was the East Wing of the Tudor house and the West Wing of the Palladian villa which followed. After the fires of 1763, 1764 amd 1765, it became the stables. Then, round about the time of Trafalgar, the ninth Marquess changed the view and this side became the front. Remember as you go round that, as you seem to walk north, you're really walking south.

The spinning-wheel belonged to Anne Boleyn. It's unused. This tapestry is a copy of one of the Raphael Cartoons in the Victoria and Albert Museum. It was worked by Queen Mary when she stayed here for a long summer holiday. Any questions? Splendid! Would you mind passing along to the right.

Good afternoon. This is the Rotunda. It was built by Sylvester Griggs because the eighth Marquess wanted something round at the foot of the Principal Staircase. I suppose you'd better follow me up. Well, this is the Royal Landing. If you're interested in portraits, all these are of the eleventh Dowager. As well as this, I have to cover the State Drawing-room, though at my age I should prefer something more limited. My colleagues seem to have managed it.

Penned here behind this scarlet rope, you can look at the room as it recedes into the distance. It was completed in the reign of George II, but instead of leaving it as it was they called in Lutyens to restyle it, which I must say he did. The ceiling shows *The Loves of Jupiter*. It's by Rex Whistler, after Rex Whistler. If you were allowed to step on the Bokhara carpet, you might notice that the panelling has four hundred and sixty-nine pomegranates carved by Grinling Gibbons, with fifteen carved by pupils.

Signed photographs of Royalty are thickly clustered on all available surfaces. The fragment of embroidery in that frame is all that was completed of a fire-screen worked by Lady Jane Grey on the scaffold. If you are wondering what that is, it's a model of the canal-cutting machine which the Family tried out and, of course, dropped, during a short-lived enthusiasm for inland waterways. It blocks the view of anybody sitting on the chair used by his Lordship at the last Coronation if they wish to watch the occupants of the Golden Sofa, not a diversion I should recommend.

Please don't overlook the half-finished game of back-gammon, the pair of spectacles laid on *The Times* crossword and the crumbled dog-biscuit. The National Trust insist on them to give the impression that the Family are in flight just ahead of you. In fact, they're enjoying life on a six-bathroomed yacht. There is a good deal I could say about that. If you have peeped your full, please move along into the Long Gallery.

Good afternoon. If you wish to take notes, do. This replaced two short galleries during the vogue for long galleries. It is used for the main portrait collection. This is the man who turned the monks out and seized their home. The effects of the curse can be seen quite clearly. The Tudor faces show the characteristics which still persist in the Family—thin lips, hooded eyes, reddish eyelashes and no lobes to the ears.

From the next century, that's Stuart times, there are our Court beauties. Like

*"About here should be all right."*

most female ancestors, they are by Lely. That gap represents Lady Clarissa. She was known as the Huntingdonshire Hoyden. Her portrait was burned by her brothers when she fled to Valenciennes with a geometry master. Everything quite clear? Right.

I'll take you along Count Otto's Corridor. The only remaining fragments of the Norman masonry are deep inside the walls. There's not actually much to see. The thing to remember is that when the courtyard was removed, the realignment threw the whole axis to the south-south-west. Now you take the three flights down the newel stair to the Chapel.

Good afternoon. I shall raise my voice slightly so that those at the back can hear me.

This was originally the Abbey wine-cellar. Cromwell's soldiers are supposed to have stabled their horses here. I do not understand how they could have prevailed upon them to enter. The interior was richly embellished in 1872. Those mosaics show *Thrift Rewarded By La Belle Dame Sans Merci*. They took the Gild of Our Ladye Dolores seventeen years. The gilt chalice and patten were the gift of the Rothschilds in thanks after a shooting party. In the side chapel are the robes worn by His Lordship at the Opening of Parliament. It is in this building that all the heirs are married. A special form of service is used in which the bride, instead of promising to obey, pays homage.

You are, no doubt, wondering what a man of obvious education is doing acting as a guide here. My trouble occurred when I was preaching the Annual Bene- factors' Sermon. I was just completing the section on the sixth Marquess when I noticed the ghost of Lady Felicia, who materialises behind those imminently doomed. She was hovering uncertainly between old Lord Edward, His Lordship's Great-Uncle, and Admiral Fitzreine, who is merely a connection by marriage. It is true there was a certain resemblance. Wishing to assist her, I gestured to indicate where she ought to stand. Unhappily my movement attracted the attention of Lord Edward's wife, who insisted that I should be removed from my post. If the Admiral had not intervened on my behalf, I should have been destitute, quite destitute.

The carvings on the font include what is thought by some to be the earliest representation in England of a plover. You now proceed up the Second Staircase, past the Bower, into the Small Banqueting Room. The Bower is never shown in any circumstances. Nor are the bedrooms, except on the annual Connoisseur's Day.

Good afternoon. No need to keep you long here. Table laid for eighteen. Service part of the spoils from the Battle of Minden. Fabergé *epergne*: there's a clockwork mechanism that waves the ferns about. Now the pictures. End wall: Turner's *Bonfire at Petworth by Sunset*. Other walls: a Cotman, a Giorgione, a Constable, a Lavery of the last Marquess—he's in uniform—and a picture by Her Ladyship's youngest sister of the House as it probably was before the reconstruction of 1823. There's the Family Motto on the chimney: *Caveat Rex*. That's the lot. Library through there.

Good afternoon. I expect you'll find the Stables more interesting. That's where I usually am. Well, the skeleton in the case is Galloping Jack, who was in the first race ever run on Newmarket Heath. The pictures are all winners. They're by Tubbs. I think that's the name. The books are Toplady Beeching's *Annals of the Turf*. I think you're supposed to go out through the Pottery and the Gift Shop; but the quickest way to the horses is through here.

Good afternoon. Mirabelle's having her secret rubdown . . . two lengths ahead when she came into the straight . . . the jockey told the trainer . . . oh, do you have to go? Turn right at the end of the lime avenue for the Kennels. If you want tea first, you can get it in the Prior's Brewery. Yes, we're having a super season . . . It's these multiple tickets with five Stately Homes in a week, you know.

39

# The Generation Gap

## by MICHAEL HEATH

"Of course I'd like to come out and chase long haired louts, but it means I shall miss 'Any Questions?'."

"The Students are coming! The Students are coming!"

"Most of them are on filth drugs which rot their minds you know. They won't be abl to last out much longer."

"Well, one of us has got to have a short back and sides and get sent in among them and spy."

"Grimshaw's the most damned awful swine— he's gone over to the other side!"

# Ill Met
# by
# Moonlight

## By ALAN COREN

*Doom'd for a certain term to walk the night—Hamlet I.v.*

Exhibition Road, SW7, 4 am and dawn the colour of a herring's belly seeping over the Albert Memorial. Ambassadorial London, this, and in a score of tall, white, faintly luminous houses, diplomatic staffs sleep smugly in their immunity, dreaming of Tripoli and Chad. The Regency streets breathe dull respectability, silent; not a soul stirring.

Except a short man in bare feet and a red woollen dressing-gown running down the road waving a ceremonial sword above his head.

"That's him!" shouted the police driver, slewing us into the kerb.

Who? Some crazed husband, chasing a lover from his wife's drainpipe? An Arab Consul bent on engraving some official oath on the Israeli Ambassador's lawn? A retired general, waking from a dream of Omdurman and sick for war?

The call that had squawked from the radio two minutes before had dropped few hints: a disturbance, nothing more. And it was that, all right. The doors flew open, and the coppers sprang into South Kensington in the textbook position with the air of men who have just found someone who may be able to help the police with their inquiries. The swordsman, surrounded, stopped.

"My Aston Martin!" he cried.

It sounded like some discreet Victorian oath.

The two policemen, one tall and cynical, one plump and keen, looked at him carefully.

"Tampering with it," gasped the man. He pointed the sword into the air, towards the block of flats above his head. "My wife . . . "

A pale blob, looking down.

". . . heard something. So she telephoned."

Not, then, a villain, but a victim.

"What were you going to do with that?" said the taller copper.

The man looked at it.

"It's a sword," he said.

"Oh, is it?"

"I had a DB5 last year," said the victim, "and they stole that."

We all looked sympathetic. Life, said our eyes, is largely loss and sorrow.

"I got a DB6 now," he said. "And they're after that, too."

Clearly, a sense of persecution lay heavily upon him. Somewhere in London, he knew, a gang lived for his Aston Martins alone: followed him when he walked to showrooms; watched him pay; trailed him home; heard him switch off the lights; then nicked his transport.

"Has it gone, then?" asked the driver.

The man shook his head.

"They were there, though," he insisted. "My wife heard them."

So the policemen crept, and flash-lighted, and searched, but there was nothing out of place; they found a broken window, though, and woke the caretaker, in case of a break-in, and he said you

41

don't expect me to mend the bleeding thing in the middle of the bleeding night, do you, I know all about that, it's been bust two weeks, but you know what bleeding glaziers are. What upset him more than anything, obviously, was the suggestion that anyone could dip their fingers into his block of flats without his knowing about it. Everyone thinks they know more than the police. Everyone's wrong.

It had been our fifth "shout" that night. We were operating out of Kensington Police Station, a huge and echoingly empty place that stands in Earls Court Road to watch over one of London's more complex and unstable acreages: on its Campden Hill boundary, it is a place of trend and affluence, where the summer nights ring to the fashionable shrieks of copywriters and Colour Supplement dollies, dining in tall thin over-priced houses and swopping one another with desperate dedication; a mile away, and the beat is an inter-racial warren of spielers and brothels, old, beat-up mansions full of transients and absconders and pimps and addicts and girls that go bump in the night. And it follows from this that the Kensington

copper has to be much more than a man with the time of day and a swift half-nelson: he has to be sociologist, ethnologist, parish priest, headmaster, bruiser, welfare-worker, and frequently father and mother both. In the lunatic insistence by *soi-disant* intellectuals who scream for a police force staffed by university graduates (and who conveniently forget that the Chicago, New York, and Los Angeles Police Departments are the best-educated in the world—and also among the most brutal, inefficient and corrupt), little mention is made of exactly where young coppers might go to learn what they will need to know. A First from Balliol might well be of use to a constable called in by All Souls' to settle a row over the tertiary meaning of a paragraph in Wittgenstein's *Tractatus;* but the chances are that three years cloistered with his intellectual peers will stand a lad in pretty lousy stead when his first shout is to a stinking basement in Notting Hill—not to take a knife off a drunk or a shotgun off a jailbreaker, that's comparatively simple, an instructor can teach you how to do that, all you risk is your life; but to settle a bitter

*"It's nothing serious, doctor. I'm just not feeling superior, that's all."*

fight between two ageing queers who want to chuck one another on to the street, to soothe a woman whose husband has just hit her with a broken bottle, to do something for a child that nobody's bothered to feed for a week, to question a pregnant teenager who's tried to open her wrists with a chisel, to pick up an addict in terminal deterioration, to stop a white landlord from braining a black tenant, or vice-versa. They send twenty-year-old coppers to do that, and if the staff of *New Society* would care to try it sometime, I'll pay their cab-fare and medical expenses. I spent six years at Oxford and Yale, and in case you think I'm boasting, let me just add that I could never handle the situations that a young copper finds himself in every night; and never would, despite the wonderful incentive of twenty quid a week, plus uniform allowance.

"She came in here two nights ago," said the Duty Sergeant, "a little old lady, very frightened, and she said that evil spirits were after her."

"Not much the police could do."

"Don't you believe it. I went along to her house, and I drew a cross on the pavement in front of it. In white chalk. And I told her they wouldn't dare touch her with that outside. And she was completely satisfied."

I laughed, and he smiled, and said:

"It's not funny at all, really. She was eighty years old, and she was petrified."

Nights at the station itself seem numbingly dull, mostly deskwork, a little tea, a few drunks and tarts to charge, and a procession of people with lost cats, lost keys, whined grievances, or foreigners looking for Wales. Activity centres on a small, rather dishevelled box-room full of switchboards and earpieces and policemen in braces, where messages are passed between stations, cars and beat-strollers; and, of course, on the cars themselves, who are most actively involved in rooting around the metropolis and nosing out such felony as dares to walk abroad. In this, routine patrol is as important as shout-answering: the atmosphere in a car is one of permanent suspicion, the eyes beneath the peaks ever on the *qui vive* for those tiny nuances which tell the expert retina that All Is Not As It Should Be. In Kensington, they're not the only patrolling wheels, either.

"Looking for toms," said the driver, as we low-geared irritatingly behind a beige Jaguar, two in the morning, an innocent-looking side-street.

"Toms?"

"Whores. They hang about round here, so the cars come looking for them. We've passed that bald bloke in the Jag three times."

"Hard up," said his mate.

"Or choosy."

*"I only have to twitch a nostril and the gun in this motor horn will blow your brains out."*

We passed him again, and his bi-focals caught the lamplight. He looked guilty. Everyone catching a copper's eye looks guilty. There was a Mini in front of the Jag, and a Rover in front of that; they might have been looking for vacant parking-meters.

"They can't sound their horns, see?" said the driver. "Or we'd have 'em. I've seen 'em drive round for three hours, just peering out of the window. You'd think they'd stop fancying it, wouldn't you?"

"There we are, then," said his mate. "Hard up."

At which point the radio crackled and threw out a few cryptic, parroty cries, and we took off, leaving rubber, howled down Kensington Church Street, sprang across Ken High Street, snaked rapidy through half a dozen back alleys, and slammed to a stop in front of an all-night launderette. A second later, another police car swooped up behind us, and shot its contents into the night. The four officers sprinted into the laundry. The casual passing eye might have been forgiven for thinking that Ronald Biggs had just turned up to wash his vest.

Not so. There was no one in the place except two skinny teenage girls in anoraks, and a young pink copper. He approached his colleagues. He had the voice, remarkably, of a prep school games master.

"They won't go home," he said.

"Oh dear me!" said a colleague.

Which sarcasm was all very well, except that what looked like a brace of errant Brownies turned out to be two-thirds of a local *ménage à trois*, tossed out by the other third for failing to come across with what he was paying the rent for. They were also equipped with nails and teeth with which, the launderette being rather cosy, they were prepared to defend their new billet to the death. It took ten minutes to evict them.

"Someone," said the driver, engaging the clutch, "has been sharing a bed with that lot."

"Imagine," said his mate.

The drunken Irishman was somewhat easier. He cried when the policemen removed him from his ex-girl-friend's flat, eighteen years old, far from Erin, and the tears running down his beardless cheeks. And stupid-drunk.

"Will you be a good boy now and go home?" they said, nicely.

But he ran, and when they caught him, he kicked one of them, hard, and swore fit to strip the cellulose off the car. And, against their original will, they arrested him. The younger policeman rolled up his trouser, and nursed his shin. I asked him if the Irishman would get charged with assaulting a PO.

"No," said the PO involved. "He didn't know what he was doing, did he?"

Whereas a gentleman whom we shall call Adrian did; we first became aware of Adrian's presence on this planet when, cruising slowly along Kensington High Street, we saw a red light walking along the pavement, some fifty yards away.

"Right," said the driver.

## The English Weekend

# Sunday with the Folks

## by GRAHAM

"Now *for* heaven's sake don't forget to tell Dad how nice his garden looks."

". . . and how's old Brucey then?"

". . . and this is your mummy on her pony—Bi... its name was—when she was just your ag..."

Adrian was six-feet-odd and bamboo thin, with hair like Veronica Lake's and a very nice beige cashmere suit, bell-bottomed, and a silk polo-necked sweater. To set this off, he was wearing a red hurricane lamp in his left hand; the deprived workmen's site stood accusingly, a few yards away. Beside Adrian swayed a lissome, musky girl in a fur coat. They both laughed tinklingly. It didn't cut much ice. They were charged with taking away an etcetera, contrary to an and so on, and Adrian became somewhat overwrought. He stamped his foot, and went into a little spiel that the coppers, one felt, had possibly heard before, concerning the fact that Adrian was a taxpayer and why weren't they out apprehending thieves, for which service Adrian paid 11s. 9d. in the £?

"We are," said the driver. And that was that. We called for a van, and it came and collected Adrian and friend, and we all went back to Kensington nick, where, amid further petulances, the pair of them were charged. Personally, I thought it was coming it a bit strong for a childish prank, and said so.

"Ah," said the Duty Sergeant, "but he's not a child, is he? And this borough loses thousands of pounds' worth of stuff like this every year. Which also happens to be taxpayers' money. And there's another thing: he wouldn't have nicked it in daylight, would he?"

He glanced up at the station clock, significantly.

"People have got to learn that they can't get away with something," he said, "just because it's the middle of the night."

"Strawberries! . . . Millions of 'em!"

"Every time we come it's apple tart!"

"Mickey Thomson's Grandad's got a **proper** swimming pool, hasn't he?"

"You know something, Grandpa . . . Daddy says you're loaded."

# Where would we be without THEM?

## By GEORGE SCOTT

I don't think we appreciate just how much we owe Them. They encourage us, They flatter us, They console us. They inflate our self-esteem, They bolster our illusions, They excuse our failings, They mitigate our sufferings.

The ancients attributed their misfortunes to the caprice of the Gods, the crossing of their stars, the sport of evil spirits, the malpractices of witches.

We say, simply, "It's all Their fault." And so, of course, it is. Whether it is that we are broke, that the car won't go, that the roof leaks, that the other man got the promotion, or the country's going to the dogs, They are always to blame.

Happily, They exist all over the world. You know Them as well as I do.

They were able to start from scratch after the war.

They don't have trade unions like ours.

They don't care about things like freedom.

They take work too seriously.

They're too docile to realise when they're being treated like slaves.

They don't have chairs to sit on at home, you know.

They don't have a forty-hour week.

They don't need as much to eat.

They're still living in the nineteenth century.

They learnt everything They know from us.

They don't care how many people are out of work.

They don't have to pay for the Health Service.

They've even got Their women doing it.

It may be all right for Them, but it wouldn't do for us.

They're terribly cruel to animals.

We were mad to think They could govern themselves.

Build a brave new world, They said.

Follow us, They said.

They've made us the laughing-stock of the world.

They must think we were all born yesterday.

I told you what would happen if They got into power.

If we all carried on the way They do, the country would be bankrupt by tomorrow morning.

They don't realise who Their real friends are.

They don't understand the first thing about economics.

They're doing all right for Themselves, don't you worry.

Work? They don't know what the word means.

We'll never get anywhere until They learn to pull Their weight.

In my young days, They'd have been given the sack for much less than that.

They're totally lacking in any sense of gratitude.

They've got no control over Them.

Who do They think They're talking to, anyway?

How They got where They are, I really don't know.

They've never had a taste of real life, that's what's wrong with Them.

I'd like to see Them doing my job.

We take the risks, They take the profits.

They're all in the same racket.

They look after Number One, first, last and always.

There's not an ounce of patriotism in the lot of Them.

*"Well, there's one astronaut who isn't taking the cut-backs lying down."*

You're too good for Them, my dear.

They just want a bunch of Yes-Men.

They take the best years of your life and then They just discard you like an old suit.

They don't want a man with original ideas, darling.

They would have turned down Winston Churchill.

They had Their knives out for me from the day I went there.

They do it all on the Old Boy Network.

My God, if only I'd had Their chances . . .

Everything was lovely until They arrived.

You didn't expect anything else from Them did you?

I knew we were in for trouble the moment They got off the boat.

Whatever They say about Them is true, I tell you.

They're just different from us, that's the beginning and the end of the matter. The way They dress . . . The way They eat . . . The way They talk . . . The way They stick together . . . The way They're always poking Their noses into other people's business . . . The way They look at you . . . The way They go on so . . .

I've always said it—you can't trust Them like you can trust one of your own kind.

You mean it was you who actually suggested your wife should stay with Them?

They wouldn't know how to look after it decently if you did give Them one.

They'd sell Their own children if They were offered enough.

But I bet you don't know how They made Their pile?

I told you They'd catch up with Them sooner or later.

They're just jealous of what we've got.

They ought to be ashamed of Themselves.

If They'd been through what I've been through, They wouldn't talk like that.

Doesn't matter what you ask Them to do, I guarantee They'll make a botch of it.

I'll believe it when I see Them do it.

You have to stand over Them the whole time— you might as well do it yourself in the end.

What beats me is how They have the nerve to advertise.

You wouldn't think They would dare to charge for it, would you?

They've no idea of how to cater for people like us.

They've no respect for anyone or anything.

They're the ones who are corrupting our children.

They wouldn't speak of Their own mothers like that.

They don't know where to draw the line.

"*Fancy taking your mind off the Common Market?*"

They're letting the side down.

They're dragging us all down to Their level.

I can't imagine how They get away with it.

It's all right if you're one of Them.

They're turning us into a nation of perverts.

Whatever will They do next?

Where They were brought up They didn't use soap.

I don't understand Them.

It's no good, They think They know everything.

They make me sick.

If They were my children . . .

You don't imagine They'll take your word against Theirs, do you?

Once you get on the wrong side of Them, you might as well start saying your prayers.

You'd think They could find something better to do with Their time than persecuting decent, law-abiding citizens.

They wouldn't speak to you like that if you had a Rolls.

They just aren't on the same wavelength with us when we talk about "fair play."

All They care about is winning.

All Their people get paid.

They take our best players.

They were lucky, that's all.

Mark you, if They had our weather . . .

They ought to be shot.

But if They were, we would have no one left to blame but ourselves.

# In Praise of Girls   by Michael ffolkes

The awfully nice thing about girls is that even if they are sometimes . . .

. . . slaves to fashion . . .

. . . lacking a sense of humour . . .

. . . less than Fanny Craddock . . .

. . . unfortunate in their choice of parents . . .

. . . idiotic at games . . .

. . . unpredictable in their tastes . . .

. . . careless about time . . .

. . . expensive to run . . .

. . . one of a large family . . .

. . . indifferent to machinery . . .

. . . over-energetic . . .

. . . they **are** *all* sisters under the skin!

"*What's come over you? You used to enjoy the rat race!*"

# Flattery in Politics

## By IAIN MACLEOD

Politician has been a rude word since Shakespeare's time, but politicians seem as pleased with themselves as ever. It just means that they have to do a lot to bolster each other's self-esteem. IAIN MACLEOD tells how.

"*We have suspended bombing, but from time to time we have air-to-ground engagements.*"

Disraeli as usual was right. At least in this politicians like being treated as Royalty: flattery should be laid on with a trowel. Wives are particularly good at this. "Darling, that was simply marvellous" is the accepted formula following any speech however short. All variations should be firmly discouraged. I once knew a political wife who used to say: "Darling that was easily the best speech you've ever made." The husband was a morose man but he could figure, and presently he began to calculate the odds against each of his numerous speeches being exactly placed in an ascending scale of excellence. The last I heard of her was that she was married to a tycoon and no doubt saying: "Darling, that was easily the biggest merger you've ever brought off." I hope her luck holds.

I do not mean to imply that politicians are vainer than the next lot. On the whole I think they are not. The good politician is somewhat like a good Creme Brulee; the outer crust is tough, unyielding and almost unbreakable: when once you pierce it, if you ever do, all is creamy consistency. Some people find speeches easy to conceive and deliver. In others the tension coils like a spring for days or even weeks before the simplest chore of oratory is accomplished. Both categories like flattery to be unconfined and they do not take it too seriously. It is in a way a mutual compliment. In *Timon of Athens* Shakespeare wrote: "He that loves to be flattered is worthy o' the flatterer," and Shaw, as usual making the same point and as usual not quite so well, said: "What really flatters a man is that you think him worth flattering." Most politicians resent and detest criticism. Few will admit it but I believe that it upsets them vastly more than praise pleases them. Perhaps I could illustrate by recording an impression of one of my weekly dialogues with my favourite but most awkward columnist when I was editor of the *Spectator*. Randolph Churchill never used to ring before midnight. It was useless to let it ring.

Randolph did too. "Hello Randolph." "Got some lovely grub for the press column this week. Listen . . ." And Randolph would start reading it to me together with a flood of views on everything under the sun so that it was barely possible to separate copy and comment. Finally it would end. "Pretty good, eh?" "Excellent. Lovely bit about Cecil King." "Thought you'd like that." "Splendid. One of the best pieces we've had." "Good." "There's just one thing . . ." "Ho! What's that?" And the temperature dropped fast. "Well the opening paragraph might be better still if you cut out . . ." "What the hell do you know about it?" Crash would go the telephone and for a day or two we were strictly non-speak.

Politicians get as much criticism as Sir Alf Ramsey or the Chairman of the Prices and Incomes Board, and they put up with it because they have to. The point I make is that it is a mistake to mix flattery and criticism. If a journalist writes an article in praise of a politician and includes in it a couple of lines of unkindly comment it will be this that is remembered and resented. It is no doubt an irrational reaction, but it is a very common one. Flattery and criticism are best kept in their separate compartments. Then a politician can read one and ignore the other. For myself I avoid reading anything about myself if I possibly can, even if I think the comment will be favourable. I tell myself that this is because I do not care about what "they" say. I suspect it is because I might.

The most engaging and unbashed flatterer in the present House of Commons I take to be Sir Edward Boyle. I have (or so it seems) frequently heard him say: "I am very glad that the Minister made that particular point. As the House will remember, Professor Beethoven in the Milton Memorial Lecture in 1923 put forward a similar suggestion . . ." The knights of the shires and the burgesses of the boroughs gaze at the good Sir Edward with a wild surmise. Here and there a head will nod as if reciting Professor Beethoven's exact words. No one ever dares to interrupt. After all if there was a Milton Memorial Lecture and if Professor Beethoven existed and did give it in 1923 then it is quite certain that Edward

*"I tell you Martha, every one is staring at us."*

really will have read it. So the House remains enormously flattered that they are assumed to be so intelligent, and Edward moves on to the next point. The essence of such an exercise is, of course, credibility. I was moved to open mirth, and so to his credit was he, when Fred Peart, Leader of the House of Commons, observed recently in the course of moving to set up a Select Committee into the allegations of a leak on Budget plans for increasing the Road Fund tax—"I have taken the opportunity of re-reading Professor Keaton's excellent *Trial by Tribunal*." It was the word "re-reading" I found risible. I will believe many things of the admirable and popular Fred except that Professor Keaton's book is his bedside reading.

Jack Diamond, Chief Secretary to the Treasury, has an unusual method which I judge highly successful. The Diamond basic speech will be heard a hundred times or so in the next few months. In Part I Jack Diamond says that he has listened with great care to the debate: that the hon. member who moved the amendment with such skill and care has put the whole Committee in his debt: that his speech showed clearly the sincerity which everybody associated with him: and that it was a privilege to be able to reply to the debate. In Part II Mr. Diamond says that the amendment is the silliest one he has ever seen. Then we vote. The process is known as the Committee Stage of the Finance Bill. It is odd how often the mover of the amendment swallows Part I so eagerly that he barely notices Part II. It is a technique that aspiring Ministers would be wise to study. If I have a criticism it is that the change of tempo is too abrupt. I do not, of course, suggest that a Treasury Minister should actually accept an amendment; we are discussing flattery, not fantasy.

Flattery in any case is an unattractive word. False praise is only part and a small part of a whole range of speech colours which lend variety to debates and to political life. The forms of speech in the House of Commons are intentionally traditional and courteous. Even the roughest and most wounding words lose something of their effect in such a setting. Erskine May is sometimes ridiculously strict in forbidding words and phrases that would be common currency in an argument outside the Chamber of the House of Commons. But those who made the rules over the centuries were wise. So flattery and sincerity, sharpness and grace blend together in a mixture that somehow manages to keep Parliament running smoothly.

*"Come on Mr. Fulsome, your appointment's for four o'clock!"*

*"English. You can tell them anywhere."*

# Two Years Hardy Perennial

## By MILES KINGTON

When I came to work at *Punch* early last year, I had one major objection to the job. Taking it on meant that I had to give up gardening.

I ought to make two things clear at the outset. One is that I did not come straight from horticulture to humour—the preceding five years I had spent as a free-lance writer. The other is that when I say gardening, I do not mean the planting, tending, nourishing and mourning of roses and chrysanthemums in a small suburban plot. I mean helping with the care and maintenance of a seven-acre chunk of rolling parkland in the middle of London.

Being a free-lance writer was not, I soon discovered, all coffee and Music Programme. A man soon gets used to the periods of black despair when the typewriter turns sullen and refuses to suggest ideas, or when the postman rings the bell because he can't get the envelopes full of your writing through the letterbox, but he never really adjusts to walking from the kitchen to the sitting-room and knowing that he's just travelled to work. Or to his wife coming home at half past five, trying to think of ways of not saying: "Did you have a nice day at the desk, dear?"

But the thing that worried me most, more even than not talking to anyone from nine to five, was the lack of

exercise, and I found myself looking more and more longingly at the stretch of green almost opposite our flat, called Ladbroke Square. It was behind railings and stretched appetisingly away so far that you couldn't see the other end. But what could I do there, even assuming I could get membership? Go for training runs? Climb trees? Nature rambles? Orienteering on a small scale?

One morning, when I was struggling with my smash-hit play about a low budget expedition to the North Pole that decides to economise by looking for it in Scotland, it came to me in a flash. The obvious thing to do in a garden was garden. If I volunteered to help the gardener two or three mornings a week, I would be physically refreshed and sit down glowing pink at the typewriter in the afternoon. My wife could ask me if I had had a good day in the shrubbery. I could put *gardener and humorist* in my passport.

Everything went according to plan. The full-time gardener, who lived in a small cottage just within the Square, put me on to the committee, the committee scratched its head and said yes, and how much did I want to be paid. I scratched my head, mentioned a random number of shillings, which was agreed to, and the next morning set off to work at the same time as my wife, she in elegant city clothes and I in gum-boots, thick sweater, windjammer, gloves and jeans.

And so began two idyllic years of hard labour or, if you put all the mornings together into 40-hour weeks, about four months. Come rain, come shine, but not come blizzard, I would be out there with Mr. Pyke, the gardener, catering for each season as it came. Hedging, hoeing, weeding and watering in summer; leaves, logs, bonfires and compost in autumn; digging, digging and digging in winter; bulbs, seeds and transplants in spring. I learnt to notice autumn a month before the rest of the family, as the first plane leaves glided down even before the football season started (have to burn plane leaves—the glossy kind don't rot down well). I mastered the art of sweeping leaves with a broom (the hands go the other way round from what you would expect, and then it's a half push, half dip, with a soupçon of pirouette). I learnt how to handle a spade, dig backwards, keep the trench in the right place and develop a sixth sense for trees looming up. I learnt that you bang a paling in with the point upwards, not downwards, so the rain runs off the top and doesn't rot it, and that if you want to grow prize

onions you are well advised to bury clippings from horses' hooves deep down near the tips of the roots.

We never actually grew onions or clipped horses in Ladbroke Square—it's just that I picked up an enormous amount of lore from Mr. Pyke, who had worked most of his life on large estates in his native north Norfolk and been so successful at local shows that he was sternly advised to enter solely for the county show at Norwich. Where, he admitted after three weeks of questioning, he had won several top prizes in his first year. If I ever have to write a cloying piece on My Most Unforgettable Character, it will be on Mr. Pyke, who is the nicest person I know and would be so shocked to be told so that I pass immediately back to the Square, which has the double distinction of being the largest in London and forming the entrance and part of the grandstand of the old, now forgotten, Notting Hill Hippodrome (1837-1840). So large that one is hardly aware of the houses behind the trees; digging in winter, with the mists down and the frost on the grass, we might have been in open Norfolk for all the people we saw or heard.

The only audience we ever had were mothers and children. The mothers said little to the gardening staff—I stabbed a hidden wasps' nest with a fork one day, came on to the lawn beating at my jersey and realised suddenly that I was standing, frenzied, in a group of open-mouthed mothers. I calmed down and said in cultured tones: "Can you remember if it's acid or alkali you put on multiple wasp stings?", but they said nothing. The children were much better value. One asked me once if I could guess what he was going to be when he grew up.

"A soldier?"

"No."

"A millionaire?"

"No, but you're warm."

"I give up."

"A policeman."

The seasons passed, the top of the spade wore a hole in one boot, I got a pay rise, the seasons passed again, two trees fell down and I joined *Punch*. It was hard work in the Square but even harder leaving it. At certain times of the year disconsolate muscles start twitching here and there in my body; just now it's the raking muscles in my shoulders and in about a month's time the part of my foot directly above the hole in my gum-boot will contract spontaneous dampness. Early next year I'll begin treading delicately round the office over imaginary patches of hidden bulbs, but it still won't really be the same. Sometimes I have to struggle hard against the urge to send an entry to *Campaign* and *Smith's Trade News*: "Miles Kington has been promoted from *Punch* to be full-time Assistant Gardener in Ladbroke Square."

PARK N' PRAY

EDWARD McLACHLAN

54

D'Arcy had been one of
st actors the world had
ever seen.

But over the years the world had not been
kind to Hugo D'Arcy.

It started with him drinking too
much and forgetting his lines, etc.

, I'm afraid, just plain old age.

Without work he was reduced to
washing up and meths. But all was not
lost. A little boy on his mother's knee
had been told of the greatness of Hugo
D'Arcy by a loving mum.

little boy had not forgotten these
rds and had grown up to be the highest
d film director in the world. And all
time Hugo D'Arcy was in the back
of his mind

At last when the right part came along, the
director found Hugo D'Arcy resting on the
embankment and signed him up

No, Hugo D'Arcy had not
been forgotten.

# ALL CREATURES GREAT AND SMALL

ALL THINGS WISE AND WONDERFUL
WE MUST CONSERVE THEM ALL

by Thelwell

*"Don't be hysterical! They've got as much right to live as we have."*

*"It's no good being sentimental. They've got to be thinned out."*

*"By the time you've got all the oil off them, you've got to retrain them to dive for fish."*

*"Over my dead body! There's a robin nesting in the sump."*

"Go on! Swipe them. There's no one looking."

"Don't hurt him!"

"Get ready! They'll run for it any minute now."

"I'm afraid it will mean destroying their natural habitat."

Until the Brooke-Kroger deal, involving such sub-items as concessions towards separated love[r]s and new rules on consular access, few of us realised the extent to which haggling played a pa[rt] in spy-exchanges. Clearly, if spying countries want to ensure value for money in future negotiatio[ns] they couldn't do better than take a page in

## EXCHANGES

**TALL WHITE SPY** available end September in exchange for short yellow similar, preferably with working knowledge of Peking sewage system. Would throw in 1 gross Stolichnaya vodka (86°) plus luxury all-in holiday for two on glorious Bulgarian Riviera (including beach cabana and wine with evening meal). Send photographs to Col. J. Kharkhov, Room 107, 14 High Street, Irkutsk.

**TREBLE GREEN STAMPS** on amusing and inventive female agent (37-24-38) own apartment, in return for any, repeat ANY, senior space research scientist. Apply, stating wig colour preferred, to ELDO, Brussels, Belgium.

**WHOLESALE BARGAIN ! ! ! EVERYTHING MUST GO ! ! ! DAMAGED FIRE STOCK ! ! !** 600 genuine Egyptian spies, £10 apiece, £90 per doz, £3,000 the lot, or would exchange for small gown business, Central London. Apply in first instance to Lance-Corporal Nat Selby, Nachas Barracks, Tel Aviv 4.

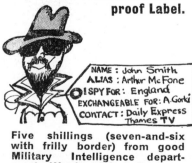
**DEREK ESMOND FILB,** 39, 5′ 6″, blue eyes, balding, own teeth. Would anybody like this desirable modern person, complete with three flannel suits, winter overcoat, and two pairs shoes? Fares paid (one-way), including sandwiches and flask, in return for Morris 1100 or equivalent foreign vehicle. Htr. and radio desirable, but not essential. Write soonest to Mrs. D. E. Filb, 17 Pretoria Villas, Woking.

**CABINET MINISTERS,** all sizes, available for immediate defection, in exchange for decent accountant or gnome. Apply in person to 10 Downing Street, London, SW1 (Rear entrance).

**ESKIMO** swapped in error. Now resident Cardiff Town Hall. Suggestions, please, to Deputy Town Clerk, Cardiff.

**PARROT,** bi-lingual (Rumanian-English). Exceptional memory. 100 gns., or would exchange Franco-Czech budgie. Box L 909.

---

## PERSONAL

**BOXER PUPPIES** all bugged. From £15. Tel. 585 1799.

**4th AGENT** wanted, share cell Lubyanka (3rd floor). Use of pail alternate Thursdays. Bridge player/baritone preferred. Refs essential. Apply in writing, stating full alias and bogus address, to ZC 676558, Lubyanka Prison, Moscow.

**KGB 100.** This desirable number, currently attached to elderly agent provocateur now working in Amalgamated Engineering Union and scheduled for early liquidation. Best offer over £50 (Swiss francs only, please) secures. Write Box 4327.

**TWO SEATS AVAILABLE** on Dakota leaving from Somewhere in England on trip over Unnamed Central European Country. Own parachute and cyanide pill required. For further details, apply in person under clock at Victoria Station, September 8th, wearing green fedora, carrying rolled-up copy of

*Droitwich Morning Advertiser,* smoki[ng] Wills Whiff and whistling the Inte[r]mezzo from Cavalleria Rusticana. N[o] coloureds.

**ELDERLY BOER SPY,** now 93, wh[o] did his country great service betwee[n] 1895-1901, reduced to selling treasure[d] collection of Kruger cigar-bands. Ju[st] one of hundreds of cases on our file[s]. Don't betray him now! Any gift welcom[e] we shall do the rest. Sell somethin[g] even if it's only a friend, and send th[e] money to Distressed Agents' Fun[d], High Rd., Morden.

**PLASTIC SURGEON,** own car, seek[s] evening work. Noses a speciality. Wid[e] range of ears. Utmost discretio[n] reasonable fees. Special reductions f[or] groups. Apply Box 4328.

The seeds, the buds, the rising sap—in Spring, the whole world is alive with lust and crazed biology! What better time, then, for all good Puritans to rally to the call of KEITH WATERHOUSE to

# Bring Back Virginity

*What, exactly, are the aims and purpose of Virgins for Industry?*

The aims and purpose of Virgins for Industry are, foremost, to restore British virginity to its former prestigious position in the markets of the world; secondly, to impress upon young men and women the economic and social advantages of retaining their virginity before it is too late; thirdly to rid Government, Industry and the Trade Union Movement of dangerous non-virgin elements whose avowed objective is to establish Great Britain as the Sodom and Gomorrah of Western Europe; and fourthly to campaign unceasingly for the removal of the iniquitous Tax on Virginity.

*Is Virgins for Industry, then, a political organisation?*

Virgins for Industry is completely unpolitical. We believe, however, that the present trend towards permissiveness is directly traceable to the folly of socialist politicians who publicly admit to being active non-virgins. We also believe that millions of man-hours are being lost each year as the result of lust and fornication on the factory floor, as well as behind filing cabinets. It is our contention that only a Virgin Government can lead Great Britain back to strength, chastity and economic sanity.

*Virgins for Industry was recently accused by a Socialist Member of Parliament of being interested only in increased production and profits at the cost of other people's pleasure. Is there any truth in this scurrilous libel?*

The socialist politician who made this vicious and cowardly attack under the cover of Parliamentary privilege is, it is openly admitted, the father of two children. Thus he publicly flaunts his confession that he has been in bed with a woman on at least two occasions. Were he to present himself at the House of Commons with a mattress strapped on his back, it could not be a clearer indictment of his direct interest in the permissive lobby.

But let us examine these groundless allegations. What is the so-called "pleasure" which it is said we seek to deny the British people? Let us make no bones about it, it is the "pleasure" of sex—which, as many doctors have testified, leads *directly* to rape, incest, abortion, prostitution, venereal diseases, adultery, illegitimacy, nervous exhaustion and like perils.

And who really wants this "pleasure"? Not, you may be assured, the Virgins of Britain. No virgin lathe operator ever approaches the foreman for half a day off so that he may defend himself in a sordid paternity suit. No virgin secretary fails to turn up at her desk because she is suffering from morning sickness. We do not see virgin company directors ashen-faced with worry, and unable to deal with important export orders, because some woman has just rung up to say that she must see them at once, and it's very urgent.

No, the British virgin is happy to forgo such "pleasures."

*Other critics, with the best of motives, claim that Virgins for Industry is impracticable. They say that if we were all practising virgins, Britain would be uninhabited within seventy years.*

Certainly there would be a marked decline in the demand for subsidised housing, free education and other perquisites of the Welfare State which (since the Exchequer does not look kindly on the single man) are largely paid for by the iniquitous Tax on Virginity.

*"But Arthur, we can't sit here at peak viewing time and not watch something!"*

But it is wrong to say that Virgins for Industry is reaching for the moon. We are realists, and we recognise that there must always be an unhappy minority who will indulge in sexual intercourse, just as there will always be drug-addicts, alcoholics, perverts and criminals. However, just as we would not expect to be governed by drug-addicts, alcoholics, perverts and criminals, neither do we wish to be governed by those who indulge in the sexual act.

*You have convinced me that criticism of Virgins for Industry is either ill-informed or malicious. Now, speaking constructively, could you outline the economic advantages of virginity which you mentioned earlier?*

Even allowing for the iniquitous Tax on Virginity, the practising virgin earning, say, £2,000 a year, is many times better off than his fornicating opposite number. Here is one case from among hundreds on our files.

As a *direct result* of losing his virginity at the age of twenty-three, John B., a chartered accountant living in Middlesex, is now the father of three girls under the age of twelve. Having kept careful records of his expenditure he has been able to calculate that the cost of this brood in the way of clothes, food, shelter, education, birthday and Christmas presents, toys, holidays, horse-riding lessons, Brownie uniforms, soft drinks, sweets, ice-cream, pocket money, subscriptions to *Jackie* and the remainder, has so far amounted to the fantastic sum of £10,700.

By remaining a Virgin a young man of equivalent income would be able to *save* £10,700 within twelve years.

*You might have added that such a sum when invested would actually appreciate over this period. But money is not everything. What are the social advantages of virginity?*

An independent survey has shown that the Virgin has *twenty-five times* more leisure than a non-virgin. Leisure in which to read improving books. Leisure to take up a rewarding and profitable hobby such as coin-collecting. Leisure to peruse the correspondence course that may rocket him to the top of his profession. He is also, from the employment point of view, a more efficient working unit, far less likely than the non-virgin to arrive at desk or work-bench with circles around his eyes, waste precious hours mooning about in the typing pool, or write pornographic letters on

# SHOW-BIZ FOLKS AT HOME

a **LARRY** documentary
on Life after the Show

the firm's stationery. Remember, too, that it is the virgin with *twenty-five times* more leisure at his disposal who is best able to serve his country in Government at all its levels.

*Twenty-five times more leisure! Surely this is a staggering figure which will come as a revelation to all thinking men and women?*

It is indeed a staggering figure, and one that perhaps deserves to be explained in a little more detail. Our argument, which is based not on theory but on fact, is that the average virgin is, hour for hour, twenty-five times more productive than the average non-virgin, irrespective of the quality, use or desirability of that which is being produced.

Time-and-motion studies show that for every fifteen minutes spent in copulation by a non-virgin, *five hours* is consumed in preparatory activities such as bathing, dressing, applying after-shave lotion and other unguents, drinking cocktails, dining by candle-light, dancing, groping in taxi-cabs and professing a mutual interest in certain gramophone records. Even then the end-product—such as it is—is not guaranteed.

In a comparable period, a virgin who has decided to spend his evening sorting through his collection of day-of-issue stamps will not have wasted a single minute. Nor, according to independent costings, will he have incurred a restaurant bill for £8 9s. 6d. plus fifteen per cent tip.

*It is clear that sex is wasteful, time-consuming, expensive and that there is no place for it in modern Britain. How do you propose to drive this message home?*

By disseminating literature such as this in schools, youth clubs, offices and factories. By setting fire to hotel beds. By spreading rumours that the Pill causes women to grow moustaches. By patrolling Hampstead Heath shouting "Disgusting filth!" at courting couples. By discouraging office parties. By taking a full-page announcement in *The Times* newspaper denouncing HM Government as lechers and forni-cators.

Naturally, all this costs money, and we exist entirely on voluntary subscriptions. We rely on *your* support.

*I would like to join Virgins for Industry. How do I set about becoming a virgin?*

# Lead and I Follow, Follow

## By PETER PRESTON

A few years ago, young and innocent, I had a harrowing experience. A big professional organisation for travel agents wondered if a reporter would like to cover their annual conference. The reporter was me. The conference was in Norway.

We heaved across the North Sea in early winter, kept sane by a bountiful bar and a whimsical agent who explained the clotted legality of his bargain trips to Australia. We waited for coaches. We shivered in chill bedrooms. We spent hours at dinner tables attending the eventual arrival of cold and minute portions of local delicacies. They—the travel agents—moaned pitifully among themselves. I—the reporter—watched fascinated, taking it all down in a little book. Here were the men who sold holidays griping about the sort of holidays they sold. Here were the English abroad, distinctly doleful because they'd got pickled herring for breakfast again.

It's a revelation one recalls whenever one meets a travel writer. I meet them regularly—usually en route to the Rocky Mountains or Japan. Where are you off to next? Oh, only Yugoslavia—but right off the beaten track. And then, maybe, the nethermost Mediterranean coast of Turkey. I met one a couple of months back in Minneapolis. What was he going to do? Hire a car and drive slap across the American mid-West; he didn't think anybody had ever done it before.

And that, alas, is the point. People go on holiday once or twice a year. The travel column goes on fifty-two weeks a year. The moneyed travel writer —with fat contract from "Holiday Magazine"—has a round-the-world ticket and, to take a true for instance, four articles to produce. It doesn't precisely encourage detailed coverage of small pensions in southern Brittany or cheap ski-ing chalets on Austrian railway lines. In fact it encourages the precise opposite: the scoop bizarre. That chunk of Yugoslavia no one had written up before turned out—to take a second true example—to be rocky wasteland, without inhabitants or hotels or even views to speak of. Why had no one chronicled a mid-West car trek before? Because the mid-West is huge, flat and uninteresting, unless you like corn on the cob.

Thus the system, born out of boredom and initiative intermingled, favours the esoteric. Who, in the sacred name of colour supplements, can go to Benidorm year after year and look Lord Thomson in the eye? Sooner or later one has to get hooked on the myth of the glossy spreads: real solitude, real wildness, real distance, twentieth-century man shedding neuroses among the (Sunday paper approved) peasants of some forgotten land. I have done it all. I fell in love with Switzerland when, at eighteen, I first discovered the

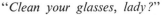

*"Clean your glasses, lady?"*

*"Sometimes, Carstairs, I wonder if it's worth it."*

efficiency of its sanitary waterworks and bid France's black holes farewell; but since then I have eaten shepherd's pie in the State Resthouse, Takoradi, removed a quarter-inch screw from ravioli in Rawalpindi, tramped the sacred cities of Morocco. I have suffered for the grand delusion.

At any cost—this delusion runs—one must escape the common herd. But the common herd, regrettably, know what's good. A friend lent me her "wonderfully quiet" shack in the south of France. It was wonderfully quiet because it was two hundred (vertical) yards from the nearest track. Water came from a near-by spring: full of lizards. Sanitation came from the near-by bushes: spiky. Wildlife burgeoned all around: rats. Forty-eight hours later, deeply grateful but infinitely wiser, we departed for a hotel in Antibes.

Even a little nearer civilisation the magnet of total normality still tugs. In a Moroccan cafe one must scrabble for fish and chips, the only dish the children eat. In a tiny Portuguese village one must hunt for tomato sauce. There is always—shamefaced and surreptitious—the long, long trail in search of an English newspaper and the glum certainty it will be a *Daily Telegraph*.

But surely—you say—somebody must relish solitude? Somebody, certainly: but damned elusive. Where do the army colonels and civil servants who superintended a distant Empire decamp to when their toil is done? To Cyprus (for example): attending the

English Church in Kyrenia, drinking at the English pub in a Greek quarter backstreet, buying frozen kippers, commuting in Mini-Mokes, forming bridge circles. What did the lone Lord I met in beach cafe in Morocco or the lonely lady in caravan on the Costa Del Sol intend? Living off British tourists. What do roving foreign correspondents do as they patrol the globe? Meet in a few distant yet notorious bars and swap Fleet Street gossip.

The desolate trails, in short, are unloved and unlovable. They are enthusiastically populated only by those writers who find professional cachet in desolation. They do, however, create a climate. They make the mundane a social burden; they make romantic adventure mandatory for post-humorous cocktail chat. And they have one substantial, mostly unacknowledged, sociological trait working for them: holiday horrors.

On that Norwegian trip the travel agents bitched constantly, but this didn't mean they weren't enjoying themselves. Everybody, tottering ashore at Newcastle, professed complete pleasure and meant it. The agonies had been part of the ecstasy. Man, returning to his lair, needed a smattering of ghoulish details to spice the colour slides with. Since holidays are mainly anticipation and retrospection, there's nothing more tedious for the remaining eleven months than bland comfort, perfect arrangements and unadulterated sun during the handful of weeks overseas.

Every news editor knows that tales of British holiday-makers camping on a building site in Majorca (because their hotel won't be finished until next spring) make riveting copy. Readers identify with such plights. Readers want to feel that holidays can still be an adventure reserved for the brave. Friends and neighbours, without supporting evidence, must be impressed by sagas of fortitude in faraway adversity.

Which is, unhappily, the reason why the long-distance master of purple prose will continue to wax and grow plump. Fewer travel agencies are collapsing in spectacular fashion. Fewer scandals are besetting Spanish tourism. Truly to suffer these days you have to cut adrift: alone in a very foreign land with all amenities as distant and intractable as possible. My richest acquaintance, having had a spot of bother in a flat-bottomed boat up the Amazon last year, is thinking of doing it again for want of anything more horrendous. My poorer acquaintances are vastly impressed with Albania's disaster potential. Meanwhile anyone seeking absolute quietude without tears might take a personal tip no travel writer would ever give: one of a dozen small Normandy resorts possessing splendid food, comfortable beds and complete peace. You need merely go in November (the month the travel writers recommend Tahiti).

*"People will always fork out good money to put up a Centre For The Performing Arts."*

# Father of the Man

## By ALAN BRIEN

The other night, after dinner, my host opened a first-floor window on to the garden, pressed into my hand a hefty, expensive air-pistol and said— "Try the watering can." Peering into the leafy darkness of NW1 at midnight, I prayed that none of his prestigious neighbours was out there taking the air, so that I would not be immortalised as the man who shot Dee Wells, or Jonathan Miller, or V. S. Pritchett, or Alan Bennett. How should I aim, I wondered. In the classical European style, over the folded elbow of the left arm, squinting along the barrel? Or like a Western gun-fighter, legs apart, arms loose, trusting to the unconscious to calculate the angle between eye and finger? What a fool I had been to tell that story earlier on about my war-time experiences as a RAF rear-gunner.

As I could not see any watering can, the choice seemed academic. So I pasted on a devil-may-care, professional grin, casually pressed the trigger, and was rewarded by the thin hiss of escaping air, then the satisfying thunk of a metal pellet embedding itself in a hollow plastic object. I should have modestly savoured my triumph, and retired from the competition. There seems to be a rule (no doubt formally spelled out in *Zen and the Art of the Air-Pistol*) that the worse you are at any sport, the more likely you are to hit a bull's eye at first attempt. I am the man who gets a double 20 with his opening dart, then never again even reaches the board. So long as I do not know what I am doing, I am brilliant. Once I have been coached, I am hopeless. The story I should have told was how I scraped through my gunnery course, when proficiency was measured by the number of holes made in a towed wind-sock, only by puncturing the canvas, with a bullet I carried in my pocket, after we had arrived back at base.

Like a fool I went on popping off the air-pistol at a much nearer target, a beer mug on a chair, only to find I was ejaculating into nowhere and contacting nothing. "It's like being impotent," explained my host, sympathetically. He disengaged the weapon from my limp fingers, handed it over to a fellow guest, who instantly shattered the mug, then snapped away up and down the garden, striking stone goddesses, plaster gnomes, kiddies' tricycles and seed packets with every shot.

On the way home, giving Dead-Eye-Dick a lift, I sneered at my host with rather more than usual asperity. "Wouldn't you know, *he* would put me down with a schoolboy toy?" I demanded. "Yes," agreed my passenger. "His is the junior size. I have the adult one, of course."

Despite my scorn, I have since found myself, whenever my wife's back is turned, gazing longingly in the windows of gunsmiths. I don't care if a pistol is a penis symbol (or is it that the penis is a pistol symbol?) this is the first dangerous, glamorous, forbidden plaything I have coveted since I was twelve. I may just treat myself to the best one that money can buy, smuggling it inside a woolly scarf and secreting it in a hidden drawer, for next Christmas.

Many more of us men than would ever admit it, I suspect, come to regret the vanished pleasures of childhood birthdays and holidays. Just what I wanted, we say, opening up a package containing boring ties

"*With all due respect sir, and without any mutinous intentions, I relieve you of your command, sir!*"

or gloves, improving books, useful gadgets, decorative knick-knacks. What we want are *toys*—elaborate, pointless, extravagant, unnecessary things which whizz and whirr and bang and light up. We want to be ordered to fold down flap A, connect terminals Y and Z, insert batteries where marked, light blue touch paper and retire immediately, on no account place near eyes, or pets, or mixed company. Why else have we survived into middle age, brought up a family, made a medium success, negotiated a mortgage, become imprisoned in routine, if we cannot now expect to be rewarded at last with the goodies our parents could never afford for us?

This is an infantile lust which women never really comprehend. Their childhood prepares them for adult charades more realistically than ours does. Men wear clothes, they dress up. Their beads become jewellery; their dolls, children; their dolls' houses, homes. Playing shops, or nurses, or mothers, or interior decorators, or dressmakers, turns out eventually to be a rehearsal for the grown-up roles in which they are cast. All right, OK, I read the "LOOK" columns in the *Sunday Times* too—I know many women rightly resent the frustration and waste and strain of their domestic squirrel's cage. But they are more often depressed than disillusioned.

Many men never get over the shock of discovering that their juvenile pastimes cannot be indulged after puberty unless they are called to be spies, detectives, racing-car drivers, VCs, astronauts, designers of robots, or Roman Emperors. Wives, mothers and daughters are indulgent towards our minor vices, our non-competitive naughtinesses, such as smoking and drinking. We appreciate their thoughtfulness, but a chap can use only a limited number of initialled holders, cases, lighters, shakers, stirrers, squeezers, pourers, glasses. Even the motor car, that four-wheeled sex substitute beloved of the motivational researchers, quickly dwindles from a mistress to a mother-in-law. All those years of apprenticeship to Meccano and you end up being a servicer of vacuum cleaners on your day off, a mechanic attendant to the mower or the washing machine on unpaid overtime.

Why do men's pleasures have to be disguised as "hobbies" before they can be entered in the family budget as a legitimate expense? If wives can spend money on make-up, shoes, handbags, hair-dressing, underwear, beyond the strict call of necessity, why shouldn't husbands splurge on model trains, construction sets, fireworks, snow sleds, science kits, jig-saws, board games, boxes of puzzles, throwing knives —without having to pretend they are intended for their children? I promise you, Madam, and you, Miss, the man in your life would rip open that tastefully wrapped, beautifully bowed parcel with much more genuine excitement next time, if he thought it contained some new-fangled toy the other men on the block had not yet been given. Like an air-pistol?

*"Don't you think it's a bit early to start running?"*

# A Monstrous Tale

## By WILLIAM DAVIS

*"We haven't seen you at Confessional lately, Patrick . . ."*

**D**ear Nessie (May I?):

I came to see you last week, but you were in. I'm told that you live in blessed darkness, deep down in Loch Ness, and only show yourself when Fleet Street begins to run desperately short of silly season stories. I called your name, but they said you don't like being shouted at. I brought some chocolates, which I dispatched into the water, and I hope you found them. You see, I came with the best of intentions. I wanted to tell you a little bit about the world outside, and warn you that it's not going to be a peaceful summer. You are going to be bombarded with sonar beams, hunted by a yellow submarine, shot at with hypodermic darts, pointed at by excited motorists, robbed of tissue samples, and filmed by umpteen pieces of equipment. An electronic eye will scan the loch surface every night, and a time-phased camera mounted on a balloon will take pictures once every twenty seconds. The aim is to prove that you exist.

I do not, of course, have any doubts myself. The sceptics are the same fools who would question the existence of giraffes and hippos if one couldn't see them at the zoo. I have never had a sighting (for some reason, you are never merely seen, but sighted) and I have no clear idea of what you look like. I am, however, confident that you are female. Who but a woman would keep everyone guessing for so long?

You may not be aware of it, but up here they refer to you as a "monster." It's not a very nice term, and you may well feel that the two-legged creatures who use it don't make a very pretty sight either. Beauty, as we know, is in the eye of the beholder. You are said to have a small head, a graceful neck, three humps and a natty tail, and to be able to swish through the water at thirty miles an hour. Issigonis would be able, I imagine, to improve on the design but I am quite prepared to accept you as you are. So, I'm sure, is the boy monster (oops, sorry) who is reported to be keeping you company.

Despite the doubters, you have come to play an increasingly important role in our dreary lives. You fascinate and intrigue us, especially now that we are running out of mysteries at a breath-taking pace. They have argued about you on television, and you are the hero of several books. Comedians find that, next to mothers-in-law, you are the best guarantee of laughter. Fleet Street relies on you to fill the long gaps between Enoch Powell's speeches, and Harold Wilson values you as a major contributor to our export drive. If you care to collect it, the Queen's Award for services to Invisible Exports is yours.

All this explains why my fellow creatures are about to launch the biggest ever "monster hunt." I do hope, Nessie, that you have a sense of humour, because it really is all quite entertaining. Let me tell you, for example, about the Colonel.

I met him last week, at the eight-caravan site, close to Urquhart Castle, where the Loch Ness Phenomena Investigation Bureau has its HQ. The Bureau is a pukka outfit, with a balance sheet, monster tie and all the other trimmings, and the Colonel is one of several ex-officers hoping to make contact with you. When I arrived on the site, he had just taken over as group commander, responsible for organising the duty watches. His name, he said, was Hugo Pyman and he was "cracking on for sixty." Colonel Pyman has been wooing you for six years, and he has had two sightings. It's not much to show for all that effort, but he forgives you. "Here I am," he told me, "a retired soldier. I have lost my main interest in life, and for two weeks I get down here, away from my wife. It's a jolly good holiday—and

anyway, it's the last great adventure we've got apart from going to the moon." He is convinced there's a whole herd of you down there, and he is in charge of a fourteen-strong team, which includes a Czech, a Swede and four Americans. They are all under twenty-one, and they get up at the crack of dawn to man eight cameras mounted in strategic positions around the loch. The Colonel is a jolly nice chap, and serves a jolly good dram. I'm sure you would enjoy meeting him. Then, of course, there's young Dan Taylor from Atlanta, Georgia. He's the fellow with the home-made yellow submarine. The sub has a small conning tower with portholes, and Dan reckons he has a good chance of spotting you. The Colonel thinks he's talking rot. "If you go thirty feet down," he says, "you can't see a damned thing. It's like peat. He says he's got lights and can see for twenty-five

*"Oh, for heaven's sake, John—the two weeks will soon pass."*

yards, but would *you* expect the monster to come up, smile, and say take my picture?"

I told him that, by all accounts, you were a kindly monster and might feel inclined to oblige. Dan, after all, is another jolly nice chap and means no harm. I also drew the Colonel's attention to the possibility that you might take a fancy to the submarine. It's not easy, after all, to tell a sub from a boy monster in the dark. The mind boggles (at least mine does) at the prospect of an actual union, but Harold Wilson isn't the only one who believes in miracles.

I gather, Nessie, that you are very shy, but if you could at least show yourself for a few minutes this summer the Colonel and lots of other people would be frightfully chuffed. And it would be fun to see the faces of the sceptics. Anyhow, you might as well get it over with because they are talking about going

after you with all kinds of noisy, monster-raising devices. They'll never give you peace, I'm afraid, until they have taken a nice big snapshot of you. If you do come up, of course, you take the risk that they will try to capture you for London's Zoo. Your daddy probably spun some yarn, when you were small, about the whole world being black and full of juicy eels, but the reality is rather chilling. Our part of it is full of people who spend their lives chasing a substance we call money. It's not as juicy as eels (in fact, it tastes rather awful) but we are all addicted to it. The way things work up here, possession of the biggest pile of it makes you king of the loch. It sounds monstrous, I know, but we call it civilisation. Thirty-six years ago, a circus owner named Bertram Mills offered a £20,000 reward for your capture, and there is still no shortage of speculators who think they could make a fortune if only you could be persuaded to go into show business. They would give you the full glamour treatment (we have ways of dealing with wrinkly skin and unruly humps) but my advice is not to risk it.

It is, literally, tough at the top. London Zoo isn't so bad if you are a tea-drinking chimpanzee, but you would find life there a bit cramped—and, besides, you would soon grow tired of being gawped at by tourists from Milwaukee and being fed quick-frozen eels at mealtimes.

The most sensible course, I suggest, is to make one convincing appearance for the benefit of Independent Television, and after that communicate only with people who, like the Colonel and me, love you for your own sake and want merely to be friends with all things bright and beautiful, all creatures great and small. We couldn't guarantee you full protection, but at least the conversation would be interesting. We would certainly be able to help you with any investigations which your herd may wish to conduct into the human phenomenon.

If you want to discuss this further, please let me know. The telephone connections between Scotland and London are not as good as they might be, but I am sure the Colonel would be happy to pass on any messages. I would gladly come up to sight you, and if you would prefer to have me bring Dover sole instead of chocolate it could be arranged. (We eat it grilled, by the way, with a sprig of parsley.) I could row out to meet you somewhere nice and quiet; just hiss, or whatever it is you do, and I'll say hallo. It would be very gratifying, of course, if our first interview could be exclusive. It's not the money, you understand, but the urge to provide readers of *Punch*—a scientific journal of some standing—with another great scoop.

Think it over, and don't be scared. We humans are not half as frightening as we look.

"*Right, clothes off everyone; this is a dress-rehearsal.*"

*"And it's very handy for the airport."*

# Uncorking my Lost Youth

## By MICHAEL PARKINSON

Football fever and cricket madness are hereditary diseases. I don't know how far it goes back in our family but I do know that my grandfather used to walk thirty miles to Bradford to see Yorkshire play, my father supported Barnsley for half a century and I consider the high spot of my life to be the day I sat next to Tom Finney on a bus. Therefore, the strain of these particular diseases is a strong one in our family, and it shows no sign of weakening, because my eldest son is already showing acute symptoms of both football fever and cricket madness. At the ripe old age of nine he has already decided to be a double inter-national when he grows up. He will play for Manchester United and England at soccer and Yorkshire and England at cricket, and with that delicious innocence of youth believes that all he has to do to achieve his ambition is to ask the Good Lord nightly to make him: "Like Georgie Best and Geoffrey Boycott . . . please, if it's not too much trouble." Well, we shall see.

The pleasure of children is that they reflect a father's lost youth and more than keep at arm's length the inevitable disenchantment that comes to every sports lover as he grows older. The simple fact about sport is that the teams and players of the present are never as good as those you saw in your youth and the older you get the more you believe it. The thing that prevents all sports lovers retiring in

# THE MUCK AROUND US

Man having emerged originally from slime, there's a certain consistency in the probability that he will end by being once more swallowed up in it. Before pollution claims him too, HEATH jots a few swift notes.

*"Trip round the bay, sir?"*

ALL THINGS BRIGHT
AND BEAUTIFUL
ALL CREATURES
GREAT AND SMALL
ALL THINGS WISE
AND WONDERFUL
THE LORD GOD
MADE THEM
ALL ♪♪♪

"*Come on in—the pollution is at a tolerable level.*"

HEATH

# AFTER THE BREATHALYSER

In common with every other motorist,
**CHIC JACOB** asks:
Where will it end?

*"Can I see your marriage lines, sir?"*

## THE WEIGHT RATIO TEST

*"You're about two badges and a sticker overweight for the engine capacity, sir."*

## THE PSYCHOANALYSER TEST
### —On-the-spot motorway-madness checks

## THE STATUTORY STATUS TEST

*"You don't appear to have a sufficient level of credit in your account to maintain a car in this servicing bracket, sir."*

## THE LONG ARM OF THE LAW TEST
### —To check rider/machine compatibility

*"I think we could pacify them if we could persuade our members to cook and eat the fox afterwards."*

# Farewell, My Ugly

## By STANLEY REYNOLDS

Staying overnight in London the other week with a redheaded actress who is one of my oldest and dearest of just good friends, I awoke in the morning, clamped a black Burma cheroot between my yellowed teeth and walked around her flat scratching the hair on my chest and looking for some place to spit. Handsome is, as they say, as handsome does. Anyway, the wandering brought me past the flat's bedroom where, after falling to my knees and peering through the keyhole, I could not help but see upon the beige satin pillow slip there lay two tousled heads.

"By Sister George," I muttered, "*Les Biches.*" But then I noticed that one of the little faces under flowing locks was badly in need of a shave. "Nancy boy," I chuckled before being reminded by the ache in the region of my fourth lumbar, just who it was

who had spent the night on a Victorian chaise longue obviously designed for a Victorian midget. Chaise it might have been, but longue it wasn't.

But that is neither here nor there. The point is, had it not been for the tell-tale shadow on his delicately etched jowls the young punk in there looked just like a girl; in fact, of the two heads floating on the downy pillows, his curls were the tousleder. This, of course, is hardly news. The Beatles have even written a new song about it with the terrifying line, *Have you seen Polythene Pam, She's so good looking she looks like a man.*

From looking like girls, the boys now have managed somehow to get better looking than them. Ordinarily, I must stress, it does not bother me. Ordinarily one merely passes these Aubrey Beardsley-looking youths, puffing out one's tremendous chest, squaring the

*"Poor fools! You seem to forget, I have the law on my side!"*

shoulders, jutting the jaw, narrowing the killer-male eyes, and one giggles over their ridiculously girlish waspy waists.

"Eeee by gum," one thinks (at least I always start thinking in a coal mining area accent when my manliness is in question), "if yon lass got shut of Wee Willie Winkie there and got in t' front parlour wi' me she'd know summat."

Actually what she'd know was that, when that bulging chest is standing at ease, it is a waist line and that I wear choo choo train print underwear given to me every birthday by a wife who knows what she's doing. As Malcolm Muggeridge, or was it the actress talking to the bishop, once said, "Some are born to chastity and some have it thrust upon them."

Be that as it may, one of the sad by-products of living in an age of youth and pretty young boys is that we men begin to court our own ugliness as a defence mechanism. Frightened by the pretty young things the imaginative man snarls back and tries to get himself looking like Lon Chaney Junior under a full moon.

I hasten to add here that I am not really ugly. Not the sort of ugly at least that you have to make an excuse and leave the room in the face of, like a *People* reporter fleeing from sin. No, if the truth were known, I am devilishly handsome, especially in the dusk with the light behind me and could at one time pull my eyebrows up into an inverted V like Peter Lawford.

But just like everybody else, I am walking around these days growing and shaving and growing and

shaving again, all manner of beards, sideburns, mutton chops, and natty little or big droopy moustaches. It is a time of extraordinary looks. People would rather look extraordinarily ugly than just plain. Normal looking people have taken to disguising themselves, so much so that it is a wonder anyone recognises anyone else any more.

This is, I think, what this whole skinhead business is about. It is an appearance backlash. A desperate fight against the uncommon number of girlishly pretty boys. In this backlash I am merely a sort of thirty-four-year-old skinhead who has grown a lot of hair in order to look ugly just as the real teenage skinheads have their heads cropped in order to look pugnacious and plug ugly. But being ugly is a difficult job. One is fighting the whole damned new and expanding male cosmetics industry and barbers who think of themselves as artists. "Listen," I told my man when I went into the barber shop asking him to give me an old-fashioned short back and sides, "I want this haircut to be a Tribute to Burt Lancaster. I'm an old movie fan, watch them all the time on TV." "On you," he said, "it'll come out like Jerry Lewis."

And it is not merely a question of appearance. Added to appearance is the role the appearance forces you to play. You have to do things like smoke stogies first thing in the morning and relish nasty dishes to go with your nasty looks. One shoves into the background the New England upbringing, the private schools, the cameos of tortured sensibility that one pens in the early hours. At a dinner party where you have been placed next to the lady novelist whose soul you have appreciated for years and whose every dear little semi-colon and comma has stirred your heart, you suddenly start explaining to her how to butt people with your head and how you sure miss not being able to get rattlesnake fritters here in England. One wonders, did Frank Harris—who was invited to all the best houses but only, as Oscar Wilde said, once—did he feel the same? Was he a tortured aesthete who could not reconcile himself to his hairy jug ears and turned himself into a hairy ape at every possible occasion just to spite those ears?

It is a mystery and one despairs over the psychological implications involved in twisting one's personality around to fit the ugly look, and quite rightly. But rising in the morning there before you is the redhead's other non-paying guest, the dolly dolly boy who has obviously *not* been sleeping on the chaise longue. Pride . . . indeed, one's very tap root of manhood demands that you puff on that damned stogie and ask if there is such a thing as a piece of thick seamed tripe in the house, all the time praying that there is nothing more hearty than raspberry flavoured yogurt.

"No, mate," the kid said in the whinnying tones

**Two pages containing games for two to forty-two players, ideas for serious discussions or family quarrels, and enough paper to make a very small party hat**

✳✳✳✳✳✳✳✳✳✳✳✳✳✳✳✳✳✳✳✳✳✳✳✳✳✳✳✳✳✳✳✳✳✳✳✳✳✳✳✳✳

## DO-IT-YOURSELF NATIONAL THEATRE

Write a short piece of dialogue based on the above tense situation, without involving anything remotely tasteless, as if it were one of the following:
(a) A rather doubtful all-male supper party debating where to move on to.
(b) The first editorial conference of the new *Sun*.
(c) A new trattoria inhabited entirely by wine- and food-writers.
(d) A *Panorama* discussion on: "What will the Battle of Hastings mean to Britain in 1067?"

✣✣✣✣✣✣✣✣✣✣✣✣✣✣✣✣✣✣✣✣✣✣✣✣✣✣✣✣✣✣✣

## MULL, EGG AND MUCK

New ideas for spicy, warming Christmas drinks are desperately needed by impoverished wine-writers everywhere. Specify the ingredients and methods for the following names:
(a) Royal Scottish Purple Brose à la Clement Freud.
(b) Ten Men's Hunting Cup.
(c) Dr. Johnson's Three Day Wassail.
(d) Borage-Gone-Mad.
(e) Mulled spiced braced laced fixed Blackjack, with seltzer.
(f) Pride of the Pyrenees.
(g) Braffle.

✣✣✣✣✣✣✣✣✣✣✣✣✣✣✣✣✣✣✣✣✣✣✣✣✣✣✣✣✣✣✣

## BOXING DAY FOOTBALL

Clear the room for action, divide into two teams and use as many balloons as possible. Score one point for a goal, two points for a show of petulance, three for accidental hands, four for charging the goal-keeper unfairly and so on up to fifteen points for being disowned by one's team-mates. A special bonus of ten points for managing to burst a balloon when the opposition has only the goalkeeper to beat.

## NO, NO—YOU'RE WELCOME TO MY SHOW

Everyone takes the part of a well-known guest star—Sacha Distel, Manitas de Plata, Lionel Blair, Kenny Ball's Jazzmen, etc.—and tries to imagine how he would behave if he were actually given his own show. The ten most convincing go through to the grand finale, where they all try to upstage each other.

✣✣✣✣✣✣✣✣✣✣✣✣✣✣✣✣✣✣✣✣✣✣✣✣✣✣✣✣✣✣✣

## MAKING UP YOUR OWN CHRISTMAS GAMES

Make up your own Christmas games.

✣✣✣✣✣✣✣✣✣✣✣✣✣✣✣✣✣✣✣✣✣✣✣✣✣✣✣✣✣✣✣

## FASHION SHOW

Dressing up with a difference. Dip into the family's old clothes, weird hats, forgotten sports items and so on, and each explain in turn why one's own get-up *must* be the fashion trend of 1970.

✣✣✣✣✣✣✣✣✣✣✣✣✣✣✣✣✣✣✣✣✣✣✣✣✣✣✣✣✣✣✣

## DO-IT-YOURSELF ADVERTISEMENTS

Write an enthralling slogan for the above masterpiece, using it as an endorsement for:
(a) paper handkerchieves.
(b) the maxi bath-towel.
(c) Inter-City Rail.
(d) The Labour Party.

of a gamin of a cockney gutter, "but we got gorgeous kippers, haven't we?"

Right away I could tell I was going to have trouble. This kid had a natural crude streak that would make Rasputin baulk. I gave him my meanest I've-knocked-all-over-the-world-kid look but he just sat there sucking his teeth. And talk about table manners. This kid would make Charles Laughton in Henry VIII look like your Aunt Bertha wrestling with a cream cake at Brown's Hotel. I could have rubbed down with yak grease and he wouldn't have batted one of those long girlish eye lashes. I was afraid of tossing in a few remarks about putting in the head and boot in street fights because I knew in my bones that this kid had cut his teeth snatching old ladies' handbags. Still, I was going actually to get sick to my stomach and give the whole ugly tough guy game away if I sat there any longer listening to him eat kippers.

"Say, Lorna," I said to the redheaded actress, looking at my watch, "I've got to get to work" and just then out of the corner of my eye I saw a hint of chartreuse discolouring the kid's otherwise unblemished cheek. "Well," I said, loading my voice with doom, "you know how it is. Married with a *wife* and *kids*, a man has got to get out to *work*" and then I piled it on, throwing in a few extra kids and some horrible stuff about pensions and mortgages, watching the kid get sadder and sadder looking until he finally pushed his plate away and mumbled something about having to lie down. I got up then and threw him the old nine to five commuter's wave and strolled out.

Of course now I had the whole morning to kill but I popped into a real barber-shop, one of those old time places with a bad tempered grouchy old barber shuffling around in a stained apron, and I got the beaver removed and one of those real wage-slave nondescript haircuts. Then I put on the old tortoise-shell eyeglasses, the kind people used to wear when they only wanted to see better and I passed the time until lunch looking purposeful and scaring the hell out of two hippies in Piccadilly Circus just by walking fast.

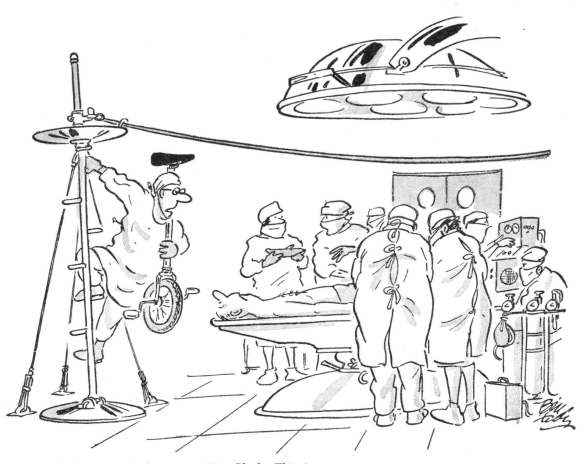

"*I won't hide the truth from you, Mr. Clark. This is going to be an incredibly difficult operation.*"

✳✳✳✳✳✳✳✳✳✳✳✳✳✳✳✳✳✳✳✳✳✳✳✳✳✳✳✳✳✳✳✳✳✳✳✳✳✳✳✳✳

# CHRISTMAS GAMES

\* \* \* \* \* \* \* \* \* \* \* \* \* \* \* \* \* \* \* \* \* \* \* \* \* \* \* \* \* \* \* \* \* \* \* \* \* \*

## OLD CHRISTMAS SAYINGS

Members of the family should count one point for each time they hear one of the following sentences on Christmas Day:
(a) "It wouldn't do any harm to look at the *Radio Times* and just see if there's anything good on."
(b) "The shop said they would exchange it if it's not quite right."
(c) "How do I carve this bit?"
(d) "Young . . . . . . has opened all his/her presents and wants to open yours now."
(e) "This cracker hasn't got anything in it."
(f) "We can't start till . . . is here."
(g) "Make sure she gets a piece with a sixpenny bit in it."
(h) "I have a funny feeling I know what this present is."
(i) "Well, it was alight when I set out from the kitchen."
(j) "I want to thank uncle for his card—can you remember which one it was?"
(k) "Isn't it nice without the papers."

## DO-IT-YOURSELF OLD MOVIES

After everyone has chosen a character from the above picture for himself, form the tableau with painstaking care, then carry on improvising from there. Anyone not catered for can burst in as Bing Crosby, Errol Flynn, Lassie, etc. The winner is the first one to prove convincingly that the discus-thrower is *either* the heroine's father suffering from loss of memory as a result of the Wall Street Crash *or* a real discus-thrower reduced to art-school work by the machinations of an international gang of art thieves.

## DISGUSTED OF EALING

Write letters of protest to the editor of *The Times* about the disappearance of the inch *or* of the real napkin *or* of loopholes in the breathalyser law, from one of these:
(a) Lady Mary Cavaunt, the Dowager's House, Fiske-on-Water
(b) Name and address supplied, Lundy.
(c) Lt.-Col. Wince, c/o Lady Mary Cavaunt, the Dowager's House, Fiske-on-Water.
(d) Shocked of Lundy.
(e) Kingsley Amis, Bernard Levin, A. J. P. Taylor, Norman St. John Stevas, Christopher Booker, Mick Jagger, c/o Lady Mary Cavaunt, the Dowager's House, Fiske-on-Water.
(f) Emigrating of Lundy.

## CLEAN UP BRITAIN'S CHRISTMAS

None of the traditional Yule trimmings has received anything like the critical publicity given to fireworks at Guy Fawkes's time. Each contestant should deliver a fierce attack on the misery caused annually by holly accidents, the moral outrages committed in the name of mistletoe, etc., with extra marks for impromptu TV documentaries or mimed *Times* leaders.

## CHARADES FOR THE 'SEVENTIES

Small groups of players leave the room, decide on a certain political development of the 'seventies and return to represent it in dumb show until someone guesses what it is. Suggestions are:
(a) President Nixon in 1972 explaining that the war in Vietnam is henceforth to be known as the Vietnamese Disengagement.
(b) The Two Day War of 1974.
(c) General Franco returning from retirement in 1976 to save Spain.
(d) Britain's exports showing a partial improvement in June 1978.

## GRANDAD ADDRESSES THE COMMONWEALTH

With nothing to do at 3 pm this Christmas, why not organise a competition to discover budding speech-writers in the family? All that is required is a one-minute oration that makes everyone feel warm, looks back at the past year with pride but not smugness, takes a look at the future with confidence but not blindness, suggests that all other broadcasts are somehow not quite so authentic, makes it plain that the orator has just torn himself away from a family Christmas to make the speech, simultaneously that the whole thing has been recorded weeks in advance and ends up by leaving the impression it has all been heard before. The winner is the participant of whose speech the audience can remember least.

\* \* \* \* \* \* \* \* \* \* \* \* \* \* \* \* \* \* \* \* \* \* \* \* \* \* \* \* \* \* \* \* \* \* \* \* \* \*

# There's Nothing like a Good Old Punch Up

By JOHN TAYLOR

Recourse to the violence of a vulgar brawl to establish the sophistry of an opponent's argument, as I always point out to men bigger than me, is utterly illogical. But, as I always point out to men smaller than me, it is sometimes the only way.

In consequence, I have received fat lips from more men than you can shake a stick at. Indeed, any time I dare to shake a stick at somebody new, up he comes and gives me another fat lip.

The ups and downs of my life of violence inevitably result in my collecting another of the downs, and it began in schooldays when being a larger and fatter than normal boy I was invariably categorised in weight classifications among older fellows for boxing tournaments.

Armed with the useful couple of years extra experience which more than balanced my unwary bulk, they all punched hell out of me—moulding me into the trembling psychological ninny you see before you; an easy target for any hoodlum aching to flex his muscles.

Over the years, nature's compensation urges one to sharpen one's wit as an alternative weapon—but it is no real road to peace. One simply incenses more people; and it is indicative of my dilemma that at the opening of the Adelaide Room Restaurant in Jermyn Street, in the autumn of 1957, the late Gilbert Harding suddenly flailed at me with furious fists because *I* had been rude to *him*. I suppose it constitutes some kind of a record.

Gilbert sent me flowers next morning by way of apology and in light of certain of his foibles the delivery was rather more embarrassing to me than the brawl; but it serves to establish with you that even he felt the blame to be not entirely mine.

What gives me more anxiety than my susceptibility to attack by itinerant toughies, though, is the growing tendency among women to arm themselves with esoteric forms of self defence. More and more, what you had intended as an assignation of nothing but love devolves into a clear physical manifestation of the war of the sexes.

If the blame is to be laid at any door, the expertise of a cavalcade of heroines in *The Avengers* comes most readily to mind. Not very long ago, the only defence a woman could muster against a man stronger than herself was strategic rather than tactical. Around their bush telegraph went the message that a man was NSIT (Not Safe In Taxis), NSOD (Not Safe On Doorsteps), NSA (Not Safe Anywhere), or H (Help!). Diminutive ladies unprepared for a struggle simply refused the date.

At least a man knew where he stood. Nowadays he cannot even be sure where

he will be lying. Too often as one is attempting to obtain one's return for the considerable expense of a couple of tickets for *Hair*, dinner at The Tiberio and a taxi to Tooting, one is as like as not to discover oneself flat on one's back on her crazy paving while she puts the kinky boot in.

There is small consolation to your pride in the fact that she has a black belt. Her belt is clearly the last thing you're likely to see. Soon it begins to occur that it may be better to cut your losses and start going out with the fellers.

Where the example of Honor Blackman has done so much harm is in its unspoken suggestion that, with training, any woman is the equal of any man. There may still be only a minority capable of applying a Flying Mare, but the general trend towards increased female belligerence needs a male primer on coping with women who are beginning to cope.

Properly considered, a woman has a variety of defensive accessories which can be brought into action at a moment's notice—and in view of the fact it is not generally realised why the wine waiter always brings the gentleman diner his cork after he has opened the bottle at dinner. Later that evening you can thank Heaven for its efficacy as you swiftly and adroitly place it in the *en garde* position as mademoiselle lunges with her hat pin.

Indeed, many protective ploys are simply a matter of previous planning. It is always wise, for example, to surreptitiously slide open the catch of the lady's handbag before embarking in the taxi for the journey home. When she raises it to belabour you, she will not only be thoroughly unsettled by its contents deluging about her ears, she will be incapable of attacking you as she scrabbles about on the pavement for the motley grotto of rubbish without which she goes nowhere.

A traditional trick of the girl who wishes to resist a pass is to start laughing. Mothers have advised this for centuries in the belief that a normal man's arrogance simply cannot stand the thought of himself as a figure of fun and will urge him to quit the field.

If her eyes aren't laughing, then all you have to do is simulate a hearty guffaw or two on your own behalf, and assure her that there is nothing you so much admire as a girl with a sense of humour. "Isn't this fun?" say.

More positive females require more positive methods, of course. A perennial two-day beard stubble will not prevent a face-slapper in the first place, but it can badly scratch her hands—and very easily dealt with is the television addict led to believe you can easily render a man helpless through the simple method of sliding his jacket back over his shoulders and pinioning his arms inside his own sleeves.

The answer to this last method is found in the judo philosophy which uses strength against itself. Don't fight back. Go along with her and continue the movement until the jacket is entirely discarded. Say "Darrrrrling—this is madness; but who are we to fight it? . . ." Then resolutely follow up her primary ploy by rapidly climbing out of your shirt and trousers.

I suppose the only defensive mechanism against which I can offer no advice whatsoever is the Biter Bit. The hell cat who surrenders far enough to allow you to get your lips close, and then sinks her teeth into them, is carrying what I have always regarded in the light of competitive enterprise into the realm of blood sports. I can think of no counter.

In my own defence, this may well be because it is a problem of which I have absolutely no experience. By the time I am able to persuade a woman to go out with me, her teeth have long gone already.

# Let us now Phone Famous Men

Just how accessible are the men who jockey our destiny? Has the telephone really shrunk the world to the point where anyone can speak to anyone? Where was the Pope at 10 am last Tuesday? ALAN COREN, just back from dialling the great, reports.

A child's game, at root, like all good things. After all, could anything match that first fine discovery of the telephone and all it stood for? That first realisation that, contained within ten simple digits, lay the infinitely possible? Out there—the information seeped into the infant brain in all its diabolical clarity  lay six billion ears, all the people in the world, available for contact and mystery and insult, unable to resist the beckoning of one small and villainous forefinger. We used, my tiny evil friends and I, to congregate at the nearest parentless house, and dial into the void, and innocent mouths would answer, and gullible ears would wait. Ah, to be only eight and wield such limitless power over adults! To fell a vicar with a practised oath, to turn bass breathing on a solitary spinster, to order fourteen tons of coal from Rickett Cockerell and have it delivered to the schoolmaster of one's choice—what could match this for delirious joy? Only the pièce de résistance of scouring the phone-book for a citizen called Dumm or Barmie and phoning him to enquire if he was. What nights we spent in illicit spinnings of the dial, tottering helplessly about our living-rooms, gasping at our own wit and ingenuity and smashing our milk-teeth on the fender in the thrashing throes brought on by such hilarity!

I wonder, sometimes, if the men who were boys when I was a boy still do it. It's not a question you can ask of bald, august solicitors, of doctors nursing kids and mortgages, of paunched executives: but do they, a quarter of a century on, creep down, perhaps, at 4 am and ring their enemies to offer six free foxtrot lessons, or scream indecencies at subscribers doomed to names like Bott and Hoare?

*"I see it's Christmas again."*

HARGREAVES

84

I thought of them last week, those tiny swine who helped mis-spend my youth. Because it suddenly occurred to me to crank the whole game up to a more sophisticated notch: perhaps it was the opening of dialling to New York, perhaps it was the acreage of puerile posters by which the Post Office whips us on to take advantage of their miracle offers, but, whatever the spur, I decided to spend the day trying to telephone the leaders of the world. Why not? After all, they had ears like anyone else, they had desks with phones on, they were put in power, more or less, by insignificant souls like me; surely they could set aside a few seconds for a chat, an exchange of gossip, an acknowledgement that the silent majority had a right, occasionally, to speak?

So I phoned Mao Tse-Tung.

"Who?" said the girl on 108 (International Directory Enquiries).

"He's the Chairman of the Chinese People's Republic," I said. "It's probably a Peking number."

There was a long silence. I could see her there, repolishing an immaculate nail, shoving a wayward curl back beneath her head-set, sucking a Polo, wondering whether she would go on the pill.

"I'll get the Supervisor," she said, finally.

"Nobody ever phones China," said the Supervisor.

"Why not?"

"I don't know," she said. Her voice was diamantine. "I only know why people phone places, I don't know why they don't, do I?"

Ruined by syntax, I pled help.

"You could phone the Chinese Chargé d'Affaires in London," she said. "The number is 580 7509."

580 7509 yielded a high-pitched moan. My Chinese may be less than flawless, but even I could tell that no human larynx was involved.

I phoned the Operator.

Who phoned the Engineer.

Whose Supervisor phoned me.

"It's NU," he said. For a moment, I felt excitingly privy to some piece of inside dope about Post Office/Chinese Legation affairs: clearly, from the man's weary voice, it was old Enn-Yu up to his tricks again, Enn-Yu the phone-bugger (I don't mean that the way it looks), the tamperer, the Red Guard saboteur; Enn-Yu, the man who had plagued the GPO for years with his intercepted calls and weird Oriental devices fitted out in the Legation basement.

"Who's Enn-Yu?" I said.

"Not In Use," he said, and a small world crashed. "They're always switching their lines down there. Every six weeks, they want a new phone number. Hang on," he said, and voices muttered in the background, and far bells rang. He came back. "It's 636 9756 this week," he said.

"Harro!" shouted a voice at 636 9756.

"Hallo," I said. "I want to know how I can telephone China."

"Why?"

"I want to speak to Chairman Mao."

"Why?"

"I have a personal message to deliver."

Breathing. Whispering. A new, more senior voice.

"Not possible terrephone China!" it shrieked. "Not possible terrephone Chairman! What you want?"

I explained again. It turned out that there were no lines between England and China. Nobody ever telephoned China. Nobody *would* ever telephone China.

"How do *you* speak to China?" I asked.

A third voice came on.

"GET OFF RINE!" it screamed. "GET OFF RINE QUICK NOW!"

And rang off. The whole thing had taken forty-seven minutes. More than enough time for thermonuclear gee-gaws to have wiped both Asia and Europe off the map. I knew Harold didn't have a hot line to Mao, and it bothered me.

I dialled again.

"Yes?" said 108.

"I'd like," I said, "to speak to Mr. Kosygin."

She muffed the phone inadequately.

"I think it's him again," I heard, distant and woolly. There was giggling. I waited. The Supervisor came on.

"Are you," she said, and the syllables fell like needles, "the gentleman who just wanted to speak to Mao Tse-Tung?"

"Yes," I said.

I sympathised. She had, I knew, a vision of this

solitary loony who had let himself loose on the telephonic world, prior, no doubt, to rape or suicide. I wondered if they were playing for time with their long, reflective pauses, trying to trace the call, trying to dispatch a van-load of GPO male nurses to my gate. But all she said was:

"Russian Inquiries are on 104."

"Have you got his address and phone number?" said 104.

"No," I said, "I thought you'd have it."

"They never send us directories," she said. "It's only them and the Rumanians that don't. Everyone else sends us their directories."

"Then how do you phone Russians?"

"You have to have their number. We keep," she grew confidential, "a list of hotels and factories, a few things like that. We're not supposed to, but we do. I've got the Kremlin number. Do you think that would do?"

"Yes, that sounds very good."

"There's an hour's delay to Moscow. I'll get them to ring you back, and he might come to the phone. That'd be nice, wouldn't it?"

"That would be very nice," I said. "In the mean-

time, as you're European Directory, could you g[et] the Pope for me?"

"Oooh, you are *awful*!" she shrieked. Her voic[e] faded, and I could just catch it explaining the situa[?]tion to the other girls. Time passed. She came bac[k].

"You're not going to say nothing dirty to them are you?" she said. "Excuse me for asking, but w[?] have to."

I reassured her.

"I'll have to keep your number by me," she sai[d] "in case there's complaints, you know, afterward[s] like. No offence meant, but you'd be surprised ho[w] many people ring up foreigners and swear at them.

I agreed, wondering who. Insights were burstin[g] in on every hand. It clearly wasn't all beer an[d] skittles, being a world leader, trying to keep up t[he] balance of payments and build new schools and ho[ld] back the opposition, with Englishmen phoning yo[u] up all hours of the day and night, shouting "Eff off!

She gave me the Pope's residential number. [I] dialled direct, 01039 6 6982. It was engaged. Od[d.] Was he, perhaps, on The Other Line? Or just on th[e] balcony, waving? I tried again, trembling slight[ly] at his proximity—five hundred million subjects und[er] his thumb, and that thumb about to curl over th[e] receiver in response to a far, agnostic call.

"Allo."

"Your Holiness?"

Pause.

"Wod?"

"Am I speaking to the Pope? *Il Papa?*"

Scuffing.

"Allo, allo. Can I 'elp you?"

"May I speak to the Pope?"

A long, soft sigh, one of those very Italian sighs th[at] express so much, that say *Ah, signor, if only this wor[ld]* *were an ideal world, what would I not give to be able to [do]* *as you ask, we should sit together in the Tuscan sunshi[ne]* *you and I, just two men together, and we should drink [a]* *bottle of the good red wine, and we should sing, ah, how [we]* *should sing, but God in His infinite wisdom has, al[as,]* *not seen fit to . . .*

"Can the Pope," I said, determined, "come [to] the phone?"

"The Bobe never gum to the delephone, signo[r.] Nod for you, nod for me, nod for Italians, nod f[or]

*"He wants you to chase him"*

ROY DAVIS

nobody. Is not bozzible, many regrets, 'Is 'Oliness never spig on delephone. You give me your name, I give mezzage to 'Is 'Oliness, 'e give you blezzing, okay?"

"Okay," I said. A blessing, albeit proxied, was something.

"Don menshnit," he said, kindly, and clicked off.

By great good fortune (or even the grace of God: who knows how quickly a Pope's blessing might work?), there was a different operator on 108 when I tried to reach Richard Nixon. He put me on to 107, who got me the White House in three minutes flat, which gave tricky Dicky a thick edge over Mao, Kosygin and Il Papa when it came to accessibility. I thought you'd like to know that, Dick, since I didn't get the chance to tell you myself. Accessibility, as Harry Truman might have said, stops here. Or almost here. The lady secretary at the White House was extremely kind, incredibly helpful and understanding; doubtless because, given American's readiness to empty magazines at those in power, you can't be too careful with nuts who phone up to speak to the President. Fob them off with a "Get lost!" one minute, and the next they're crouched on a nearby roof and pumping away with a mail-order Winchester. The President, she said, was down in Florida, at Key Biscayne, where his number was 305 358 2380; someone there would speak to me. They did, and they were just as syrupy and sympathetic, and who knows but that I mightn't have got into the Great Ear if I hadn't played one card utterly wrong? What happened was, the call from the Kremlin, booked, you'll remember, an hour before, suddenly came through on my other phone, and I was mug enough, drunk with bogus eminence, to say to the American voice:

"Sorry, can you hold on a sec, I've got Kosygin on the other line?"

It was a nice moment, of course, but that's as long as it lasted. America hung up. Tread carefully when you step among the great, friends, their corns are sensitive.

I rather liked the Kremlin.

"Is that Mister Coren?" they said.

It's no small thrill to think one's name has echoed down the corridors of Soviet power, from room to room, while nervous men, fearful of the punishment that follows bureaucratic cock-ups, have tried to find out who one is, and what one wants with the Prime Minister. After all, so much is secret, so much unknown. I might have been anybody, even the sort of Anybody whose whisper in a top ear could send whole switchboardsful of comrades to the stake. Who was this Coren, this cool, curt international voice who seemed to be on such good terms with Alexi N. Kosygin that he thought nothing of phoning him person-to-person? For men who remembered Lavrenti Beria, no kindness to strangers was too much. Which is no doubt why I actually got to Kosygin's private secretary, who was himself extremely civil.

"I merely want to present the Prime Minister with my good wishes," I told him.

He was heartbroken that the Prime Minister was inextricably involved at present, but swore to me that my message would be passed on immediately. And I have not the slightest doubt that it was. It's a long way to Siberia, after all, and the cattle-trains leave every hour, on the hour.

Which left me with just two numbers in my little black book: Havana 305 031 and Cairo 768944. It took me a day to get through to one, and three days to reach the other (all calls to Egypt are subject to censorship), and when I finally did make contact, Fidel and Gamel were, needless to say, busy elsewhere. Both, however, promised faithfully to ring me back, which is why I leave them till last. Courtesy I like. Not, though, that they actually *have* rung back, but who knows? Even now, the dark, dependable forefingers may be poised over their respective dials, groping along the cables for a chance to chew the fat and swop a joke or two. If not, and if they read this first, don't worry about it, lads. It's nothing urgent

I just wanted to say hello.

# Absolutely Everything There is to Know About the Afghan Hound

## By FRANK MUIR

Afghan hounds are so called because they are hounds and come from Afghanistan. At least, they are supposed to. Mine came from just outside Chelmsford but you'd never know.

They are large dogs when observed talking to, or niffing, one of the smaller breeds like the Pekinese but not as large as the really large dogs like the Irish wolfhound. Female Afghans are slightly smaller than the male and stand about three feet high which they don't do very often as they much prefer lying down or dashing about. When prone on the floor, having a stretch, they measure about fourteen feet long by three inches wide, with curly edges.

The Afghan hound is an achingly beautiful piece of nature to look at, for all the world like a greyhound in a fun-fur. The coat is very woolly and long to protect the occupier from claw wounds when hunting snow-leopard in Kabul, or Chelmsford, and is some two sizes too large. This means that when the dog breaks into a run its skeleton has accelerated quite a few inches before the coat starts on its way. This accounts

for the beautiful rippling waves on the fur of an Afghan on the move.

My specimen is female and eighteen months old. I named her Casanis, for sentimental reasons, after a Corsican drink compounded of aniseed balls steeped in equal parts of meths and marine varnish. She is mainly golden in colour, the non-golden parts being her tummy and her face. Her tummy is a subtle off-white, not unlike pineapple yoghurt. At some inquisitive period of her infancy she seems to have lowered her long, graceful nose into a vat of black dye, the ends of her ears just dipping in also, as they still do when she investigates wet paint or drinks from the loo. Her eyes are a soft, metallic gold colour only found elsewhere in a partially sucked Olde Englishe Humbugge.

House-training an Afghan is as simple as training a normal dog; it just takes longer. For the first month or two that she was our guest, Casa's score averaged out at fifteen pools inside to one outside. At puberty this fined down to about three to one, and the line on the graph is levelling out encouragingly. I don't think I am being over-optimistic when I say that I believe she will be bone dry by the time she is ten.

One of the difficulties in any sort of training is that these dogs are shy, sensitive creatures who react to any harsh word, or admonitory action, by expressing themselves. You only have to tap an Afghan puppy lightly on the nose, or upend it, and it behaves like a fire-extinguisher, releasing a steady flow of about a gallon and a half, sufficient to extinguish most medium-size domestic blazes.

If you intend to own an Afghan start by taking up all the carpets on the ground-floor. Then go to your nearest builder's sundriesman and order a sheet of stout polythene the same size as the ground-floor. Also order six cubic yards of sharp sand. I think blunt sand would do just as well but ordering sharp sand makes you sound knowledgeable, i.e., undiddlable. Tip a wheelbarrowful of the sand in the corner of the room furthest from the back door, smoothing it out until it is about a foot thick. Carry on until the whole floor is covered with sand. Then scrape away the surface until the sand slopes gently towards the door. Saw the bottom off the door an inch above sand level. Continue the process in all rooms until you reach the back door. Lay down your polythene sheet. Cut a flood-gate in the back door. You may now fetch your Afghan puppy, secure in the knowledge that your home is self-draining and will only need a weekly hose-down to keep it fresh and wholesome.

It will come as no great surprise that this ancient marque of hound, bred for centuries to leap up and down the Hindu Kush, is athletic. Casa can touch a speed of nearly thirty knots upon sighting (and removing herself from the presence of) an enemy, such as the dustman, or an unexpected piece of paper. She also practises levitation. By some Oriental alchemy of the mind she can achieve a vertical-off from a standing position, rise to a height of six feet and land on top of the privet hedge. There she will sit for hours, looking aristocratic and soignée, protecting the pass from leopards and dustman; occasionally getting up and parading the hedge, a difficult operation calling for a kind of straddling walk not unlike the gait of a wild-fowler struggling through estuary mud.

An Afghan needs brushing every day. Getting her up on the table need present no problem if you are gentle with her. When she sees the brush and goes rigid do not on any account fetch her one with the poker. Just croon an Indian love lyric and swiftly tape a castor to each of her paws. Then incline a plank against the table and push her up the slope. Do remember to put chocks under the castors before you start vigorous brushing or you will have her through the window.

It was in the presence of food that Casa first revealed to us what an aristocrat she was. While our two elderly poodles went through their disgraceful exhibition of rolling about, sneezing, doing hand-stands and giving impressions of each other in the hope of getting an off-cut from the roast beef, or at least a bit of the string, Casa just stood aloofly to one side, looking intently at a framed print of Cockspur Street. Then, when I stooped to toss a poodle a slice of burnt outside—whoosh! A golden flash and there was Casa, on top of the hedge, with the whole joint.

If you intend to own an Afghan it is essential to have all food above Afghan level. This means raising all the working surfaces in the kitchen to a height of six feet. Do as I did and nail twelve-inch blocks to your wife's gum-boots. She can then slip these on

*"The crowds don't make my mouth water now like they used to."*

89

*"Be reasonable, madam—we can't have one pedestrian occupying
enough space for six units of off-street parking."*

when preparing food. Quite a good idea is to sling the dining-room table from the ceiling on chains so that it is six feet above the polythene carpet. Our dining-room chairs are positioned on amusingly painted tea-chests which bring them up to a convenient height. The new look to our dining-room not only makes a conversation point for guests but has cured my wife of sliding her chair back from the table.

Apart from stolen food and her official rations Casa much enjoys eating boiled eggs, Brazil nuts, jig-saw puzzle pieces, sofas, any valuable book whose binding has been treated with British Museum Formula Leather Preservative, grapes, sand-paper. Which is interesting. One has always been led to believe that life was sustained on the North-West Frontier on a diet of curried goat and rancid yak's butter. Has our N-W Frontier literature been living a lie? In view of this new evidence of materials dear to an Afghan hound's heart, should stories read more like this?

"Akbar Khan smiled wolfishly as he reloaded his ancient jezail with a Brazil nut. Below him the remnants of the gallant 44th struggled through the snows of the dread Khyber Pass. 'Kill them!' he snarled through grape-stained teeth. 'Kill them all and there will be a feast tonight for all ghazis! There will be boiled eggs, curried sand-paper, jig-saw puzzles and as much British Museum Formula Leather Preservative as you can drink' . . . (etc.)"

And what of the famed Afghanistan Manual of Love, available in paper-back near every secondary modern school, "The Scented Pass?"

"If your lord and master is still off-hand and has his mind more on beer, then cause him to recline on a sofa and fan him with sand-paper. Whilst he lies bemused creep upon him and massage the back of his neck with a handful of British Museum Formula Leather Preservative, at the same time shoving a lightly boiled egg into his ear. As his breathing becomes laboured crack a Brazil nut between your . . . (etc.)"

You might well ask at this juncture what exactly is the point of acquiring an animal which is almost permanently incontinent, is a food thief, nervous, scruffy unless brushed daily, and a hedge-squatter. The answer must be that owning an Afghan is illogical and not to be encouraged.

But then one evening, as now, I will be alone in the room with her. And, as I type, she will settle herself gently on my left shoe and look up at me, her chin on my knee, those golden eyes wistful and wise and unfathomable. And suddenly a warm, friendly glow spreads through my whole being. Or, to be more accurate, spreads over my left ankle and suede shoe. And it is starting to go cold . . .

Casa is at it again.

# I Remember the Drawing but not the Caption

Some personal highlights of cartoon nostalgia
from WILLIAM HEWISON

UPPOSE a kid of seven can be nostalgic about the marvellous golden summers there were when he was a kid, but in the main this affliction hits hardest at those who are freewheeling down the vale of their later years; at the balding of the pate and the going of the mind, we will remember all. So if nostalgia is a sentimental longing for times past, I think the little thing below just about sums it up. It seems that somewhere along the line the nostalgia virus bites and thereafter the symptoms are plain to see: a bias towards the old and familiar and a fuss about anything new. Just reflect on the carry-on over the excellent 50p. Mr. Paul Crum, who did this cartoon in 1936, suggests through it that he would probably have liked that coin. Incidentally, his "signature" is that little rescue drawn on the plinth, and to complicate matters further, his real name is Roger Pettiward. A great original cartoonist, he bent pictorial humour into a new, zany direction—a goon before his time. Perhaps his most famous

drawing was of the hippo who kept thinking it was Tuesday; I testify that this is still going the rounds even today as an interminable shaggy-dog story.

As Art Editor I get the occasional letter, crabbed and wavery, from the reader who complains about present-day drawing, and who wheezes the praises of Charles Keene and Du Maurier. Keene, I agree, but Du Maurier, no. He is renowned for his women, or rather, woman. For he drew only one woman—chocolate-box, wooden, unreal. But to show I am not totally against, here below is a cartoon in which Du Maurier has a go at Unisex and the Maxi at the same time.                    [1891]

His main output was at the turn of the century, when fighting cockney spouses and drunken Irishmen were thought to be highly risible as subjects of fun. Below is an example of the genre. [1901]

Dooley: *"What's the matter wid ye anyhow, Mick—all tattered an' torrun an' bitten all over?"*
Mick: *"Ay, an' me own dog done it! I want home sober last noight, an' the baste didn't know me!"*

Taste, good and bad, seems to bother a lot of people when they look at cartoons; humour, they appear to say, does not cross all frontiers. When this drawing by Mathias was published in 1958, some readers were offended. The blind, they wrote, are not a subject for humour. Yet the Guide Dogs for the Blind Association were delighted with the cartoon, and I believe they still have the original.

*"Well, which is it, Sam—a lovely old vase or a hideous modern one?"*

*"Hullo, Gerty! You've got Fred's hat on, and his cover coat?"*

*"Yes, don't you like it?"*

*"Well — it makes you like a young man, and that's so effeminate!"*

Now, Phil May—here was someone who did draw real people, and multitudes of real people, in a spare, fluid line, the whole thing bursting with exuberance.

While we are still on about taste, I wonder what the Mathias objectors would make of this cartoon by G. L. Stampa. There is an underlying callousness shown here concerning the poor that is probably objectionable by today's standards. [1911]

Clergyman (*taking friend round poor parish*): "*Yes, a nervous little fellow. I remember his father was highly strung.*"
Woman: "*Ye remember wrong, then. 'E got orf wiv ten years!*"

Yet J. H. Dowd in 1931 can show the opposite side of the coin. Is this sweetly sentimental? Perhaps, but it strikes to the heart, nevertheless. I suppose to a lot of people this is an example of "good drawing." I would agree up to a point, but my definition also includes Quentin Blake and Steadman.

Hospital patient (*one of large family in poor district, given a glass of milk*): "*How far down can I drink?*"

92

Young cartoonists are burrowing ou between the cobblestones of Liverpoo and points north, still influenced by th early work of André François. Françoi moved on from cartooning into th higher reaches of graphics and fine ar some years ago, but he left behind notable collection of unforgettable draw ings. He certainly wasn't everybody' meat—test yourself on the example below.

"*Don't trouble. I've found it.*"

Some of you might have forgotten tha Gerald Scarfe, that master of th chopped intestine, once drew very funny cartoons e.g.:

"*Can he borrow the bike?*"

Another gag that has lingered long with me is one by Ronnie Searle, published in 1947. This is early Searle, but the idea is on a par with Crum's hippos.

"*Careful—that stung!*"

I have kept off political cartoons, but this one shouts for a place because it has a certain topical interest.     [1846]

## A CASE OF REAL DISTRESS

"Good people, pray take compassion upon us. It is now nearly seven years since we have either of us known the blessing of a comfortable residence. If you do not believe us, good people, come and see where we live, at Buckingham Palace, and you will be satisfied that there is no deception in our story. Such is our distress, that we should be truly grateful for the blessing of a comfortable two-pair back, with commonly decent sleeping-rooms for our children and domestics. With our slender means, and an increasing family, we declare to you that we do not know what to do. The sum of one hundred and fifty thousand pounds will be all that will be required to make the needful alterations in our dwelling. Do, good people, bestow your charity to this little amount, and may you never live to feel the want of so small a trifle."

I suppose it is time for a real oldie. This one by John Leech appeared in 1852, when most artists drew the happening and then explained it at length in the caption below. In this one Leech draws the happening *before* the happening, and credits his readers with some intelligence.

Contemplative man (*in punt*): "*I don't so much care about the sport, it's the delicious repose I enjoy so.*"

I mentioned Charles Keene earlier on; this example of his work (below) demonstrates two things—his strong gutsy drawing, and a Victorian middle-class attitude to workers who strike (probably not much different today). It also shows their liking for the dialect caption; this one must be a fairly rare attempt at 'Geordie'—the Durham miner epitomised the militant worker fighting for improvement.     [1889]

## THE LABOUR QUESTION
*Mechanic:* "HULLO, JEM, NOT AT WORK! WHAT'S UP?"
*Collier:* "OH, WE'RE OUT ON STRIKE."
*Mechanic:* "WHAT FOR, THEN?"
*Collier:* "AW DIVEN' KNAW, BUT WE'LL NOT GIVE IN TILL WE GET IT!"

Does anyone know who drew the first Desert Island joke? Or Psychiatrist's Couch joke? Or Trojan Horse joke? (Probably George Morrow, this last one.) These innovators must remain unknown and unsung, but to end on a personal note, I stake a claim on being the first with the Excalibur joke, though it wasn't a very good one.
A very early Hewison, shown below, is perhaps a bit better.     [1954]

"*Boy! What a party!*"

# Make Fat Not War

## By WILLIAM HARDCASTLE

*"Everywhere the same story, man— nothing but student unrest."*

I give you this slogan for the 'seventies. I will grant you that, though he couldn't see his jackboots except in the mirror, Herman Goering wasn't exactly what you would call cuddly. Sidney Greenstreet showed that girth and gruesomeness can be menacingly combined. Yet I am convinced that the world would be a better place if we all proceeded to unloosen our girdles and make these the non-slimming 'seventies. Let calories be unconfined.

I must declare, as they say, an interest. I have been chubby since an early age. I was known on the block as the boy with his shirt tail always hanging out; the shape of my bottom had some curious unsettling effect on my underwear. Since then I have never looked back. Over the years I have managed to tame my shirt tails, but otherwise I remain, as they say in the more polite men's shops, portly.

I have achieved this against constant and excessive brainwashing and propaganda. Another such exercise is being mounted at this moment. As regularly as Christmas trees shed their pine needles, the Dames of Fleet Street give up their space around this time of year to post-holiday slimming diets. They assume their readers have blown themselves up over the past few weeks and conceive it as their duty to help them deflate.

It isn't as if they ever had anything new to say. They just get out the old cuttings and switch things round a bit—two leaves of lettuce, instead of three of spinach, for Wednesday lunch, and so on. As if, to any intelligent person, such advice was necessary. Anybody knows how to get thin—you just stop eating and drinking. But *why*?

When Mae West said, "Come Up and See Me Sometime," one knew that, if one did go up, there would be plenty to see. I'm delighted to note that that splendid lady is operating to this day on the principle that you can't have enough of a good thing. By contrast the poor brain-washed modern girl's main aim is to become the nearest thing to a blood-drained corpse this side of the municipal mortuary. Her partner's desire is for his ribs to be seen pushing through his unisex blouse. This benighted couple are flying in the face not only of Miss Mae West but also of historical fact. This has established beyond peradventure that to be fat is to be content and jovial.

There are, as I have said, exceptions to this rule. Benito Mussolini and Nikita Khrushchev were both broad of beam but neither can be said to have been plumply endearing. But take Winston Churchill—never a man to neglect his mutton chops, his champagne or his brandy.

I am glad to see that both the main political leaders in Britain today have a tendency towards avoirdupois. Edward Heath may have been unloading ballast lately in pursuit of his East of Suez (or West of Tasmania) policy. But I can't help feeling that he shares a similar metabolism with Harold Wilson, and that both have a built-in leaning towards corpulence. Only poor Jeremy Thorpe maintains a fashionable cadaverousness, a fact which, I feel sure, bodes no good for the Liberals at the forthcoming elections.

The main argument against fatness, of course, is that it is bad for your health and leads to an early grave. You will get this information from doctors who, as any underwriter will tell you, are among the worst risks that ever gave the Man

"Have you got any caviar?"

from the Prudential a sleepless night. If you'd taken the doctors' advice a few years ago you would have laid off sugar and been swilling cyclamates day and night. Now where would you be? The fact is that in modern life there is danger in everything, and one of the dangers which, in my view, is not sufficiently stressed is that involved in dieting.

To summarise briefly, it can ruin your business career, destroy your marriage, and send your children cowering into a corner. This is because dieting makes you bad-tempered. It is the happily plump peddler who pulls off the big sale. The well-fed spouse keeps the home fires burning. It is the hungry father who snarls at his offspring. And I speak only of the domestic scene. On the wider stage it has been as often as not the haggard scarecrow-like statesman who has earned most of history's demerits. Rather than rush out and pick a fight, the portly politico is much more likely to put his feet up and doze a bit while matters simmer down.

In all charity I should say that incurably thin people deserve our sympathy. I once had the bright idea of running a get-fat diet in a paper I was editing and instructed a woman writer (I think, as a matter of fact, it was Olga Franklin) to map it out. We ran groaning menus every day for a fortnight, but the result was a total flop. As I say, getting thin is easy; you just put the stopper back on the light ale and confine your intake to small lean steaks and lettuce (with no olive oil in the dressing). But to get fat is a blessing that is forever denied to some.

There's a fellow in my office who you can practically see through. Every day he has three buttered buns for elevenses. Yet he still looks like an advanced case of kwashiorkor. To somebody like him, one's heart goes out. But that is no reason why Betty Banting of the *Sunday Excess* should try to get us all to look the same.

Aesthetic arguments are used in support of slimming, and truthfulness compels me to admit that the picture which appears weekly in Punch is fairly accurate. But Rubens wouldn't have picked me for a model, anyway. There were plenty

*"It's been a good life."*

twentieth century translations of this archaic non-war cry.

"The tape must roll."

"The film must be processed."

"The cameras must be manned."

"The lights must be set."

"The copyright must be cleared."

"Let the dog see the rabbit."

True, all true. How even the poorest of us hankers to be poorer still. To have the comfort of a cruel master, the refuge of someone else's decisions. The inherent indiscipline of show business *needs* the discipline of superstition, the myth of tradition, the protective freemasonry of "being a pro."

There is, of course, no such thing as a pro. But that, as the ancient mariner said, is another ship.

In the warm show-must-go-on fairyland galley, Judy Garland, the late lost Judy, must be forever the preserver of it in Hans amberson. "I was Born in a Trunk," said the song. Born in a trunk. The aching exclusivity of it. A thousand rotund Mrs. Worthingtons come to mind searching anxiously, and every moment more urgently, for trunks, as turtles for islands.

Alas, the facts are much more factual. No impresario cares, and—more hurtfully—no audience cares whether you were born in a trunk or a casket.

The show is hanging on a thread. Heartbreak. Heart attack. Comeback. Ingenue. Whatever the tightrope, the close-up is always on the wrong face. The trembling lip, the bead of sweat that matters are not in the spotlight. They're in the wings. Or round the corner at the back. They belong not to the brave actor but to the investing impresario. The message is simple.

"No play. No pay."

Aching though the face in the spotlight may be to play, it takes two to tango and a helluva lot more to get the music going. The audience owns its arrogance in shouting the show must go on and is entitled at the same time to its ignorance. This is the price you pay for magic.

The magic is only partly for the audience. Most of it is for the actors. They—desperately—even in this day of tape-measure talent, want the show to go on. Heaven help them, they would want it to go on even if *they* had to pay the audience. Don't take advantage of them. Don't humble them on hearsay. It's only an opinion.

The real drama. The real drama. The real climax. The real phrase—can only now be heard. The first night audience is as incidental as the actors. The investors, the angels are the ones. Scattered, and not only over the West End and the East End but far afield among the co-ops and the butchers' shops of the midlands and north, the clubs of the east, the off-course bookies, the widows and the widowers. Linked by two-way television, they can at last be heard even as the first night curtain falls. They can voice the new legend, the words someone else will have to explain in the 70's:

"The show must come off!"

Schnozzle has no answer to that one.

*"Should Britain join Europe? Why, is it falling apart?"*

# THE SHORTER THE BETTER

Samuel Beckett's new play lasts a mere thirty seconds, setting a trend without which we could never have presented seven complete new works on one page.

## BROADCASTING IN THE 'EIGHTIES

(i) Talks, music, drama, news and light entertainment will now all come under one department—Radio.

(ii) The experiment tried in 1979 of having as many as three or four programmes a week was not a complete success. Listeners generally could not remember when to switch on and as a result did not switch on at all. From now on there will be just one easily remembered programme, on Sundays, from 1 to 2 pm.

(iii) If listening figures fall much below thirty-four, it may prove necessary to make this programme entirely canned laughter.

(iv) Will the head of Radio please come and see me after lunch?

## DESMOND MORRIS
### The Tax-Paying Chimpanzee

However far man has come from the world of the primates, there is still one characteristic that marks him as unmistakably ape-like—his intense desire to hold on to what he has obtained. The gorilla with his piece of fruit; the baboon with his piece of fruit; the best-selling author with his gross profits. Sex, power, territory, all have their part to play, but they pale into insignificance beside the £80,000 I shall earn from this book. From close study

of myself I know that I would go to any lengths to keep that sum intact, even if it means avoiding the tax on books by stopping this dissertation at this point.

## THE DUKE OF WELLINGTON— volume ii
### by Lady Longford

Thomas Creevey relates how, shortly after the Battle of Waterloo, he encountered Wellington walking in Albemarle Street and stopped to talk with him.

"I greeted him and enquired how he intended to spend the years of peace he had fought so hard to obtain.

'Oh,' replied the Duke, 'I have half a fancy to enter Parliament and listen to the clashing of swords there.'"

Not ten years later he was Prime Minister of England. Was he, as some have claimed, less successful in the political field than on the battleground? Or, as nobody seems to have claimed, vice versa? Whatever the truth of the matter, not thirty years later he was dead, to be awarded a grand funeral at which Thomas Creevey, had he still been alive, would made some illuminating observations. But Creevey was dead, Wellington was dead and England was, from many points of view, a different place.

## IN THE CORNER
### a new novel by Kingsley Amis

Jerry Chadwick was good with women, in the sense that he could usually get them to do what he wanted. He was also bad with women, in the sense that he didn't particularly enjoy it any more and wished he was somewhere else. It wasn't that he didn't enjoy the simple things of life, like putting his feet up in taxis or re-designing the Union Jack, because he did. At least, he had done until he met Tulip Bentley, who threw his previously settled outlook on life into confusion and left him feeling bitter and unhappy in a small sort of way.

So it came as a welcome relief when Jerry fell off the pavement in front of the bus. Or rather, it would have done if the bus driver hadn't braked in time. Jerry just lay there, shouting: "Keep driving!" He felt so silly.

The End.

## THE BREAKFAST PARTY
### a new play by Harold Pinter

*Act I. The scene is a suburban dining room. Janet is pouring tea. William is reading the paper.*

**Janet:** One lump or two?

**William:** According to this morning's paper, at the bottom of the front page we all have to turn to page three.

**Janet:** Perhaps you prefer to call them cubes.

**William:** It's extraordinary. "Turn to page three." I've looked everywhere else in the paper but there's no other mention of it. Perhaps they're making it up.

*Act II. The Same.*

**Janet:** I knew a man once who took seven lumps. Seven!

**William:** What were you saying?

*Act III. The Same.*

**Janet:** He once kissed me between the third and fourth lump. But he didn't lose count.

**William:** There's a picture of daffodils on page four. I suppose they're daffodils. It's difficult to tell with the *Guardian*. I suppose it's the *Guardian*.

**Janet** (*suddenly screaming*): I've never told you what happened after the seventh lump!!

*(Silence. Curtain.)*

*A scene from the only sequence in Fellini's new film, 10⅔. It lasts seventy seconds, not counting credits and intermission, and sums up the entire range of Fellini's intellectual thought*

# Hail to Thee Pre-Militant Alma Mater

## By RALPH SCHOENSTEIN

The latest student revolt at Columbia University was a D minus demonstration: no really decent looting, not one relic nicely destroyed, and not one dean locked in his study. The poor young rebels of Students for a Democratic Society still have plenty of relics and deans, but they're running out of issues. Columbia's new president has been hitting below the belt and granting their demands.

"We just can't find a programme for mobilizing the campus," one SDS leader told me, retreating towards his homework. "You see, SDS has so much spirit that sometimes it runs a little ahead of the issues."

"Sort of anticipatory revolution," I said. "But do you plan any protests for things that have really *happened*?"

"Well," he said, "some professors are still doing secret research for the Pentagon."

"What a rotten business: freelancing national defence. Well, at least they're doing it for *our* side."

"... and then there was our collection
of Van Goghs, Utrillos, Renoirs ..."

"And the boys are also protesting Columbia's evictions from some of its buildings. People are being moved to make room for an old age home, a school and a lot of urban renewal."

"An old age home? A school? *And* urban renewal? How low can the Establishment get!"

I wished I could have lent this lad an issue or two from my own student days at Columbia. I went there in the early 'fifties, when the Battle of Morningside Heights still meant a clash with the sergeant-majors of King George III, not the English majors of Brooklyn and Queens; when Ho Chi Minh was an avuncular ally; and when SDS to me meant a struggle to win the heart of Sandra D. Schenck. In those pre-revolutionary days, we never had to invent campus issues because real ones were always at hand. None of us was checking to see if the physics teacher was doing secret work for the Boy Scouts or if the math teacher was drawing pentagons because we were much too busy with such crusades as the panty raid. There was some fierce combat in the spring of '52 when we stormed the gates of Barnard in a lust for lingerie; but we were no mere transvestites gone berserk, we were rugged young patriots hunting a little Yankee lace before going off to Korea.

In addition to the battle for ladies' underwear, there were other campus issues that kept the boys aroused. There was, for example, the ever burning question of whether or not grass should be planted in a big brown stretch of campus that was known as Van Am Quad. It was a horticultural hullabaloo, with the allergic leaning towards dirt and the lovers of Wordsworth yearning for a little lawn in the naked city. A few years after I left, the lawn finally came; but then Vietnam eclipsed Van Am and grass became something that students started to smoke.

Lace and grass were issues that belonged to everyone, but I also had my own private war with Columbia College. In a ludicrous effort to make me a Renaissance man, the dean had demanded that I meet a science requirement.

"But I don't want to waste a course by taking geology," I told him, turning down a crack at the easiest science. "I transferred here for the English because I want to be a writer."

"Well, son," he said, "there may come a day when you'll have to write about rocks."

*"This is the life, eh?"*

"But I can look it *up*. By that logic, sir, I should study sodomy in case I have to write about Oscar Wilde."

When I threatened to leave the school rather than go off shredding cliffs, the dean finally made me the first student for whom the science requirement was ever waived. I became a minor campus hero, but I didn't exploit my fame the way Mark Rudd has done in his cross-country trips on behalf of SDS. Right after my triumph, I should have sallied forth on an intercollegiate lecture tour to inspire the boys into beating the science requirement. I might have discouraged some men who are making missiles today.

Although I conquered the science requirement, I did lose a battle to Lionel Trilling, one of the school's most famous teachers. In asking his permission to take a special English course, I was so unnerved by Trilling's icy demeanor that my request finally emerged as a feeble, "Well . . . I really just wanted to . . . get your thinking."

Like a judge delivering a sentence, Trilling froze me with his eyes and then slowly said, "Get my *thinking*? Never use a cheap Broadway cliché in here."

It wasn't a Broadway cliché, it was one from Madison Avenue, but his error was understandable, for those were the days when Columbia sat like a Vatican on the Hudson. You no more expected a professor to know Manhattan streets than you expected the Pope to know the films that were playing in downtown Rome. I felt comfortable in the ivory tower, comfortable with the feeling that when their classes were done each day, Mark Van Doren and Joseph Wood Krutch didn't go out into the local jungle but to some English country garden. "O who owns New York?" we used to sing. Well, we knew that Columbia held some very impressive deeds, but we never stormed a classroom to make them lower the rents.

When I went back to Columbia, on a recent sentimental journey, I roamed about the campus like a man from another age. For long melancholy moments, I stared at the field where I'd played football with boys whose draft cards were not for burning. Only two young squares were tossing a football now. All the other boys were lying on the lawn, some with long hair and love beads, some in undershirts and cowboy hats. A few were dozing; one young couple were cuddled by a tree; and all the rest were on homework breaks between disruptions. I felt uneasy to see them lying in the sun, reading the quotations of Chairman Mao, the disciples of Mark Rudd confronting a disciple of Mark Van Doren. Some of them looked up across the generation gap and into my face, searching for middle-class morality.

All I wanted to do was cry out, I may be wearing a shirt, but I blazed the trail you're on. I marched on the unmentionables and I smashed the science requirement and how I bugged that Lionel Trilling!

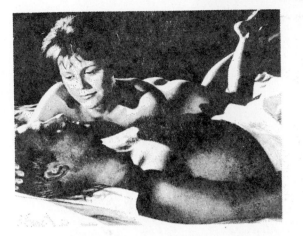

As the film opens, Sven Svensson is discussing the meaning of life with his sister, Erika, who has a summer job working as a boots in the decaying Venetian palazzo of . . .

. . . the alcoholic Duce di Fozza, the deranged psychotherapist and Mafia boss, who is tired of life, fast cars, money, women, and heroin. Why is Sven impotent? Is it . . .

. . . his Catholic upbringing, rare in a Sw which persuaded him that all women mere objects of and for degradation? the Vietnam war? His stepmother has

. . . Sven flees to a hot Greek island, where the incensed colonels force him to strip and confess his membership of the Communist Party. He is rescued by an English nympho . . .

. . . maniac, who deserts her package tour in order to initiate her new lover in diabolic rites that destroy his faith in the Trinity. Fearful now for his sanity, Sven . . .

. . . attempts to write down his story, but turns into a gull. O he? At this point, fantasy and reality interlace; was Sven a g along? Is he the Devil? Has there been . . .

. . . to a friend in the Dordogne. Sven and the girl romp in slow motion for an hour or so, and we see a number of sunrises symbolising the Creation, then the couple . . .

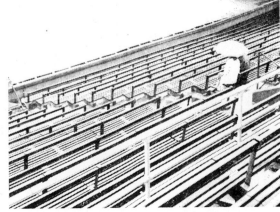

. . . drive around Europe in fast American cars, laughing, despite the fact that Europe is utterly deserted. Life is good for Sven now. In Saint Peter's Square, however . . .

. . . they pick up a hitch-hiker on his way to being defrock tells them that all is vanity faints, and when he wakes up

...ast, after years of wasteful overlapping, the moviemakers of Europe have been persuaded ...unch to collaborate on the all-in European film! Scandinavians, French, Italians, Spaniards, ...e all got together in a spirit of brotherhood and greed, and it's with great pride and pleasure ...we present a few clips from their mammoth production.

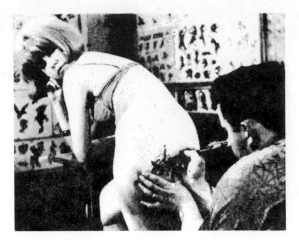

...ttempted to show the pubescent ...that family love may transcend ...er difficulties (she is an ex-Nazi ...sexual marquis), but Sven rejects ...fection ...

... and turns to their chambermaid, a failed Spanish nun, who has fled to the permissive fjords in search of spiritual solace and a cheap abortion. She makes the mistake of ...

... allowing Sven to tattoo her—to a background of Vivaldi—thereby lowering herself in his estimation. Distraught at this further revelation of debased womanhood ...

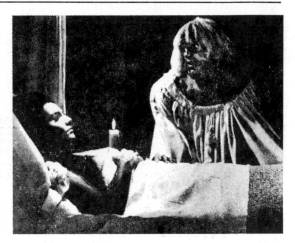

...murder at all, or is it all in the mind of Mlle. ...e Escalope, the oldest ornithologist in France, ...e classic work *Gulls et Hommes* inspired the ...or ...

... in the first place? Or did it? Is he in fact the director, or is he The Director, symbol of the evil genius that has brought the world so close to thermonuclear war?

Sven, baffled by all this, poses as a travelling candle salesman, and visits his father's latest mistress, Norma the lovely Turk. She can give no answers, but sends him ...

...ere is his Aunt Beluga, short and Flemish-speaking, ...island of meaning in an incomprehensible universe. ...lls Sven that action is all, and he becomes a ...

... bullfighter. Or is he still a gull? Either way, he is horribly gored by an Episcopalian sexton. Given three weeks to live. ...

... he goes off to St. Tropez with a friend. Is she wearing a tin hat because of the imminence of World War III? Or because gulls, for some strange reason, hate her? We shall never know.

# Bring Back The Good Old Songs!

COME, come, come and protest with me
Down at the old Bull and Bush,
        (*Ta-ra-ra-ra-ra*)
Come, come, start some unrest with me
Down at the old Bull and Bush,
        (*Pom, pom*)
Bash . . . up all the fixtures there,
Then we can move along elsewhere,
Boot any fuzz in the mush—Whoosh!
Come, come, come and be a pest with me,
Down at the old Bull and Bush.
        (*Bush! Bush!*)

---

I'm Burlington Bertie,
I never talk dirty,
That's why I'm not working today:
My elegant passes
At the once-upper classes
Are hopelessly stale and passé.
My tails and my topper
Just put the dead stopper
On box-office business, you know;
It's not economic
To be a clean comic
Like Burlington Bertie from Bow.

---

Any old iron, any old iron,
Any-any-any old iron?
Buy on tick,
Scoop up quick,
Flog it to the Arabs for a wad that thick:
Bren-gun here, tank-tracks there,
Trouble-spots your eye on,
It's the metal of the scrap that appeals to a chap,
Old iron, old iron!

---

I strolled along
The Bois de Boulogne
With a stocking around my face,
I saw the very place,
And I rapidly played my ace:
A crash of glass and a vitriol spray,
The manager coshed—another good day
For the man who broke the bank at Monte Carlo.

---

We've been together now since Friday night,
And it seems like a night too much;
These long-drawn relations never work out right
—And the bill, by the way, goes Dutch.

See . . . my . . . Rolls an' Jag an' Minimoke,
Hi . . . Fi . . . Colour-tellies fit to choke,
Grub . . . served . . . by a Chinese butler bloke—
Property development's the way!

Pent . . . house . . . Stately home in Somerset,
Swim . . . pool . . . Florida by superjet,
Some time . . . bound to be a baronet,
(Bought another yacht the other day). Oh!
*Chorus*
"Wot . . . cher . . .," all the neighbours cry,
"You was destitute, mate,
How'd you get the loot, mate?"
"Sim . . . ple . . . suckers," I reply—
"Knockin' down the Old Kent Road."

---

My old man
Said "Bring round the van,
And wait in the shadow of the wall:
The Scrubs is bad, but the Ville's much badder,
So don't make a cock-up with the old rope-ladder . . ."
But I dillied and dallied,
And dallied and dillied,
And waited till the warders hued-and-cried,
'Cos you can't ask a wife to fix her old man's bust-out,
When she likes him best inside.

---

Two bleary black eyes,
Oh, what a surprise,
All that I got
For a weekend on pot,
Two bleary black eyes.

---

Has anybody here seen Kelly?
K-E-double-L-Y,
Has anybody here seen Kelly?
We're huntin' far and wide.
He said he'd come along with us
And help set fire to a Belfast bus,
Has anybody here seen Kelly?
Kelly from the ould Bogside.

---

Old Macdonald had a farm,
Ee-i-ee-i-o,
Grew such crops upon that farm,
Ee-i-ee-i-o.
Grew a tax loss here, a tax loss there,
Here a loss, there a loss, everywhere a tax
   loss,
He'd be sunk without that farm,
Ee-i-ee-i-o.

*"Isn't it a shame . . . his naughty old mower won't start."*

# Oh Come All Ye Trendy

## By ALAN COREN

**"Mr. Noble has no doubts about the civilised way to drink at Christmas. 'A long glass of ice-cold champagne in my bath. It's expensive—66s. 6d. a bottle. When people come in for drinks, I shall offer them a pétillante Blanquette de Limoux, at 25s. 3d.' "** *Harpers Bazaar*
**"This year, why not a whole roast ox?"** *Esquire*
**"We always give our parties a topical theme, and dress and act accordingly. This Christmas it's going to be Student Rebellion."**

*American Home*

Well, Mr. Noble, we've come a long way from the manger, you and I. I have it on irreproachable authority that it would have been possible to go through Bethlehem with a fine-toothed comb a mere 1969 years ago and still not have come up with more than a handful of citizens who were drinking champagne in the bath. It's not taken long to get us civilised, all thing considered.

Not, however, that your own plans for a fun-filled Yule leave nothing to be desired. I have no objections to your mounting your Christmas thrash among the perspiring tiles, chacun à son wassail, but it strikes me as something less than hospitable to retire to the suds with three gnsworth of vintage bubbles, leaving your guests with only a *pétillante* Blanquette de Limoux to take the enamel off their teeth. For readers currently too dazed by this glimpse of la dolce Christmas to grope for their Harrap's Shorter French, *pétillante* comes from *péter*, to break wind, and 25s. 3d. derives from the English *cheap*. Now that you've broken the story in *Harpers*, my personal advice would be to shelve all thought of a Christmas binge and see the season out in some quiet Eastbourne retreat, twelve quid all-in, including free cracker and choice of mince pie or nut. Trendy it ain't, but it's safer than being nudely besieged among your own porcelain by a platoon of enraged Blanquette drinkers, incensed by the song of a popping cork behind the bathroom door.

The question posed by *Esquire* will be fraught with unanswerability for those readers whose demented efforts to separate a small turkey from one or other of its extremities has resulted in a turnup full of stuffing and a slashed jugular. For such scarred and apprehensive carvers, the thought of matching wits with a whole roast ox revolving sneakily on its spit will leave the brain ringing and the palms clammy. Especially since the aforementioned whole roast item is considerably larger than the average dining recess and the net result of trying to feed off it would leave most families smaller by two or three spitted children, not to mention the odd elderly relative crackling in the flames and casting a pall both literal and metaphorical over the entire Noël. Bedsitter-dwellers seduced, in spite of all this, by the *Esquire* offer, would be well-advised to start small and work up; a whole roast mouse, say, would bring a touch of *ton* to your solitary proceedings. It's hell to stuff, of course, but it turns a treat on a knitting-needle. Forty minutes on a low candle, and don't forget to baste.

That's the trouble with Christmas among the glossy set. As with anything else for which life is worth living, Lamborghinis and chinchillas and emerald tooth-stoppings, fierceness of competition is the bugbear, the coloured person in the woodpile. Up here among us trendies, it's Christmas red in tooth and claw, friends, and don't you forget it: how can we help one another, this Christmas, to make the world a more envious, greedy place, and knock spots off the finks in the neo-Gothic penthouse opposite? It's not the thought, it's the gift in front of it. Leafing through the shimmering pages of *Queen* in search of something for the little woman, as well as a present for my wife, I find such uplifting sales-pitches as "Christmas at Cartier begins at £50," a message calculated to bring cheapjacks sprinting from all over the realm in search of stocking-fodder. It's "Where Christmas Starts" *apud* the Cartier copywriters, and who will say them nay?

There's a hard time ahead for us pace-setters, I don't mind telling you, and a glance at the harrowed faces moping along Beauchamp Place and South Audley Street will bear instant witness to the hell of trying to keep up with, and preferably get ahead of, the Harpers. Noble's bath booze-up, for example, is so old-hat, it's not true: this year, my wife and I are throwing our first party on Christmas Eve, before anyone pinches our idea of filling our swimming-pool with pre-phylloxera Mouton Cadet and chucking our guests in at the deep end to guzzle their way through to midnight. Anyone failing to bring his or her sable bath-towel will be forced to drink in the paddling-pool with the kiddies, and no second helpings on the quail patties!

Christmas Day, of course, we shall be having the traditional dinner, an old-fashioned family do, just a few pages of *Burke's Peerage* invited at random, with a Redgrave or two to pass round the paper hats. We've hit on rather a splendid main course, we think: why, of the two traditional Christmas animals, should it always be a whole roast ox that everyone eats? This year, we're having a whole roast ass. We're getting round the problem of carving by taking as our Christmas Day party theme the Pleistocene Era: everyone's coming in Mister Fish okapi-skins, and we're just going to tear bits off the ass and gnaw them in the time-honoured way. It may not be topical, but we did Vietnam for our Hallowe'en Ball and

"*Of course I've got a ticket—just a minute.*"

*How about a rabbit, no?*

*Coloured silk scarves, no?*

*White doves, no?*

*A crystal ball, no?*

106

Biafra for Poppy's coming-out thing, and one tends to run out of newsy motifs, doesn't one? After dinner, all the chaps chuck their clubs in a heap, and the wives have to pick a club and go off with the owner; it's going to be an absolute hoot! Apicella designed our caves specially.

Boxing Day's always a problem, isn't it? It's partly the inevitable feeling of anti-climax, partly the irksome task of initiating divorce proceedings, but mainly it's the money. There never seems anything left to spend it on. Still, we've come up with rather a good wheeze this year—we've hired Cardiff Arms Park for the merest of king's ransoms, and we're taking as our theme the Springbok tour. It's a Boutiquiers XV against the Frost Script-writers Second Team, kick-off 3.15, floodlights by Cartier and half-time lemons by the Clement Freud Citrus Ensemble. Of course, we're frightfully nervous that the whole thing will turn out an utter shambles: it's Snowdon's first time as a referee, and since his entire sporting life to date seems to have been coxing the Cambridge boat, there's every likelihood that the game will end up with both scrums running backwards up the A40 at thirty-two strokes per minute and going like the clappers for Putney Bridge. Still, we've hired the South Wales Constabulary to drag guests off to the nick, so there should be something for everyone.

We've not forgotten the kiddies, either. After a *pétillante* gripewater cup at Alvaro's, they're all off to Holland Park Comprehensive for Ken's super new nativity romp, *Oh! Bethlehem!* Then it's back to Tiberio's for the gala Rusk And Gerbers Fork Supper, leaving nanny with an hour or two to herself to thank daddy properly for the monogrammed underwear.

Saturday, of course, we're holding our Mini-Moke Rally, starting off with mulled vodka at Kenny Palace and ending up with tobogganing on Harrod's Simulated Snow Slope and a refreshing mixed sauna at David Morgan's, before settling down again to roast something whole in time for our al fresco party on Hampstead Heath. The theme is the Normandy Landings, by the way, in case you're from ITN, or know anyone who might be.

Which leaves only Sunday to be got rid of. Sunday's the most terrible day of all, really, because that's when all the Supplements come, and you have to go through them, heart banging away like a trip-hammer—they'll all be doing their post-Christmas stuff, you see, and sure as God made little green banknotes, you're bound to find that someone's been doing something you didn't, something more In, something more Now. That's the worst about Christmas—with all the effort and all the excitement and all the beastly in-fighting and everything, you often come to the end of it all only to find that you've completely overlooked something terribly, terribly important.

*A sizzling blonde—ah yes!*

*And presto!—my ticket."*

*"Just a moment—your ticket please, miss."*

# PICASSOPROBE

As the Picasso bandwagon rolled into London with its 347 engravings, we asked six of the passengers for their comments on the show.

"Oh, it's all so marvellous it's difficult to describe it. To me it's a beautiful portrayal of the artist's relationship with his model, or rather, it's a humorous chronicle of his old age and emotional . . . not humorous, really, more realistic, but the crucial thing is that Picasso has finally come to terms with life. At least, he's come to terms with art. Or with his model, anyway. What do you think?"

"It's not at all what I thought it was going to be. After all that build-up you find it's not a patch on Soho, money on false pretences really, because the people in the pictures aren't doing anything, are they, not what you'd call anything much. But the funny thing is that when you look closer you can sort of imagine some very odd things going on, and that's nice. He certainly makes you work hard for your money, mark you. Still, that makes a change."

"I don't trust modern art much on the whole, but with Picasso I always feel one knows where you are. It's all there in the sales rooms records, after all. Mind, I think he's pushing it a bit with 347 engravings at the same time—it's the fallacy of market saturation and a quick turnover—but old Picasso has always stood up to the market before and he should again. I think I'll have a little flutter on number 94 over there."

"I came to the exhibition because I am totally against all forms of censorship, as well as apartheid and hanging, and an artist should have complete freedom to depict life as he sees it. Between you and me, Picasso sees life in an odd sort of way—half the drawings don't seem to be about sex at all—but we must remember that a great artist is a law unto himself. The thought of police officers going round looking for dirt fills me with blind fury. Which ones do you think they'd seize?"

"What I really love about Picasso is that he's such a screaming bore and knows it. For the past thirty years he's been churning out these ghastly cartoons, a mixture of Cocteau and Osbert Lancaster, and watching people go mad about them. That's a tremendous achievement in anyone's language. I'd never miss a Picasso show, any more than I'd miss a David Frost show."

"I haven't actually been to a modern show for years, not counting the Cecil Beaton of course, but I felt I definitely had to come to this. Well, he is the greatest living artist, isn't he? And so marvellous for his age. And the Nobel Prize, I think. Anyway, I'm really glad I made the effort, even if the actual drawings are just a little disappointing. Do you know if they do tea here?"

# They Don't Make Endings Like They Used To

## By STANLEY REYNOLDS

Happiness may after all be egg shaped, a warm puppy, the light shining in my sweetie's eyes or, like the old song says, a thing called Joe. The difficulty in defining it may perhaps come from the fact that when you look at one of the traditional places for finding it, it just ain't there no more. I refer, of course, to endings, Happy Endings. *Three dozen Busby Berkeley Girls and Dick Powell singing in the middle of them . . . Do you see those Spitfires up there Miranda, well, that's where I belong, up there making sure Nosher and Pongo didn't die in vain . . . Wipe your tears, my dear, there's a clinic in Zurich that can . . . And so Tom Sawyer and me was home again with Aunt Polly and the reward money . . . I can (see) (walk) (talk) (dance) (sing) (love) (live) again . . .*

Is it, I ask myself lying awake at night, blinking in the darkness, waiting for that spark of inspiration like Don Ameche had when he played Alexander Graham Bell or Cornell Wilde had as Liszt, some kind of a goddam plot or something? Some vast conspiracy perhaps on the part of the entertainment industry to keep us all in our ordinary little places by showing us, on stage, screen, and printed page that not only does life no longer have the possibility of a happy ending, but also it often has no ending at all, merely a finish of the whimpering just before the credits roll. The consumer of the mass produced dream life sits huddled before television, silver screen, or over the printed page eager to be carried away on fantasy's winsome wings and inevitably as the play, film, or novel closes he is smacked in the face with the flannel of damp apathy when he is not sloshed over the head with a bucket of icy despair. It was not, I hasten to add, always so. *Betty Hutton marrying Eddie Bracken . . . Dick Powell marrying Mary Martin . . . Jimmy Stewart falling into the arms of June Allyson . . . You remember those old stocks and shares Uncle Albert left in his trunk, well they're worth a cool . . . Ziegfeld was*

*out front tonight and he's coming backstage to . . . It is a far, far better thing I do . . . I'm saving these last bullets for Effie and the kids, if those murderin' devils—hey! is that the sound of a bugle? . . . But it was you I really always loved, Margie . . . And Scrooge was as good as his word . . . Gad, Holmes, you've done it again . . .*

Your average TV play comprises, in these days of tightened production budgets, maybe four characters. If two of them are male, two female, or anything closely resembling either, and the play is going out in one of the prestige drama spots, you can bet your hard-back copy of *A Christmas Carol* that if relationships all around don't break up before the sixty minutes are done your set must have broken down or

*"It needs adjusting. They should go blue when they're strangled."*

109

maybe you dozed off and who can blame you. The only thing looking like an optimistic sign that I can make out on the mist shrouded horizon of TV drama is the modern alternative to the miserable ending which is, of course, no ending at all. You know the sort of thing. After some poor wretch has been through everything hellish that the modern mind can devise—lack of communications, his secretary sniggering at his new flared bellbottoms—the play will end with him staring or walking into the distance with the theme music slamming home the message about how uncertain this whole life business is. Gone is the definite finish, the real end that we grew up with in the older more stable world of depression, hunger marches, world wars, and no drip dry stay-pressed lightweight fabrics. *Free, free at last of this terrible curse of turning into a wolfman every time the moon is full . . . Dead, yes, but his (music) (poetry) (painting) (books) (electric light bulb) will shine forever . . . He was yellow, the dirty stinking rat was yellow . . . Gosh, Mickey, you do . . . Perhaps it is old fashioned and stuffy of me, Miriam, but I think that England, and the ordinary men and women of England, stand for something bigger than Herr Hitler and Il Duce and their . . . The moon belongs to everyone, Eddie . . . So, obviously it could not have been Cartwright, and Lady De Villiers says she saw Dr. Jergens in the conservatory at nine o'clock, and so the murderer is . . . I do . . . And that is how Nicely Nicely Johnson is squaring it with the bookmaker, plus throwing a little something in the way of the old doll's home . . . It's ours boys! It's one of ours! . . .*

As far as the reader or viewer is concerned, the non-end is perhaps more satisfactory because he is able, with a little imagination, to provide his own happy finale as he drifts off in the arms of nembutal. The writer may have shunned anything as nastily bourgeois as a funeral, a wedding, a birth, or a volcanic eruption to put paid to his puppets but the imaginative consumer of today's packaged dream life can change all that, imagining for instance that the sinister man who came in to read the gas meter was in reality a long lost uncle who has made a fortune in Australia and has come back disguised as a sinister meter reader just to see if that niece of his has real character. "Wipe your tears, my dear," the

*"You can't rely on professionals like you used to . . ."*

110

sinister meter reader says, suddenly changing into Charles Coburn who made a fortune in Hollywood in the old days playing these parts, "we'll get Tiny Tim a new crutch; and there is a clinic in Zurich, and if they can't cure you—what the hell! Heroin grows on trees when you've got the kind of money I've got."

With your actual miserable and unhappy ending, however, there is no such escape. The consumer of the sorry dream life is stuck. Grim and dreary shades haunt him as he climbs the stairs to bed or puts aside the bedside book and blows out the lantern. The best advice here is to stop reading or viewing at that point where a happy ending looks at all possible. It is not much of a suggestion, but it may bring some relief to fellow escapists who are sick and tired of being left with a sinking, if not decidedly sunken, feeling at the end of a work of contemporary fiction, left miserable and wondering what ever happened to the supply of happy ends. *I thought, Belinda, if you knew that I were a King, you wouldn't . . . And I saw J.B. this morning, Sue, and he did . . . Free, free from the terrible curse of that monster my father, the Baron, created . . . And we'll be known as the folks who live on the hill . . . And there's four or five million more little people out there, Mayor McGinty, who are sick of being taken for suckers by political bums like you . . . And on the third day He . . . And then maybe Europe will be safe for free men to . . . It's oil, oil, oil, Miss Charlotte, gushin' up black and beautiful . . . O.K. copper, you got me dead to rights . . . And Yes, I said, Yes . . . And now maybe Dodge City will be a safe place for a . . . And just as soon as your leg is better, Dad, and you're out of hospital, Mr. Green wants to see you back at the plant . . . You do, Ginny, you really do? Sure, silly, I always have . . . That is the Zulu warriors, tribute to brave men . . .*

The trouble with modern fiction, however, is that the characters just seem to amble along, veering from apathy to boredom with only the occasional outburst of anger and tears to punctuate the disillusion and world weariness. What can you do with or for characters like that? They aren't vampires, they don't get attacked by Red Indians, they aren't trying to invent the electric light bulb like Spencer Tracy or ride the winning horse in the Grand National like twelve-year-old Elizabeth Taylor. The psychotic plots they are wriggled through are all neuroses and nothing money can cure. In fact, somewhere writers have picked up the idea that money doesn't solve anything. Where they got this idea I don't know, unless it drifted in along with the tax demands on the fat fees they earn. Now, unfortunately, all the most miserable people in novels or big or little screen dramas are miserable in the highest style of comfort, with wall to wall carpets, central

*"You mustn't trouble your pretty head about world peace, my dear. Leave it to us men."*

heating, dream kitchens, and the latest in fashionable clothes. They are even all healthy. Just ask yourself, when was the last time you saw a character whose old mother needed an operation or whose kid brother would never play the violin again? Or, for that matter, whose little stockholders would all lose their life savings? Whose daughter was being forced into a loveless marriage? Whose son had let the regiment down? Whose great uncle, the Baron, had unleashed a monster on Transylvania or even the North Riding? Yes, there's the nub. It isn't so much the demise of the happy ending, it's just that they don't make misery like they used to. *Dead, dead, and never called me mother . . . Atlanta's burnin' Miss Scarlet . . . This is ruin, United Consolidated down another five points . . . All these years I've secretly hated you . . . So you von't talk, eh? . . . My God! The Thing! It's eaten Professor Charters . . . It's every man for himself now . . . I give up . . . I'll never (laugh) (love) (dance) (play) (sing) (walk) (write) (invent) again . . . ARGGGH! This is poisoned . . .*

# WHAT'S ON

*Thos. Cook's Mayfair branch is picketed by the Schools Action Committee, not because they are discontented tourists, but because the Chairman of the Governors of a school which sacked some of their supporters works there. High Court case about wartime convoy is disrupted by Welsh language enthusiasts. Cambridge hotel windows are smashed as a blow against the Greek Government—PUNCH's Bulletin lists other openings for a bit of fun.*

**SMUTS STATUE** Meet for mass daubing. Jan Christian Smuts (1870-1950), South African premier, philosopher and architect of the League of Nations was an undergraduate at Christ's College, Cambridge, where students are forbidden by reactionary dons to make love on the lawn. Expose this setup for what it is by mucking up the memorial to one of its famous sons.

**COWDRAY POLO** Marbles under horses' hooves can bring any chukka to a halt. The tactics you have learned to use against mounted police can be used against polo ponies. A few extra polo balls thrown on to the field can make quite a difference too. Cowdray is the tycoon who owns the *Financial Times*—the only British newspaper to be printed on pink paper. Make your protest against this watered-down Marxism by bringing your ferret to the next game.

**NATIONAL GALLERY** Smash the glass in all the pictures. The Gallery is supported out of taxes paid by armament firms. Patronising it means backing the sale of death-dealing missiles. Teachers, when you have finished striking over your just claims, strike against School Visits to the Gallery. Remember: every time anybody passes through the door, they are condoning aggression.

**PICKET TEA** Join Mrs. Whitehouse in a picnic picket at the British Museum, where the Director is Sir John Wolfenden, author of the infamous Wolfenden Report. Wives and Mothers wishing to strike a blow against permissiveness towards homosexuals, join forces to make visitors to the collections think twice.

**SNAGSBY & KENT** 206 Commercial Avenue, Wapping West. Pickets wanted. This firm displays the Royal Warrant, earned by supplying Buckingham Palace Mews with nosebag stiffeners. We must make a stand against flagrant support of a Monarchy which has consistently snubbed the Outer London Republican Movement, twice returning complimentary tickets for a Love-In. No violence before midday in accordance with the *Three Ducks* Compromise.

**FIGHTING FATHERS** Priests wanted to volunteer for mass chaining to parking meters in the Piccadilly area in protest against the refusal of Cardinal Heenan to curse the Reverend Ian Paisley with bell, book and candle.

**NUMBER 10** Throw a brick through a window to mark your disengagement from the policy of paying a salary to the Leader of the Opposition. Why should bankers' pal Heath get his booze on us? Make the Prime Minister stop lavishing Our Cash on crypto-Powellites.

**Reformed Spelling Commandos Drawing Lots for the Tomato before Enoch Powell Meeting.**

# The PUNCH Demo Bulletin

**Putting Finishing Touches to Bomb at Hands Off Rutland HQ. When completed it will be slipped into Hatfield.**

**ALL-IN WRESTLING** Start fires under seats. Saw through the centre of the ring. Blow anaesthetic darts at wrestlers. Shout that the contenders aren't the advertised ones but ringers. Introduce swarms of bees. Drown grunts of pain with songs. JOINT PROTEST:—Anti-South Korea. Nationalise the National Trust. Legalise Incest. Make *Panorama* Drop Hussein.

**SACK WINCHESTER** Crossman's Old School.

**LSE** Take over the London School of Economics by Action Teams from London Arts Schools. To economists, Art is a commodity. They must be re-educated. Mural artists badly needed. Also tattooists.

**HORSEGUARDS** Cavalry horses could help to feed our Belgian neighbours; instead they are wasted in warlike display. Give them LSD on sugar. Spray pipeclay and brass with aerosols of concentrated smog. Play tunes on your harmonica which the horse will associate with dressage.

Don't forget how valuable itching powder can be.

**THE SHELL BUILDING** This South Bank monument to International Oil Capitalism represents British bourgeois architecture at its most debased. Strike a blow against it by moving homeless families into the Royal Institute of British Architects.

**THE TIMES** Why are sexy ads secretly banned from the Personal Column? Teach it a lesson by mobbing its more profitable companion *The Sunday Times*. Meet in Gray's Inn, down the road from the office. Bring your boots.

**KIDNAPPING** Volunteers wanted to kidnap Eirene White, Minister in the Wilson Government and daughter of the Whitehall lickspittle Thomas Jones, the man who encouraged Baldwin to sell out to the mine-owners, Hitler, the Mary Webb lobby, etc. A bash at White is a bash at Unemployment.

**LORD CHIEF JUSTICE** There is no law in Britain for the poor. Attack the Top Judge where it hurts. His Kentucky wife has been busy turning the church in Smith Square into a Concert Hall. Make sure no note of music is ever played in it—except by you.

Every pianist silenced is a revenge for the sentences on the Train Robbers.

**SOTHEBY'S** Any firm which has a New York Branch is supporting the Pentagon. Wreck their auctions by swamping them with scores of simultaneous bids, putting off other bidders by jeering at them and heckling the auctioneer about selling fakes. Give false names if you win anything.

**GUILDHALL** Move into Guildhall and defy the Aldermen to throw you out. This ancient building belongs to us all, not just to a small, unrepresentative clique. Use the Banqueting Hall for feeding impoverished members of London Borough Councils. The project is under the patronage of the Home Counties Committee for Friendship with Albania.

**SWEDISH NEUTRALITY** Make the Swedes stand up and be counted. Take over any theatre performing one of Strindberg's plays and hold a Nude-In.

**THE THIRD PROGRAMME** One of the BBC Governors is Mary Green, Headmistress of Kidbrooke Comprehensive. Picket the school! Bring the kids out on strike! Warn off the staff!

**Next Target of Anti-Union Action Group.**

# Expel the English

## By GEORGE MIKES

*"My wife has never re-programmed her initially faulty, negative data on me, Miss Ploemsch."*

It is a painful subject I have to raise here today; unsavoury and disturbing. It is certainly not my own choosing. I am a kindly and scholarly man—actually very fond of tigers, leopards and a few other animals as well as of children under three, but I have never been a man to flinch from duty. Many people will ask: how do I have the right to inflame feelings? The answer is that, having looked around and seen what is going on in this country, I do not have the right not to do so. Because the situation is worse than alarming. We must be mad, literally mad, as a nation just to watch these happenings. It is like, if I may borrow a metaphor, watching a nation busily engaged in heaping up its own funeral pyre.

There is an obvious danger of over-population for which—I shall not beat around the bush—the English are primarily and overwhelmingly responsible. But before I come to the details and to my suggestions for a remedy, let me tell you a few facts. Yes, facts, because all I am going to say is based on sound, scientific evidence.

A few days ago an immigrant from Jamaica remarked: "Oh, those bloody English . . ." These were his very words, I have witnesses to it but, naturally enough, cannot reveal their names. Another immigrant from Barbados said this: "Too many bloody English around . . . They always take the best jobs." Things have come to a pretty pass. Here are two decent fellow-immigrants who in broad daylight, in my own town, complain that they cannot get proper employment because of the English.

These are the scientific facts which cry to heaven. They create an extreme urgency of action *now*. Just that kind of action which is hardest for a politician to take because—I am fully aware of it—it may not be popular in certain sections of the electorate. The natural and rational first question is to ask: how can the dimensions of this explosion be reduced? Some

*"Which particular starving people is this gathering in aid of?"*

people speak of coloured immigration, of immigrants' descendants and dependants, of inflow and outflow, but actions connected with them will not help, they will not amount to more than taking out a drop from the Ocean. It almost passes belief that no one thought of the obvious solution—or no one dared to utter it— EXPEL THE ENGLISH!

It has been generally accepted as a principle by the fairest and noblest spirits in this country that it is fair to expel the immigrants, and I say this as a coloured (white) immigrant myself. But it is only fair to expel the first comers first. They have been here long enough. It is only equitable that they should give way to those waiting to come in. The English have always been great believers in the queue.

Those who are the English of today came from Normandy, in 1066, causing no end of troubles to the Welsh, the Scots and the Irish—the lawful possessors of these or neighbouring lands. They all came without permits; without any certificates whatsoever.

They behaved with complete disregard to local customs and laws. They practically took over the country.

And then—I am trying my best not to become offensive or discourteous but hard scientific facts must be faced—well, then they started breeding. They never really *liked* breeding; they have never been very fond of the procedure and the paraphernalia that go with it but they have always been clannish and did their patriotic duty. What are the facts? In the eleventh century only a few hundred thousand came. In the twelfth century, a mere seven hundred years ago, the day before yesterday in historical terms, they numbered a bare two millions. Under Elizabeth I their number rose to five millions and at the time of Malthus, who made such a fuss about population, they still numbered eleven millions only. And what do we find today? There are over fifty millions of them (not counting the more recent, post-William immigrants) *and they go on breeding.* A very

*"They don't cast spells like they used to."*

eminent philatelist (I cannot, of course, disclose his name) told me that on present trends there would be more than seven hundred and fifty-six million English in this country by AD 3525.

Such is the magnitude of the threat. I do not wish to speak of the impact of this immigration: the complete disruption of the original, traditional Scottish, Irish and Welsh Way of Life. But life is just not the same as it used to be before 1066. I do not speak of their refusal to mix on equal terms with others: there are still, in 1970, large, completely white areas in the country. But I shall ask, I have to ask, *what is the use of the English*?

They are not very good workers; they keep organising strikes; they come forward claiming higher and higher wages and set a bad example to more recent immigrants. In business they are chasing higher and higher profits. After football matches they behave like vandals. And—it is a painful question but I must ask it—which race supplies most of the criminals? Who are the predominant race in English prisons? The English.

They are not really necessary either. The two last Prime Ministers, before the present one, were Scots; the Treasury used to be run by the Hungarian Mafia, supervised by a true Briton, Sir Eric Roll, who was also born in Hungary. Business is getting American, the restaurant industry Italian and Greek, huge chunks of the press are in Canadian and Australian hands. And so on. They contribute little. Yet the English behave as if they owned the country. Not long ago I received a letter from an old lady, a Trinidadian old-age pensioner, living in my own constituency. She lost her husband fighting for Britain and then came here, opened up her seven-roomed house to boarders in a purely immigrant neighbourhood. With growing fear she saw one house after the other taken over by the English. The once lively, cheerful and noisy street, alive with guitar-music and calypsos, has become a place of funebrial silence, inhibited tranquillity and the stiff upper lip. The English today give her nasty looks and one man actually turned after her in the street and murmured: "Really, I say . . ."

The English themselves are not too happy here. They keep complaining about economic conditions, low wages, bad business and, most of all, the weather. There is a better climate in France whence they came from. I know that some people like talking about helping distressed Englishmen, to alleviate their sufferings, to be kind and humane towards them but I tell you: to improve their lot is positively harmful unless it formed a part of the policy of their voluntary or enforced repatriation to France.

This is the only course open to us. The English themselves will feel better and enjoy life more among their own people, their own kith and kin, the French. Besides, they have given up India, South-East Asia, Africa, the so-called White Dominions and—the most tragic mistake of all—granted independence to the United States of America, so it would be utterly pointless to make a fuss about a tiny island on the peripheries of Europe.

Yet I do not anticipate such a policy to be carried out entirely without opposition. Some of them will try to cheat; others will try to dig up spurious Scottish, Welsh or Irish ancestors; others again will pose as foreigners. It is rumoured that handbooks to teach them the tricky and crafty ways of foreigners are already in the bookshops, doing brisk business.* But I wish them well and in my humane and scholarly fashion I propose ways to alleviate hardships. They should only be banned from settling over here. I stress the words "from settling." This has nothing to do with permitting English-born people to come to study (to learn English, for example), or to gain some qualifications, or come as tourists just to see what is going on—they might be interested, after all.

Nobody can make an estimate of the numbers which, with generous grants, would choose either to return to their country of origin, Normandy, or go to other countries (Jamaica or Pakistan perhaps) where their skills, such as they are, might be welcome.

But do not dilly-dally, act without delay! I must seriously emphasize not only the importance but also the extreme urgency of the required measures. Judging by the rate they emigrate to Canada, Australia and a few other lands, in a few years' time, it seems, they will have left of their own free will.

* An obvious reference to *How to be an Alien* by George Mikes.

# Stoned in Public

## By LORD MANCROFT

I don't know who was the model for Epstein's statue of Rima in Hyde Park, but my grandmother thought nothing of her at all. "Dammit," the old lady remarked as we were passing by on our Sunday stroll, "I'm nearly eighty myself, but if I couldn't strip off better than that, I'd cut my throat."

Most people, however, do know that the model for the statue of "Justice" which used to stand to the left of Queen Victoria in the House of Lords was the Mistress of the Robes, and the model for the statue of "Mercy" on the right was the mistress of the sculptor.

I myself, though this is not generally known, have also been in the business. I was the model for three inches of Winston Churchill's right trouser leg on the Oscar Nemon statue in the House of Commons. I happened to be in Mr. Nemon's studio one morning when he was having a little trouble with the hang of Winston's trousers, and he asked if I would oblige by posing for a few minutes. Bursting with pride I obliged, and have thereby passed into history.

But Winston's statue, grand as it is, has already given rise to controversy. My bit of trouser is on a level with Lloyd George's coat button on the opposite side of the Arch, and the Welsh Liberals don't approve of Winston towering over their hero.

However much the pigeons may regret it, I am beginning to wonder whether the day of the statue isn't over. A statue, even one like that of Alderman Rufflebottom's in front of the local Corn Exchange, must be cast in the heroic mould, and the days of heroics are drawing to a close. Look at Nelson in Trafalgar Square. Splendid! But is anyone seriously thinking of a similar carry-on for Monty, or Alex, or Admiral Cunningham? And in any case, if you'd taken a vote in 255 Battery RA, you'd have been told that their real war hero was the chap who invented self-heating soup. A couple of tins of that elixir might make an interesting subject for Henry Moore, or Anthony Caro, but the result would give rise to debate, and somebody would be sure to come along and daub it with red paint, or better still try to blow it up.

That's the trouble with statues; they're like Embassies, provocative. Next time

*It's no use worrying lad, if it's got your name on it there's nowt you can do . . ."*

*"Excuse please, how do you spell Simpson?"*

## Mothball

**by TEICH**

you're in Winchester Cathedral, have a look at the gaudy statuette of Joan of Arc up by the Lady Chapel. It wasn't until it had been unveiled, and the notables had said their pieces and departed that someone noticed that the Maid had been put looking straight into the tomb of Cardinal Beaufort, one of the men who had voted her on to the stake. Understandably, there was trouble; mutterings in the Close, narky letters in the *South Hants Advertiser* and so on.

Statues are now becoming even more controversial, and this worries me. Easily though I am able to contain my admiration for Karl Marx, I wasn't pleased when they recently blew up the old brute's bust in Highgate Cemetery. What next, I asked myself? If the Comrades don't get proper satisfaction they'll have Disraeli off his plinth in next to no time. Then somebody will take a long hard look at the statues in the curtilage of the Palace of Westminster; there are only two of them, and they are, oddly enough, of Oliver Cromwell, who tried to abolish Parliament, and Richard the First, who never summoned it. So the King Charles Society will try and heave Old Noll into the Thames, and the United Arab League (mindful of the Crusades) will put a bomb under R. Coeur de Lion. Then we shall really be down to basics and somebody will turn up the record and find out all about the row that Alderman Rufflebottom had with the Safeblowers Union in March of 1886, and the Corn Exchange will be in for trouble too.

Foreigners arrange these things more calmly. The Indians, for instance, pull the statues of British generals and governors from their plinths with a gentle Oriental decorum. For my taste, however, they recently went too far. At the very moment they were hauling some viceroy off his horse in Bombay, they were asking us to subscribe to the erection of a statue to Gandhi in Bloomsbury Square.

Come to think of it, what are the Indians actually doing with all our generals and governors once they have got them down? Are they storing them in a Generals' and Governors' Museum, as the GWR have done with the Cheltenham Flyer and its mates in the Railway Museum at Swindon? And are they planting their horses and elephants out in the open like the dinasaurs and pterodactyls that used to mope around the Crystal Palace before we burnt it down? I suspect so, because Our Dumb Friends lobby is powerful the world over. Just you watch. When the boys from the London School of Economics eventually have Nelson off his plinth, I bet they won't dare lay hands on the Landseer lions. It was for this reason, I'm sure, that the Sudanese let Gordon on his camel come back intact from Khartoum, and who's to blame the children of Camberley for thinking that Gordon was the name of the camel? When I was a child I used to admire the two greyhounds that stood guard on either side of the gates outside the Beauchamp home near Norwich. They were, I now realise, the supporters from the family's coat of arms. Under them was the family motto, "Toujours fidèle" but I thought, in my innocence, that this was the name of the dogs, "Towzer and Fido." I hope these splendid animals have been well treated by the Regional Beetroot Board, or whoever it is now occupies the house.

On reflection I no longer want, nor, unless I am accompanied by some animal, deserve to have a statue erected to myself. Winston's trousers will suffice.

There was a time when I had my eye on that empty plinth at the North East corner of Parliament Square, but I presume that this is now reserved for Himself sculpted in comfortably fitting shorts, puffing his pipe and gazing in calm solitude past all the photographers and out over the Scillies.

When I left my home in Montagu Square I did go so far as to suggest to the LCC that they place on the house one of their round blue plaques saying "Lord Mancroft, Poet and Dreamer, born here." They replied by return of post explaining in some detail why this could not be. A previous letter from me complaining about the rates had on the other hand taken them nearly a month to answer. Next time I am worried about our dustbins I shall write, of course, to the Council, but I shall also propose by way of a postscript the erection of a statue to myself in Eaton Square. I bet the good fellows will reply to the whole letter within the day.

# Yours profitably

Job lots of letters from the famous fetch tidy sums these days (recent victims: Napoleon, Bonnie Prince Charlie, Florence Nightingale) but it could really be a boom industry if only it was properly organised. Miles Kington dips into the Punch catalogue of postbagiana.

*Dere Will Shakespere,*

*It seemeth to me proper not to conceal from thee the talk that plagues the whole town this year, namely, concerning the true nature of the author of the plays appeared under thy name. Some say they are penned by Marlowe, some by me, some by the Earl Oxford and God knows what noblemen else. Does this not tickle thee? When posterity shall know without fail or doubt that they were all composed by (word indecipherable).*

*Francis Bacon*

(£10,000)

---

*To George Washington:*

*A storm at sea, corruption among the public servants and some trouble with the horses have, it appears, conspired to prevent my last communication from reaching you. I earnestly pray that you may not have set anything on foot which might ruin matters between us, as in my letter I have made known my Government's secret decision to grant all the sundry requests of the colonists. I trust that when the present groundless unrest is past we may see you in these islands.*

*North* ($500,000)

---

*Chère Joséphine,*
*Demain soir?*
*Ton Napoléon*

(£500; reductions for orders of more than ten)

---

**Dear Mr. Findlay,**
**Please send 1 lb potatoes**
**2 pork chops**
**1 tin of beans**
**yrs**
**Mrs Beeton**

(£50 or nearest)

---

*Dear Mr. Robinson,*

*Some day when I am less hectically involved in business I would welcome the chance of meeting you. As a matter of fact, I do not remember ever meeting your father, though I did know your mother quite well.*

*Lloyd George* (withdrawn from sale)

---

*Dear Sir or Madam,*

*I have not yet had the pleasure of a reply to my prospectus of house painting services and would appreciate soonest response.*
*yours faithfully*
*Adolf Schickelgruber*

(Upwards of a hundred copies of this letter available, prices varying as the later ones are feverish to the point of illegibility.)

---

*To Thos. Chippendale.*
*Dear Sir,*

*I write to thank you for the suite of furniture ordered from your workshops but six years ago, and also to impart that I am confined to the house by my doctor for an ankle broken as I fell through your Gothic chair, which otherwise pleases me well save only the sharpness of the legs on which my dog ran and died. The divan looks well in the saloon and I trust the feet will soon arrive. Kindly furnish with your bill a short description of the method used to assemble your looking glasses.*

*Chesterfield*

(£5,000)

---

*My Darling,*

*my darling, darling, darling! I never thought it could be so beautiful. This is true love, true everlasting passion. It is even more splendid than I had dared hope.*

*your very very own*
*P.S, Could you move over? Your knees are sticking into me.*

(From Queen Victoria to Prince Albert. Also from Queen Victoria to Sir Arthur Sullivan, Sir Arthur Sullivan to Sarah Bernhardt, Sarah Bernhardt to Bernard Shaw etc. etc.—please state desired correspondents when ordering.)

Dear Sir, I have studied your revenue form but am baffled by its wilful obscurity and private jargon. which way what next?

James Joyce

Postage Due 2d

TAX INSPECTOR
Dublin
Ireland

*"Turn her round and head for the amusement arcade."*

# Where are the Wits of Yesteryear?

## By BASIL BOOTHROYD

Owing to an accident of birth I never heard Oscar Wilde wowing those smart dinner tables, and even if I'd been available they weren't the sort I'd have got asked to. Come to think of it, how many even dowdy dinner tables do I get my feet under these days? The social practice in my circle tends increasingly towards unobtrusive get-togethers in the late mid-evening, with the dishes washed but enough coffee left over to masquerade as hospitality. Friends newly back from foreign parts may lend tongues a faint wag with a snort of duty-free Cointreau, but that's about it, and by ten-thirty one of the breadwinners present will be winding his wrist-watch. Tomorrow is another day, with the shadow of the 7.59 already looming. Time to cut short this enthralling discussion on whether the moon is made of tin, or who's going to get custody of the Falklands.

Oscar, if you ask me, wouldn't have come up with a crack fit for the back of a match-box under these conditions. It isn't only that he'd miss the white-gloved footmen, the procession of soups, fish, birds, sorbets, joints and soufflés, all with matching bottles, which appear, mysteriously, to have coaxed funny remarks out of people at that time (myself, I'm a write-off for repartee after an averagely well-farced omelette), but the chat's less fun-prompting. Wilde, I admit, hadn't much chance to be witty about the colour problem, high-rise workers' flats, the ethics of teachers' strikes or the effect of systemic fungicides on brussels sprouts. But if he had I can't see him coming out with anything very memorable. Such smart lines as "A really well-made buttonhole is the only link between art and nature," or "One man's poetry is another man's poison"—apart from the feeling that we could have done better ourselves anyway—are hardly likely to convulse the modern dining-recess getting its heads together over a current talking point.

**Host:** What about this book of Harrison Salisbury's, all about the war we're going to get between Russia and China?

**Hostess:** It's scary stuff, all right. They say that even if we keep clear, the fallout could kill half London. What do you think, Oscar?

**Wilde:** (*after a quick hard think*): I have nothing to declare except my genius.

**Host:** I don't see what the hell that's got to do with it. When you've only got a four-minute warning——

**Hostess:** I thought it was fifteen now, darling?

**Wilde:** Meredith is a prose Browning, and so is Browning.

**Hostess:** Oh, well, let's change the subject. You see the dockers have rejected the offer of thirty-six pounds for a thirty-one and a half hour week?

**Host:** No, let's talk about the split in Mrs. Gandhi's Congress Party. Unless Wilde here has any views on the Bar students' sit-in?

**Wilde:** The unspeakable in pursuit of the uneatable.

**Host:** They are? Right. (*Rises and winds wrist-watch*) Well . . . long day tomorrow, what?

A riot, the whole thing, and you can't really blame poor old Oscar. He did his best with his natural gifts, and went home with a few useful lines for *Lady Windermere*, and you can't do more in a society suffering from instant communications and a preoccupation with the countless unfunny aspects of twentieth-century life.

You can't help wondering how some of the other legendary wags and pundits would have shown up these days. I was never in a pub with Sam Johnson, and the chances are that nobody else would be, once they looked in and saw he was there. He was probably all right for his times. "I am willing to love all mankind, except an American" may have gone big when there was nobody around, as usual, but Boswell, and a landlord who thought all Americans wore feathers in their hair, but you can't see him as a show-stopper today in the Cock, Fleet Street, saying that "criticism is a study by which

men grow important at very small expense." Too many critics in the bar. And too many lawyers, from the Law Courts over the road, to sound off in anything like full voice with the one about not liking to speak ill of strangers, "but I am afraid he is an attorney." In our own times, in any case, he'd be expected to be comically pungent about Pinkville, the Springbok squatters, and Barbara Castle's agonies over containerisation disputes at Tilbury. Well, to be fair, he might have uttered on containerisation, but it would just have been something about the state of the language, leaving the larger situation, as seen by the PIB and the Conservative shadow spokesman on transport, virtually unscathed.

Nor, gag for gag, can I see Canon Sydney Smith trading fun with today's Most Reverend His Grace the Lord Archbishop of Canterbury. Or, at the other end of the scale, any representative swinging vicar. Smith got into the treasuries of humorous quotations all right by pronouncing digestion to be the secret of life, or saying—with less than immortal wit, I can't help thinking, "When I take a gun in hand the safest place for a pheasant is just opposite

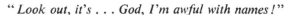

*"Look out, it's . . . God, I'm awful with names!"*

the muzzle," and it was great stuff in the seventeen-nineties or thereabouts, when the Church was all set on a steady course and nothing likely to worry it this side of the Second Coming. You could go frivolling on about being preached to death by wild curates, or the delights of breakfast "because no one is conceited before one o'clock," and the rock of religious conviction remained more or less unchipped. But put Sydney on *Ten to Eight*, or the late-night TV God talk, asked either to report on the state of play in oecumenicalism or face a grilling on the Virgin Birth from some sharp BBC agnostic, and you're not going to get enough aisle-rolling epigrams to make a sheet of cracker mottoes.

And all this is to say, of course, that the old days were a pushover for wits. They found life agreeably larky. The global anxieties didn't crowd in so much. Sam Johnson may have had it called to his attention that Frederick II of Prussia had seized Silesia, or Clive conquered Bengal, but what was there to say about it that that toady Boswell would trouble to note? Sydney Smith, for all his preoccupation with the pleasures of breakfast, may have read the occasional six weeks old dispatch saying Bonaparte was loose again, or Stamford Raffles had founded Singapore. Where was the fun in that? Take Wilde. The Zulu War left him commentless, likewise our annexation of Upper Burma. A quip about the importance of the well-tied tie, or divorces being

"*I know we've been here for four hundred years, but we'll certainly pull out as soon as the Britons show they're able to defend themselves.*"

made in heaven, yes, but tell him that they've opened the Manchester Ship Canal and he just couldn't care less—not even worth a cuff note for *Dorian Gray*.

Oh, yes, they'd have their work cut out today, trying for a belly-laugh on the Redcliffe-Maud report. And you can ditch the theory that they could turn their talents to remunerative one-liners for David Frost. They'd never go down with the mass ratings. Come to that, they never did. Amusing remarks about the digestion were OK for an audience with something to digest, and the Canon's vision of the hereafter, with paté de fois gras and trumpets, may have circulated well among archdeacons taking their madeira-break, but a Tolpuddle comic pinching the material for next week's smoking concert would have died the death. Work-house rafters, it's safe to say, wouldn't have been endangered much either.

It brings us back, sadly, to a conclusion already hinted at. That possibly all this good stuff wasn't all that good anyway. There it is, in the records. But you have to wonder. When you think that, under the crushing pressures of modern life, you and I have produced some rare little old gems in our time: and just because of the Boswell shortage we're thrown back on the degrading necessity of having to repeat them ourselves . . . They certainly had it made, those old clowns. Didn't know when they were well off, if you ask me.

"*Just remember, son, power corrupts and absolute power is even nicer.*"

*"You were lucky, being away.* We've *all had 'flu."*

# The Weather Forecast
# Will Continue Variable,
# Subject to Sudden Disasters

### By GEORGE LUCE

It isn't everyone, is it, who walks out of a job one week, and finds the Heir to the Throne dropping into the slot the week after? And I was gratified to notice, reading the proceedings of the Dryden Society of Trinity College, that some of the gags that in the past had squeezed a smirk even out of TV cameramen, had raised a laugh in Cambridge (troughs of low pleasure?)— which says something for the indestructibility of the material. I have to confess, though, to a fleeting moment of tooth-grinding, eyeball-popping frustration—for so long had I nursed this secret craving to slip one or two gems from the repertoire (preferably the sub-Whitehouse ones), deadpan, into the middle of a straight spiel, just to see what would happen. Nobly, in the interests of the public service, I repressed the impulse (well, nearly always) and blow me, not five minutes after I'd shuffled off into obscurity, glowing with rectitude and Reithian principles, someone else swoops in and carries off my pet ambition. There's privilege for you.

I must nevertheless submit a small correction at the point where HRH is said to have lost his lines—"What the hell comes next?"—ad libbing his way out of the crisis—"This doesn't happen on the BBC."

Not so. This is *exactly* how it happens on the BBC—the incident itself has the

123

*"I think there is some mistake—I only wanted to borrow five pounds."*

ring of total authenticity. In order, then, to remove any similar misconceptions, I'm going to offer a few armchair tips on broadcasting in general and the weather-wrangling lark in particular, which may serve to enlighten the curious, or to confuse the aspirant after the guards and glories of the mass media.

First of all, there are two kinds of broadcasting, Live Broadcasting and Other Broadcasting (and that ought to bring a few producers yapping and baying out of the canteen). Live broadcasting is mostly to do with Cues and Clocks and Programme Links and never quite having your material square by airtime. In horse-opera terms, it's a kind of Trail of the Lonely Goof; it's strictly for people who positively enjoy being miph. Kaolin. morph. cases, because the possibilities of disaster, including those generated by your own incompetence, are limitless. Half the time it's just someone yanking the wrong switch, and, say, cutting off your head-phones so you find yourself squeaking "Can you hear me" like Sandy Powell into what's known as a dead acoustic and jiggling every key in sight while an eager nation is tuned in to every breathless curse; or someone cutting you up into vision just as you are trying to untangle your legs from the mike cable.

Pardon me (you say *dulcissimo*) while I unwrap the parcel meantime shall we look at the caption chart WHICH WE SHOULD HAVE HAD IN THE FIRST PLACE (*sforzando*). Simultaneously, at the back of your mind, you've scripted an elaborate medieval fate for the button-pusher in the gallery.

If it's not the people at the back, it's your own personal maladministration, or Not Paying Attention. For example, if you don't check your notes, some nasty socio-geographic disturbances can happen, such as hill-farmers in Birmingham or coastal areas of the South Midlands. If you don't go through the drill like an airline pilot, you can wind up very spare indeed.

Here's a cautionary tale that I'm still reminded about. Those magnetic rubber symbol things for the weather chart?—if you want to use gadgets like those on air, you must sort them out logically beforehand, otherwise you get into a hellish tangle with everything in the wrong place and left hand behind right ear. On this day, I thought I'd sorted, and, wading into the routine with a few throwaways, was happily hurling two or three hundred miles of rain into the West, when I observed the horrid little discs were dribbling down the board, ricocheting like pin-table balls and falling about my feet. Uh-huh, wrong side, flip 'em round. More skidding discs, a bigger pile on the floor—My God, I've been de-Gaussed! Breaking into a sweat, talking a blue streak, mind racing like a catherine wheel, I recollect sifting very deliberately the bits I had left, leering sickly into the camera murmuring something about "Let's try that again before Flags-of-All Nations," noting there were eleven seconds left to knock off most of the UK, and scraping home with half a second to spare for a flash of the Ipana and a triumphant never-thought-I'd-make-it-did-you gesture before I was faded. Kind people said it was the best comic turn on the box that week, but it induced a severe case of what the engineers would term overload distortion. (Another engineering phrase highly applicable to the software as well as the hardware is "Wow and Flutter"—there's a lot of that about.)

The networks *appear* to be relatively goofless because operators eventually develop a built-in double-check early warning system, and the whole scenario is then reduced to a custard-pie production—you learn to anticipate the trajectory of likely trouble and duck, and it's astonishing how often you bob back a mere second ahead of cue. So, any time your favourite presenter looks a little glazed over, you can reckon there's right pandemonium going on in the background. (This is where the real excitement lies—anticipating the snag and covering fast enough for no one to notice. It's a dull day if you're not frightened at least once.) The next time you are talking to a genuine all-wool, kite-marked broadcaster, observe closely—nine-tenths of him is relaxed, comfy and with you; the other tenth is whizzing round in close orbit Looking for Something to Go Wrong.

In the matter of technical meteorology, there's no problem that five or ten years' experience won't solve. Nowadays, the vast output of the communications net-

*"Be reasonable, guv—where can I find the Chief Rabbi on Early Closing Day?"*

work is shovelled into the computer, which in turn regurgitates the basic answers. Inspect briefly to guard against total derangement in the machine, and do a crude blacksmith's job hammering what it says into some sort of three-dimensional form. And you are there. At least, if it's sound radio, there's just about time to knock up a script before, about five minutes to deadline, someone comes puffing into the studio with the glad news that there's an amendment to the story, or it's snowing in Northampton.

Telly is a little more complex. There are tedious hours rigging all those synoptic graffiti on the backdrops, but I'd rather not dwell on that. The pregnant message you are about to deliver must be crammed firmly between your ears, because there's no autocue, no jumbo board, and no time to think anyway. You are either working flexible duration to a fixed time-out or vice-versa, and you are cueing your own camera cuts off the floor and as like as not someone else's telecine feed as well.

One of the great paradoxes of television is that the shifty looking character is the one who is working off the top of his head, darting between clock, monitor, props and script, and occasionally remembering to gawp down the lens; the steady chap with the frank and sincere gaze is cudding away on autocue. With any luck

*"I'm not quite sure how to put this darling, but ever since we've had the house modernised, you don't fit in any more."*

*"Sorry—we make it 11,075,423 vehicles on the road. Recount, please—over."*

it breaks now and again, but cheers for the very old hand, who, when his autocue *did* break, threw up his arms and said so, beaming at the viewers and adding "Bear with me a second until they bring me a script, and then we can go ahead again." Great stuff, but not quite so great as the front-man who dried solid (no studio aids at all) and continued mouthing silent gibberish for a full forty-five seconds while the whole building went berserk slamming in stand-by mikes, amplifiers and what-have-you in an attempt to clear the apparent breakdown in sound. If you've got that kind of wit, you're probably earning good money in the trade already. (You may not think so, but the speed with which technical snags are cleared behind the scenes has to be seen to be believed.)

The full-time prognosis-pedlar, has, of course, to surmount a number of hazards peculiar to the business, including a certain inconsistency in his material, and a much wider inconsistency in the reaction of his consumers.

Most of all, he must be comfortably reconciled to earning a living on a total vocabulary of about three hundred words. A talent for pools coupons helps—on the other hand if you announce "perm any three from five" there are liable to be Questions Asked. In the matter of style, if you follow the advice of an Elder Statesman of the BBC and make it like "Talking over a pint," there are shrill protests from the preservation of archaic English lot—these can be routed with a whiff of Fowler as a rule—keep it orthodox and there are howls from the other camp who want to know why you can't use everyday language. Either way, just look out of the window at the kind of westering sky that comes straight out of Constable and has inspired the marmoreal phrase all the way from Shakespeare to Tin Pan Alley; then think of a new way to say Cloudy with Rain at Times. I'm prepared to lay fifty to one in pints (the only currency I understand) that, for example, not one of the present constellation on the "Punch" roll would last a fortnight. Like me, after the thirteenth day of bright periods and shattered scowers, they would be discovered, cringing in a dark corner, only to be gently led away under the lights, daubed with brown cement, and told firmly—You must be out by seven seconds to the minute.

Perhaps it's all for the best—there was a time when it was handy to be mildly eccentric if you were in the weather trade—the image now is crisp, electronic and white-coated—but that's another story. Still, it's sad to think we shall probably never hear the Cloudy-with-rain-at-times theme beaten out on 'cello and bagpipes.

The average Briton's typical idea of a typical scene of an ordinary street in an average American town based on the average content of typical American books and ordinary American motion pictures.

Real life as lived in a real, typical British living room as lodged in the typical mind of the average American, who sees typical, real British cinema and reads real, average British novels.

# Here Today and Still Here Tomorrow

## By VINCENT MULCHRONE

I hear the words every year, but still they hit like a cricket ball in the belly. I lift the phone, and the voice at the other end says "Nah *then*?"

Thousands of Northerners living in the South will recognise the panic-stricken drill that follows. Because he's sitting up there in the North waiting for your first words, to hear whether your vowels have gone soft. Answer with something like "Oh, hullo Charles" and he's put it on the village tom-toms that another one had "gone over." With an exile's cunning you re-tune your ear in a trice and answer with the required "*Nah* then," possibly adding an ingratiating "yer daft bogger."

In the back street where you both grew up, standard, unaccented English is still held to be unforgivable snobbery. The visiting exile has to beware of such simple words as "you" and "yours" which, in the *tutoiment* of the Heavy Woollen District, must be rendered as "ta" and "thi."

He talks a bit more Ilkley nowadays. Even so, a Southerner, judging by his telephone voice alone, might think he hadn't fourpence to scratch his arse with, as the saying goes—though I doubt it goes much further South than Sheffield.

The fact is that he is squatting in baronial comfort in Wharfedale and ringing you from the phone in his master bathroom. "We're off again," he announces. "Same place. Costa Gastronomia. So we thought we'd stop with you on the way. Well, it makes a nice break in the journey. And you know we can't stand them West End hotels . . ."

You are about to pay the annual penalty for living in the South. You look at the window sill which does duty as the bar. Some sticky vermouth. A bottle of tonic waiting hopelessly for gin. The seemingly inexhaustible bottle of Angostura bitters, its label faded with the years.

Now, what was it his wife was drinking when they broke their journey with you last year? Was she on gin (she frequently is) or did she go all posh and ask for sherry? (The rules against going all posh don't apply to women, in whom it is dismissed as a weakness to be expected.) Better get both, anyway. And some beer that he can complain about. Two bottles of wine for dinner, and not our usual supermarket *vin plonk* either. He can price any wine offered him and frequently does so, out loud. Then Scotch. He'll want to sit up late telling your wife how he used to thump you at school.

So far, you are down about a tenner. "They're always starving when they get here," says your wife. "What'll we give them?" You are about to say fish and chips when she solves it, as she solves many problems, with the words "Better make it a fiver." A fiver is a sum from which there is never, ever, any change.

She puts the kids in a spare room, where they fall through camp beds throughout the night—and go to school next day in shocking tempers. The visitors' bed linen won't cost more than about a pound at the laundry.

Still, it's good to see them. He plonks a bottle of whisky down on the hall table with a look that says he's not a man that expects owt for nowt. She gives your wife a little parcel. If it's hard, it's table mats. If it's soft, it's napkins. There must be a thriving table mat and napkin industry in Wharfedale, catering solely for situations like this. Still, it's good to see them. You find yourself repeating this to yourself quite a lot. And they are going next day. They *are*, aren't they?

The ones who stay a second night have a habit of saying "What about the West End, then?" They are chilling words. You know rather less about the West End than you know about the Sea of Tranquillity.

Given a bit of warning, you shyly approach more sophisticated friends for the names of places which look as if Princess Margaret might pop in but which are, well, sort of safe. And, well, not too expensive.

*He* enjoys himself. You can tell by the way he insists on paying for the taxi home, even though all his money is already in travellers cheques. And by the way he insists on finishing his bottle of Scotch before going to bed.

By the time he announces that we're all going to bed because he's forgotten to mention a 6 am start in the morning, your bar has been reduced to its familiar complement of bottles.

Next morning, while your wife is packing for them all the available bacon—"It's the one thing you can't get on the Costa Gastronomia"—he threatens massive assaults on your sobriety next time you're in the North. He expects your face to light up at the thought. He feels sorry for you, stuck here in the London rat race. Still, he realises he has been a breath of fresh Northern air for you, which should put you on until good fortune next takes you up the M1.

When it does, the anticipation builds up right to the saloon bar of The Hermit, where he is lording it over the "early doors" crowd. The hubbub of greeting is composed of affectionate insults.

Knowing the Yorkshireman's tight-lipped canon, it is enough to unman a chap when he is awarded one of the highest expressions of warmth and friendliness —"*Nah* then, yer great fat git."

He turns to the landlord. "Give him a pint. He likes his ale, don't you lad? Can't get decent ale in London, can you, kid? And give him a pork pie while you're at it. The wife's away, so we'll get fish and chips tonight. You like pork pies, don't you? Can't get decent pork pies in London. They don't get the meat down there.

"Do you know, he bought us a steak dinner in London the other week I wouldn't have given to our cat. I don't know how they've the cheek to charge them prices.

"Sup up, lad, it's your round next. You enjoyed that, didn't you? Can't get ale like that in London. I don't know how you can stick it down there."

There are times when I don't meself.

"Well, what did you learn?"

# Bethlehem

## By JAMES CAMERON

O little town of Bethlehem, how still we see you lie; above thy dark and dreamless sleep the silent stars go by.

Bethlehem is your Tour Day Number Four; who can resist the lure of the Fount of the Faith? Lunch will be provided; your bus leaves at . . .

Doesn't it *do* something to you, Angela? When you think of that little joint being where it all began . . .

Papers, please. Dokumenti; papiers, rakoshah. No of course be welcome, but stay this side of the street. There is troubles.

Eppy Chrismus, lord; you need guide to holy things? Okay, lord, come back glad.

The town was fortified by Rehoboam, and the Inn of Chimsham here was a rendezvous for travellers to Egypt—to *Egypt*?—In the historic, ladies; is not travelling to Egypt now. In West Bank different situations now. But good old Saviour just the same; let us now visit specially holy place. We are still friends, thanks God; you and me and Jesus Christ. Now on the left . . .

O little town of Bethlehem, how still we see you lie.

What—still lying, even now?

You might think it would take a hell of a man to make funny stories about Bethlehem. You would soon think otherwise if you had ever done the pagan patronising pilgrimage that was the lot—and maybe still is—of spare foreign correspondents and TV crews obliged to do the rota story of Christmas at the grassroots, as reliable a story as Oxford Street, and almost as squalid. As an assignment it ranked with the Cenotaph or the Boat Race: an inescapable dead loser. Unless there was a war there was virtually nothing whatever to say about Bethlehem that you couldn't equally say about Blackpool Pier. Of course you could milk the old originals—Matthew, Mark, Luke and John, who at least had some first-hand advantages, though long ago deprived of copyright—but even the pinching of archaic phrases couldn't disguise the emptiness of the argument. Bethlehem was the worst PR the churches ever had. Was a bus-load of blue-rinsed ladies from Wisconsin supposed to herald in some sort of return to God?

"*You and your memory—we could have had burglars.*"

*"**Isn't** life simple when you know you're right all the time?"*

Bethlehem was for years a traditional Arab town dedicated to the pious exploitation of Christians. It is now an Israeli dominion—protectorate, colony, cordon-sanitaire, afterthought?—dedicated anew to the old Arab folk-craft of exploiting the Christians, with the difference of a nominal rake-off and a noticeably sterner efficiency. The big difference is that hardly anyone goes now, and for good reason: the travel-agents have chickened out. That the Arabs should run the Christian heartland was one thing; that the Jews should supervise the Arabs in conning the Christians is another. Religion is nothing to do with it at all (since despite so many illusions religion in the Middle East is the one wholly flexible thing) but *management* is all. The situation of the Israelis supervising the Arabs' concession to fool the Christians is highly complex. I don't say it can't be fixed, but we aren't there yet. The Israelis may be militarily tough, but they are full of sentimental scruples, especially as far as Jesus Christ is concerned. He was, after all, one of their chaps. For anyone to make a supermarket job out of Christ is profoundly offensive to all good Jews; it attacks their sense of the aesthetic. Now, at last in Bethlehem, the Jews can tell the goyim how to behave.

Bethlehem is probably one of the nastiest little towns in the Middle East, and by God that is saying something. Even for an accredited unbeliever like myself there is something pretty awful about this Butlinisation of a subtle and splendid story. Were I Billy Graham's understudy I would feel ill at ease in what the Jordanians made of Manger Square. Manger—what Manger? They abound. Descend upon it and you will be beset by toothless prophets, in very serious competition, who will contend to escort you to any one of four birthplaces, each one equally authentic, and equally improbable. Nevertheless this must be Bethlehem; is not every alley lined with anointed boutiques, vying with each other to sell you Madonna Egg-timers, the Three Kings Holy Calendar, the Authentic Star-In-The-East Underarm Deodorant, small timepieces set into crucifixes only one remove from the original article, cufflinks in the image of the Dead Sea Scrolls; can you not have a drink in the Bar of the Magi or the Star In The East

*"You should have made an appointment with my secretary here, I'm giving an interview to the Observer colour supplement at eleven."*

Saloon or, even simpler, The Birthplace? Have you ever heard of a pub called The Stations of the Cross? As far as I know it isn't there yet, but it won't be long.

Once upon a time there was a small township called Bethlehem, which in Hebrew means The House of Bread. It sits on a limestone ridge six miles from Jerusalem on the road to Hebron. If you read the book of Ruth, it sounds more romantic than it appears today. It was famous as the birthplace of David but—as the old books say—"it received no special favours from his hand." The big deal for Bethlehem happened when Mary found no room in the inn and there, in the stabling annexe to a travellers' tavern, gave birth to the world's most famous Jew, who was executed on the Roman cross in his thirties, thus inspiring some nine hundred million followers today all over the world, and providing a livelihood for a multitude of chancers to ride the waggon on his myth. As in Bethlehem today. I think they do no especial fault; there is indeed a sort of merit in consolidating a belief that rarely does harm, and often good.

O little town of Bethlehem. It was desecrated under the rule of the awful Hadrian. It has convents still under the orders of the Greek, Latin, and Armenian Churches. Here did Jerome work in an unremembered room translating his Scriptures. It was taken by the Crusaders in the eleventh century. The bus will be leaving in half an hour for the Tour of the Four Authentic Birthplaces. There will be a brief stop-over at Gethsemane for Bread and Wine. Lady, lady: do you not want a fragment of the True Cross? I put it to you: the security of the State demands an extension of its boundaries. Do you never read the words of Minister Dayan? I give you my word as a true Hadji: this is exactly where Christ was born; everybody else lies, and alas for money. How can Israel behave this way to our people, who ask nothing but human rights? I am sure you are right about the Scriptures, but last week someone bombed our supermarket and Mrs. Levinsky's daughter lost her leg; what were you saying about the Manger? Yes, it's just up there; you can see by all the police. Bethlehem is a nice place to live; do you see that view over the hills? Oh God how can you say it could start again; haven't we had enough? Now, ladies and gentlemen, here is the truly attested location where He who came to save us all first saw the light; I dare say it was brighter then; still you know how it was for the Prince of Peace. Haven't we had enough? Listen: stop it, stop it; what matters is today. Lady I insist: a fragment of the True Cross for a mere fifty piastres; I mean pounds. After all for God's sake this is Bethlehem, isn't it? Allah-illah-Illah: O give me somewhere to live, where I shall not be hurt and harried. Did you hear about Mrs. Cohen's son: called up *again*, and on the tender edge of marriage? Attention, everyone: the bus for the hotel is about to leave.

O little town of Bethlehem, how still we see you lie; above thy dark and dreamless sleep the silent stars go by.

Do you hear that, Fatimah? Do you hear that, Rachel?

Lucky for the Christians; they got Bethlehem, at least.

*"This is absurd. It's nothing but a rat race."*

# PIN-UPS IN THE NEWS

"I hope to follow in Daddy's footsteps," says Tertia, the serious member of the Lestrange-Talbot triplets. Their father has just become Major General in the Guards.

Svilde Hôst, an au pair from the Arctic Circle, is writing a novel about the Webbs.

Cherry McMahon, one of the Science Museum team who are investigating the early history of the parachute.

Here's one girl who thinks that Shakespeare's plays were written by Shakespeare. "They're full of anagrams that prove it," says Drusilla Deb-Ramsgate, Lord Plantagenet's lively daughter, who is seen here retrieving *Macbeth* from a computer.

Mrs. Henwick, the Streatham housewife whose Clean Up *The Encyclopaedia Britannica* campaign has snowballed recently.

Mary Barn was buying lunch for her poodle the other day when her hat caught in the door of a Mini. Subsequent recriminations led to a long dinner with Arthur Hawksey, the property-valuing heir to the Da Gamba fortune. His grandmother told *Punch* that she had never heard of Miss Barn. Viewers soon will, as she expects to be offered a part in the new Children's Serial "Will of the Witanagemote."

... giving the headmaster any ... excuses, so can we ...

# Daughter in the House

## by GRAHAM

"... *And your family place in Berkshire ... that's where your fath keeps his polo ponies?*"

"*Of course, if you'd rather see your daughter going about in rags ...*"

"*That's got an Honours Degree in Philosophy?*"

# Notes for a War Novel

## By MILES KINGTON

*"The Ministry of Defence has decided that, as a matter of principle, every suitable qualified officer should be able to take a university degree before or during his service career. . . . Army cadets will undergo a new two-year course at Sandhurst in which one year will consist of uninterrupted academic study. It is hoped that this will then become the first year of a three-year university course for all officers who reach the required standard."*

*The Observer.*

"Name?"

"Morgan, sir."

"Good. Now, why do you want to join the army?"

"Mostly a sense of adventure, sir, but I also want very much to bear arms for my country. And I've always been terribly interested in marching."

"I see. Well, Morgan, I'm going to be frank with you. Those qualifications might stand you in good stead in some careers—rural preservation or something like that—but it doesn't really add up to what we think of as officer material. I'm awfully sorry. Next?"

"Lewis, sir."

"So you want to be a soldier, do you, Lewis?"

"Oh no, sir I want to continue my researches into late nineteenth-century French literature. For a start, it's time we re-evaluated Verlaine's religious phase and . . ."

"Yes, yes, maybe, but do you *really* think the Salop Regiment is the right place for it?"

"Well, sir, I do realise that your unit is basically a classics and political philosophy outfit, but I think it would be well worthwhile building up a small modern language section."

"That's the spirit! Just the sort of man we're looking for. You'll have to take a medical test, of course, but as long as you remember to take your glasses along to it I think we can safely say you're in."

\* \* \*

Autumn prevailed. The sodden west wind blew the leaves across the hallowed barracks square, whipped them into a lonely whirlpool and went on to ruffle the ancestral ivy of 1st Battalion HQ. A major, walking smartly across to the regimental library, shivered, once. In their quarters, Lewis and Morgan honed their minds on a point of semantics while the wireless in the corner keened Monteverdi.

"You see, Sam," said Lewis, "when John Knox talked about the monstrous regiment of women, he used the word in the original sense of ruling. He meant Elizabeth I and Mary Queen of Scots."

"Yes, I know," said Morgan, "but do you think the word 'regiment' still has overtones of domination, unfair privilege, working under duress? And do you think the men sense it?"

"I hope so," said Lewis. "I spent three hours this morning trying to get my section to tell the difference between an undistributed middle and an argumentum ad hominem. God help them if they ever come under fire from a well-trained German logician."

They both laughed. Then Lewis grew serious.

"Sam, there's one thing I've always meant to ask you. How did you ever get into the regiment after

*"About time too! He's going to America to clear his brother's name."*

137

making such a bad impression on the recruiting officer?"

Morgan grinned.

"Simple. I went to him afterwards and explained that my profession of military virtues had been purely satirical, even a piece of gratuitous Dadaism, and that all I was really interested in was the army as improvised theatre of cruelty. Artaud for Artaud's sake, I told him."

At that moment the Monteverdi faded and the news was announced. The two men stiffened.

"Synchronise watches," said Lewis. "It is now . . . 2300 hours. In exactly ten minutes Professor Wilkinson will be attacking the influence of Flaubert on the novel. Ready?"

"Ready."

Ears pricked, the two officers sank back into their chairs and on to the alert.

\* \* \*

Summer came, and with it the golden days of strolls along the parade ground, corned beef lunches on the lawns and river-borne expeditions with the water lapping timelessly round the assault craft. Bittersweet days, though; the shadow of the final passing out exam was always there, as was the fatal moment when they would venture through the ancient portals into that other world of drill from nine to five and gentlemen's khaki suits. Lewis took to his books viciously as if his life depended on it. Morgan wrote to a highland regiment which, he had heard, needed a skilled

*"One thing I did notice—he wore turn-ups."*

instructor in French verse formation. He never received a reply and later learnt they had been transferred to Germany.

"Mr. Lewis," said the Major-General, "how would you distinguish a Racine tragedy from a Voltairian pastiche at long distance?"

"Inferior prosody, sir. The Voltairian model also has religious doubts, which make for greater flexibility but less power."

"What is the method for locating and destroying a Nietzschean proposition?"

"Basically, spotting the Schopenhauerian camouflage and then proceeding to cut off the intuitive supply lines. If there's still trouble, five minutes intensive Bertrand Russell will silence opposition."

"Excellent. Now what is this?"

He pushed something across for Lewis to examine.

"It's a fourteen-line Gautier poem, sir. Effective at close range but no good for sustained bombardment. Also, it has been wrongly assembled."

As one man, the examining board rose and applauded.

\* \* \*

Two years later Lewis ran into Morgan in Shaftesbury Avenue.

"I heard you were in London," said Lewis. "Seconded to the Phonetics Research Division of the Guards, isn't that right?"

"That's right. We've been working on a new approach to parade ground commands—increased comprehensibility and all that. And you?"

"Postgraduate work at Aldershot. It's meant to be top secret, but I can tell you that we're trying to crack the Russian plosive system."

There was a silence, as each waited for the other to broach the unmentioned topic. Morgan was the first.

"Well, it looks as if the peace is going to come to an end. It's hard to believe, but if what they say is true, it's war at last."

"Yes," said Lewis not looking at Morgan. "And that means they won't be needing us any more. Who wants an army officer when it's back to the daily routine of shooting and fighting?"

"What will you do, then?"

"Don't know. Drift into film work, I expect. You?"

"Advertising, probably. I have a few contacts."

They didn't say anything for a moment.

"We'll keep in touch, though," said Morgan.

"Oh yes, we mustn't lose contact."

"See you around, then."

"See you."

Seconds later they were lost in the Piccadilly crowds.

# Letter to an Old Flame

## By ANGELA MILNE

Hollowood

*Now at last, thirty years later, Angela Milne can tell her side of the story.*

Dear Terry,

Remember me? The nice little English girl who was staying near your place in Connecticut that summer more than thirty years ago?

Of course you do/don't. It was the summer before you got married, which could have blotted me from your mind. Equally, though, it could have jelled me there as part of a magical time when the world was young and you fell in love. And that, dear Terry, would make two of us, because it describes exactly how I still think of you.

Did I imagine, as I stood alone at the front end of the *Georgic* one dark May night and saw a single tiny light prick the black horizon (a supreme moment surely denied in its full glory to air travellers), that I was sailing to Romance? Actually no. As far as I knew, I was sailing from it. The boy friend in England—you must remember him, Terry, I used to give you letters to post to him on your way home. At first. The one you forgot, and kept in your pocket for days, probably began: *"I am sorry not to have written for so long but life has been so gay. David, I think it would be fairer to you if I . . ."*

Don't think you broke anything up. Even as David and I said our last farewell in London we somehow knew we were doomed. There was I, tearing myself away from Stamford Bridge (don't believe what you hear about British football matches, Terry, David and I found the crowds perfectly well-mannered), the Marx Brothers films, the rambles round dreamy old Chelsea, my job as a fifty-bob typist, leaving all this because some inner force was driving me to seek a newer world. I mean, the Hattons had asked me over to spend the summer and I'd be an idiot not to.

So now, a pioneer, I watched the twinkling lights multiply and had mixed thoughts. It was marvellous but what was I doing here, knowing not a soul in America but Jenny the Hattons' daughter? Why had I left my loving family, and London, and—idiot that I was—David and Stamford Bridge, or, as it would now be, David and Lord's and Wimbledon?

In such a mood, Terry, I reached the Hatton home on the pine-clad hill. It was lovely, a real ranch atmosphere, the swimming pool was heaven, the Connecticut country was beautiful, everything was fun, yet the high spots of my day were the

139

Arrivals and Departures of Liners in the paper, and the visits to the post office to post or collect the letters those liners bore. Geared to the homeland, that was me before I met you.

We've got a young man to come up weekends and play tennis, they told me. The idea was that you'd make up a four not only for tennis but for the summer, with Jenny and her fiancé Pete and me. They also told me, meaningfully, that your father was a tycoon and you were working your way up in the family business.

"Oh yes," I expect I said, "how nice. Jolly good show." I used to find myself saying things like this in America, as you may remember. One fine day Jenny asked me what I'd be doing if I were in London.

"I might be at Lord's," I said wistfully.

"Gee," said Jenny, "if you aren't the most English person I ever met."

This might explain why, when you drove up in your little car and your white flannels, I thought how nice and English you looked. Nice and thin, nice ordinary length hair, nice face, nice smile. I bet when they asked me afterwards what I thought of you, I said, "He's awfully nice, isn't he?" and dear Mr. Hatton—wasn't he a pet?—put his arm round me and said it was sure swell to be reminded so often of his beloved native land.

On Monday Mr. Hatton went back to New York and you were in the home town ten miles away, dutifully bottle-washing. Mrs. Hatton and Jenny and I were living our customary weekday life until the next Friday. I thought how you'd be up again next Saturday, and how the Hatton household was getting a settled, familiar atmosphere. Jenny and I drove to the post office, which was also the drugstore, for the post and our fifteen cent boxes of marshmallows, then on to the real estate man for a block of ice. We roped this on to the car bumper and took it home to the icebox. We swam, and pottered about, and made grapefruit and cream cheese salad, and drove to New Haven to do the shopping, past your house. Roll on Saturday! What would I wear? My best white Aertex shirt and flapping green linen trousers. *Now* do you remember me?

Saturday came and went and the next week flowed by, some of it at the big weatherboard house where Uncle Bob lived. I can't remember his surname. He wasn't really Jenny's uncle, Martha was his real niece, she'd come to stay from Detroit. Funny how one does remember some things. Well, Uncle Bob, or rather

*"Always been his trouble—just can't delegate."*

*"Not fleas?—again?"*

Auntie Bob, had an electric sewing-machine, and Jenny and I spent the week making dresses. I machined mine at deadline speed because next Saturday after tennis you were coming to one of our weekend porch suppers, and it was utterly essential that I should be wearing orange with white trimmings.

I must tell you also about the skunk in the wood opposite the drugstore. We got a great whiff of it every time we drove to Uncle Bob's house. I've never had the chance to smell one since, but I know it would smell as marvellous as it did then.

So one way and another, Terry, it was no surprise to me when as you climbed into you little car that next Saturday afternoon to go home and change, and you put your hand over the door to slam it shut, I saw the uniqueness of that hand, its fantastic assemblage of four fingers and a thumb, and knew myself a goner.

Do you know what I think the best definition of the moment of falling in love? It is when one can say of somebody those monstrous words of Juliet's—

*Take him and cut him out in little stars,*
*And he will make the face of heaven so fine—*

and find them to be solemnly true. You slammed your car door, and lo! they were.

So you rattled down the drive and came back in a white suit and we all had a lovely party on the porch. I should think. I can't remember.

But I remember how from now on the life about me had intensified. I mooned about the Hatton property noting how mistily the far hills dreamed, how deliciously the path to the swimming pool wound past the luminous red tennis court and through the shimmering birch wood; and how this pool, which, you remember, was a large pond really, now became a pine-shrouded vista of wonderment. I won't say the Harmless Snake and the bullfrogs the swimmers shared it with became my friends, but they were distinctly more lovable. And the sunlight which so frequently poured over our hill-top paradise grew ever hotter, and I thought I had never lived before.

As for your tennis, Terry, that got even better while mine got even worse. It now seemed presumption to partner or oppose such a demi-god, and I preferred to sit at the side and gawp at you. Not that my emotions showed, I imagine. Back at the ranch the Hattons would drop dark hints about my British reserve and I got the impression they thought I was missing my chance.

Well, look how the summer had been going. Week after week you turned up for the tennis parties and the suppers with us and Pete and the Yale Professor of Stage Lighting and the Russian emigré and the Uncle Bob lot and all the jolly people who filled the place at weekends. And there were the foursome parties we went on, the picnics, the movies, the dances at the Country Club with you glorious

*"Oh, is that you Ethel? I was hoping it would be a wrong number, so that I needn't stop and talk."*

141

*"It's an emissary of the Church."*

in your white tuxedo, me ravishing in floor-length chiffon. But what, passionwise, had happened between us?

Nothing.

Then, one tennis afternoon when Jenny and I were sitting on those long deck-chairs with our feet up, something did happen. You came off the court and sat on the end of mine, and to make room you gave my feet a courteous yet playful shove with your tennis racket.

It was almost too much for me, Terry, though you wouldn't have guessed from my cool smile. From now on I dared, yes, I dared to hope. I wandered round the woods reasoning that strictly nurtured New England boys did not bang similarly inhibited Old England girls' feet with tennis rackets unless they meant to get somewhere, and it was in this dizzy mood that I received the news that you had suddenly gone away. Off somewhere for a fortnight.

Well, everyone needs a break. We were off ourselves to the Middle West. I wasn't a sightseeing foreigner now, but a New Englander homesick for Connecticut. When we got back you were still away. It was late August and we'd been picking blueberries one afternoon when Mrs. Hatton met us at the door. "What do you know?" she said. "Terry is going to marry Martha."

"I say!" I expect I exclaimed. "How awfully nice for him!"

Then I walked down to the sad swimming pool, and sat looking at a bullfrog for quite five minutes. A few days later I was on the boat, all excited at going back to England.

What with finding that David had another girl (a genuine sports-lover) I'm afraid I never really thought about you again, Terry, except to wonder how deeply I had disappointed the kind Hattons. But I've always remembered how falling for you gave me Connecticut on a plate, and I thank you.

Yours ever,
Angela

# PRINCE PHILIP—A NEW SCANDAL
## Has He Gone Too Far This Time?

**The Duke yesterday: unrepentant**

**So the Duke of Edinburgh has got himself in another mess!**

Yesterday, as all the world must know by now, an American newsman was chatting with His Royal Highness and commented in passing that it was a fine day. The Duke agreed; but then went on to add: "though I think we're going to have some rain tomorrow."

### Dear oh Dear!

Dear oh dear oh dear! It's this sort of reckless off-the-cuff comment that has begun to make us doubt whether he ever thinks before he speaks. What right has he to stand up and pontificate on climatic conditions? Did he think for a moment what the constitutional position would be if, for instance, the Queen had thought the fine weather would continue?

Make no mistake. We have often applauded his bold statements. We admire his bluff Hello's, his urbane and witty How Do You Do's. But when it comes to making rash meteorological predictions he should be reminded that tolerance of the monarchy demands some responsibility on their part. We tremble just to think how the Americans felt when they heard him ride roughshod over their isobars.

### Don't Forget

So remember, your Highness. As a hand-shaker, you are unbeatable. We would give our eye teeth to be able to smile like you. But when you open your mouth and try to talk like an ordinary human being, it is the duty of the British press to try to make capital out of distorting anything you say. That, your Highness, is how democracy works.

**Punch says—watch it!**

142

143

# FLAT CAPS COME TO TOWN LARRY (from Birmingh

It must be what they call "sophistication." If you live in the capital, you learn to ignore all the queer sights around you.

There isn't the same warmth in the Londoner as you find in Blackpool or Manchester. You try to break them down but there's no response.

London's the only place I know where they pay a lot of fellers pots of money for doing nowt.

If they fancy a night out at flicks, they go to Odeon, Leicester Square, and stand in the pelting rain . . . watching other folk going in.

But what gripes me most is the fact that everything in this bloody country centres on London.

# THE SOUTH STRIKES BACK!

"Oh, my God! I haven't packed the Entero-vioform!"

"He says I can't go in without cap, or you without shawl!"

"You can't understand the jokes! I don't even understand the language!"

"Shut thi' face when our Ena's deliberating!"

"By gum, lad—hasn't tha' got round to wearin' collarless shirts wi' big brass stud in t' South yet?"

"I don't believe it!"

*"Ee, great to have you back, Jonas lad. We swapped them a General of the East Kent and Surrey Light Horse for you, lad."*

*"You'll have to speak your lines a lot louder— Batley folk like to hear every word, loud and clear."*

*"Surrey 456 for two, Edrich not out 257—rain stopped play."*

*"Look, dear, I wanted lots of gorgeous squalor, and this just isn't gorgeous enough!"*

# Great Coffee Stains of the Renaissance

## By KENNETH ALLSOP

**Monday** Lunch with Crispin Calf-Binding, publicity chap at Chatup and Windbag, at the new Soho trattoria where they flambé everything. Even the hors d'oeuvre was roasted in blue fire—most novel, a remark which creased Calf-Binding, who thought it wittily apt as lava splashed, spitting and smoking, from the fried caviare on to the stack of advance copies he'd brought along for me. Main purpose of lunching was to let me in on their new publishing plans under the Leisureflick imprint. Idea is to maximise the coffee table book trend to its full potential. As Calf-Binding said, publishers so far have been shifty about the non-book trade. All busily pretending to be making contributions to high culture with desperate albums of *Early Victorian Fly Swats and Vintage Roll-Your-Own Cigarette Machines* and *The Great Gothic Footscrapers of Our Civilisation*, with enormous margins, lots of big chapter heads and medieval prints, and the artwork colour you get on baked beans billboards. Calf-Binding is convinced that Leisureflick can make a great com-

mercial breakthrough by rethinking the entire coffee table book supply-and-demand. They've been quietly studying some consumer research done for them by MAKE (Modify-and-Activate-Kinetic-Engineers), the American people-improvers. Time-and-motion spot checks in The Boltings, Boar's Hill and the Span village at New Ash Green show that in a coffee table environment hand-to-book contact averages a daily thirty-five seconds; each individual "book approach," as it's termed, is confined to three sporadic dips at most and often one-and-a-riffle. Logical recommendation MAKE has put forward is economically to slenderise by jettisoning the old-fashioned convention of commissioning, say, 60,000 words of text and paying for reproduction rights on a hundred illustrations. Quite simply, the new Leisureflick series will look as fat—and each one will be as fat, but it will consist of the same paragraph duplicated as often as needed to fill the space left for typography, likewise with the half-dozen pictures. Statistics prove that this will

WHY DECORATE?
INTRODUCED BY MALCOLM MUGGERIDGE

never be noticed by the "reader." Brilliant. He also guardedly suggested that I might contribute to the series. Shall think it over. As I waited at the Haymarket bus stop on my way back to Fleet Street, saw Lindsay Anderson walking on the opposite pavement. What an incredibly glamorous life I lead.

**Tuesday** Rather specially sparkling lunchtime gathering of the in-crowd today. After finishing my column about writing last week's column, by foot along Ponders End High Street, savouring the early spring sunshine, like gobbets of fried egg through the burned bacon rind of the plane trees' bare branches and all encircled by the polished frying pan sky, if that's not too ridiculous a way of describing it. In the Withered Vine had drinks with Les Judd, Ponders End's wittiest estate agent, Dennis Toole, just back from a BEA flight to Manchester, and Dick Carper who always seems to me, with his corner shop wallpaper displays, to capture the savage social parody with which George Grosz illuminated the Berlin of Brecht. I had been twitting Les about his window display of properties ("unique bungalow homes near golf course"), suggesting that smart though the photographs might be on their wooden easels they had a shallow, mechanical decadence. But his little black eyes were fixed along the bar on a girl with dirigible superstructure. "Ghorrrrr," he said, once again reminding one that he wasn't nicknamed the Noël Coward of Winchmore Hill for nothing, "I bet she has to throw some of those sandbags overboard to get moving." Suddenly it hit me: the blockage was weight. Immediately rang up Calf-Binding. He thinks I'm on to something important, perhaps comparable to the moment when Crick and Watson cracked the DNA structure. Thought a great deal today about my bowel movements. Utterly objectively, I know of none so fascinating.

**Wednesday** Why do people pile their cripplingly squat, hernia-administering casual tables with oddly shaped volumes about Krautstrunk glass, Flemish ivory combs, Isotta-Fraschini and Panhard-Levassor

HARGREAVES

cars, eighteenth-century bronze clocks and Chinese porcelain? Because (a) they won't fit into normal shelves and (b) a languid supremacy is conveyed to callers, the air that these arcane subjects are the everyday coinage of the culture which bred their owner. As their high-veneer covers shimmer in the dancing glow of the Rainbow Fountain Lamp, they are like an extra pile on the wall-to-wall carpeting, an urbane jab in the ribs for the Joneses next door who have only the *TV Times*, the latest part of *Man, Myth and Magic* and *The Reader's Digest Book of the Road* on their bark-rimmed lozenge slice of natural knots. Next stage: so what limits the number of these ornate status cymbals clashed so resoundingly under neighbours' noses? Heaviness alone: sheer tonnage. How can this be overcome? I have a notion. Checked the index of Curzon's *Modern Parliamentary Eloquence* (1915). My name not there. Inexplicable.

**Thursday** Telephoned an old Oxford friend, now one of the young lions in the Department of Weights and Measures, earmarked (it's murmured around Whitehall) for office of glittering distinction in that austere but discreetly powerful world of metric scholarship. We lunched at White's, not the same without Randolph and Evelyn, although my stories about them are. Gathered most useful data on non-shelved books, and wear and tear on structural fabric of buildings. Apparently, nationwide, each living unit has an average of one-quarter-ton of deadweight of Redouté's roses or *Our Heritage of Landscape Paintings* bearing down upon rafters and foundations, until buildings on all sides are sagging in the middle like badly cooked cakes. A theory rapidly gaining respect around Westminster is that the rush by an industrial "society of rising expectations" for portfolios of antique pistol paintings may not be entirely unconnected with the crumpling of high-rise flats. Am in no doubt about next move re Calf-Binding and the project, and I dropped him a note on way to preview of Les Judd's *Genitals* at Southgate's off-High Street Little Theatre. Of course one can keep up the pace, yet at times I fret about the loss of stillness in my life—it's a good year since I read any Dante or a line of Kant's *Groundwork to a Metaphysics of Morals*. I miss it.

*"Listen, Tovarich, all that talk about escaping to the West is nonsense. I was just as locked up in the London Zoo."*

# The Only True Horoscope!

Parliament wants to know how astrology will fare under the Trades Description Act. The answer is in Kington's Stars (formerly Madam Kington's Stars), which offer predictions *nobody* can challenge.

**TAURUS** April 20-May 20. One day soon your friends will clap you on the back and ask you how old you are, though your innate truthfulness may not always govern your answer. You can expect a cake from loved ones. International relations will worsen in some areas, but this should have no effect on your work prospects. If you play correspondence chess, it may be your move.

**GEMINI** May 21-June 20. If your marriage partner shows signs of independence, even secretiveness or complete withdrawal, it could all be for the good—who knows what the stars foretell? Financially, this is as good a time as any to start a lavish musical based on the discovery of Saturn's rings. You will remember something you forgot to do. Avoid the monsoon season.

**CANCER** June 21-July 20. A chance remark in a pub may lead to a glass being placed in your hand. If people show an inability to understand and listen to your problems, it might be because your shaving cuts form the name of someone they hate. Don't worry if you fail to communicate with a friend—dial again. Not a particularly auspicious week for taking up the mandolin.

**LEO** July 21-August 22. The world will come to an end on the 8th, though not on this astral plane. Carry on as if nothing has happened, paying especial attention to health, success and happiness. Any attempts to wallpaper your home on the 14th may well be followed by a telephone call to a professional decorator. Avoid berserk orchestras.

**VIRGO** August 23-September 22. Affairs of the heart continue to go well, if you take exercise, eat wisely and sit up straight. Don't worry about impending lawsuits unless you are a neurotic criminal and don't be afraid to force a show-down with world leaders—they will respect you for it, even if they don't say so. Weekend shopping will be a drain on resources.

**LIBRA** September 23-October 22. This week, try to look at life afresh and make a new start in your dealings with others. If possible, sell all that you have, give unto the poor and be even as a little child. If this is not practicable, render unto Caesar the things that are Caesar's. Prune roses now.

**SCORPIO** October 23-November 21. You will read a horoscope in Punch which claims to be proof against any claims for wrongful promises. You will do your best to find a flaw in it, but fail. You will now redouble your efforts. Attempts to regain Britain's lost Empire should be postponed for the time being. Work worries will ease off at the weekend.

**SAGITTARIUS** November 22-December 21. There will be a sustained attempt, involving millions of pounds, to pressure you into making certain purchases, notably petrol, chocolate and detergents. It will succeed, but not on a large scale. While you are asleep on the 9th, you have a sudden blinding insight into the identity of Mr. WH.

**CAPRICORN** December 22-January 19. You will encounter a tall dark stranger named Arnold Winschutt, a referee who always guarantees himself one draw in his pools entry and is still trying to get seven other referees interested in his scheme. You pass within feet of each other on the pavement then go your separate ways. This evening is a particularly good time for supper. Avoid traffic pile-ups.

**AQUARIUS** January 20-February 18. Financially the future looks fair to disastrous, though if you invest with a touch of genius you should avoid all but the worst debacles. A close relative agrees to spy for the Russians, in conditions of the utmost secrecy, and a letter from a long-lost relative goes astray in the post. There will be some very good news, though not necessarily for you.

**PISCES** February 19-March 20. Your windfall of several thousand pounds from a grateful madman is concealed from you by a firm of unusually dishonest solicitors. You ought to make small repairs in the home now, rather than postpone them for years and find the place disintegrating round you. Someone at work falls desperately in love with you, but there are reasons why you must not know.

**ARIES** March 21-April 19. Although this again won't be your week for master-minding a South American coup d'etat, you are well shot of the financial and legal problems it would have entailed. Instead, concentrate on earning more money than you spend. You will go on what seems like a long journey across tarmac, though you should be back the same day. Avoid falling trees, elms especially.

**ON HER MAJESTY'S
SECRET SERVICE**
GEORGE LAZENBY as James
Bond and The Other One

# CINEMA
ffolkes

**ANNE OF THE THOUSAND
DAYS**
RICHARD BURTON as
King Henry VIII
GENEVIEVE BUJOLD as
Anne Boleyn

**CACTUS FLOWER**
WALTER MATTHAU as
Julian Winston
GOLDIE HAWN as
Toni Simmons
INGRID BERGMAN as
Stephanie Dickinson

**KING LEAR**
FRANK MIDDLEMASS as Fool
MICHAEL HORDERN as Lear

# THEATRE
Hewison

**THE APPLE CART**
JOHN NEVILLE as King Magnus
MAURICE DENHAM as Proteus

**THE WHITE DEVIL**
JOHN MOFFATT
as Monticelso
GERALDINE McEWAN
as Vittoria
DEREK GODFREY
as Bracciano and
EDWARD WOODWARD
as Flamineo

# The Father is Manager of the Child

## By MICHAEL PARKINSON

Andrew, my eldest boy, is nine years old and will one day captain the England soccer team. I am as certain of that happening as I am that Nicholas, the six year old, is going to be the best fast bowler since F. S. Trueman and that Michael, who is two, will one day win Wimbledon and marry a rich and wealthy American oil heiress thereby keeping his mother and father in the manner to which they would dearly love to be accustomed. The child is the mirror of the father's sporting ambitions and it is a terrible position to be in. In my own case I realise that my father regards me as an awful failure because many years ago I joined the *Manchester Guardian* instead of Yorkshire County Cricket Club. The fact that the *Manchester Guardian* offered me a job and Yorkshire had shown no inclination to support my father's theory that I was the best opening bat since Len Hutton, did not alter his opinion that I was mad to prefer journalism to cricket. Looking back I can see that he had invested a lot of time and money in me in order that I might one day play cricket for my native county and give him the pleasure of sitting in the crowd, nudging the man next to him and saying, "That's my lad tha' knows." (Looking back it seems that from my very early childhood I measured off my years in new cricket bats. I would have one every birthday and was never allowed to play with it until it had been properly "broken in." This ritual involved days and nights of oiling the surface of the blade and then tapping it gently with an old cricket ball until father decided it was seasoned enough to withstand a real game.)

Similarly the summer nights of my youth were spent in diligent practice. Nothing fancy you understand. Just learning the classic rules of the Yorkshire game: defence first, fancy stuff later . . . much later. By the time I was eight or nine I was well on the way to becoming the most boring batsman in the world, a guaranteed emptier of cricket grounds. I could stay there all day but I didn't possess a single scoring shot. This depressed me and delighted my father who always believed that any fool could hit a six but it took science to stay at the crease for an hour or two.

As I grew older I developed my own tiny repertoire of scoring strokes. My father approved so long as the shot did not require the bat moving out of the perpendicular. For a time I played the game according to him and then I started a bit of clever stuff like the occasional late cut. By this time I was playing in the Yorkshire leagues and feeling that I had done

*"Can't I plead with you, Helen? It isn't my wish that our marriage should end like this."*

*"Haven't the Bobbie and Doreen Proudfoot Formation Dance Team got a wonderful sense of the dramatic!"*

pretty well, but even so there was no escape from father's influence. At every game, home or away, he would sit behind the bowler's arm and watch me play. He would assess every stroke I played by either nodding his approval or, if he disapproved, standing up and demonstrating to me what I should have done. The only time I saw him lost for alternative suggestions was when I made my first late cut in his presence. I was rather proud of the shot. I picked the right ball, everything went well and the ball sped between first and second slip to the boundary. I experienced that delicious feeling that comes to all sportsmen when they have accomplished something difficult. I looked toward the boundary to see what father thought. He was standing there shaking his head in sorrow. Afterwards he said: "I don't know where you're getting these bad habits from."

It was the same with soccer. He took me to my first game when I was five and reminds me that after twenty minutes I told him: "Well it's all right but I finks we'll go home now." To which he said: "Well

I don't finks we will." In that moment another soccer fan was born. He didn't have lofty ambitions for me as a soccer player but that didn't mean that he left me alone to discover the game for myself. Being a lifelong supporter of Barnsley Football Club he believed that soccer was a shin kicking contest played with a ball. Ever since the day I first saw Danny Blanchflower I had different ideas and our philosophical conflict about the game was real and deep seated. He wanted a son in the great tradition of Barnsley hard men whose approach to the game was simply to reduce the other side to rubble. I wanted to be a Blanchflower or a Shackleton or a Finney, a player of wit and charm. This ambition was eventually destroyed by a series of young men in the Barnsley and District League who had obviously heeded what their fathers had told them, and who kicked me black and blue into a premature retirement from the game. "Too soft, our Michael" is all that father said.

At the time I scoffed at his disappointments believing them to be extreme symptoms of someone

*"I only carry traveller's cheques."*

who was merely football daft and cricket mad. Nowadays with children of my own I sympathise with him and damn myself for being so insensitive. The trouble with children is that they won't listen to their dads. Only recently I had occasion to discuss the future with my nine year old after he had arrived home from school with legs so bruised they looked like mottled rhubarb.

"How did you get those bruises?" I asked.

"Playing football," he said.

"Child, the idea of football is to kick the ball and not the man. Who was marking you, Nobby Stiles?"

"No, Big Danny. You see every time I got the ball and tried to beat him he just kicked me," he said.

"What position were you playing?" I asked.

"Oh I was playing up front. I'm always Georgie Best when we play," he said.

I tried to be calm.

"Look son. How many times have I told you that it's not wise to try and copy Georgie Best, not unless you want a wheelchair for your tenth birthday. The sensible thing to do nowadays is get yourself in the defence where you can do the kicking and not get kicked," I said.

"But I like being Georgie Best. He's smashing," he said.

"But don't you see child if you are to fulfil your promise as a footballer and satisfy your father's ambitions for you to captain England it would be sensible to play like Bobby Moore. Look at him.

Never gets the knocks, never breaks sweat. He'll go on forever," I said.

It was no good, he just started sulking. I decided on a different tactic. "Let's forget about soccer. Let's see how the cricket is developing," I said.

We went outside and erected the plastic baby bath which serves as a wicket. For a time things went well. He had obviously remembered all that I had taught him, playing forward and back with an impeccably straight bat. Then it happened. I bowled him a good length ball on the leg stump. He dropped on one knee and swept it in to the garden shed. I was appalled.

"What was that?" I asked him.

"Garfield Sobers sweeping Ray Illingworth for six to win the match," he said.

"That might well be so in your mind, but in fact it was a cross batted swipe that no true Yorkshireman would even contemplate and for doing it you can now go and practise playing forward and back defensively in front of your bedroom mirror," I said.

"That's boring," he said, and went indoors.

"Boring or not it's what will get you your Yorkshire cap," I shouted after him.

I was upset at the time but I'm over it now. I don't despair. I know that one day he will play for Yorkshire and captain England at soccer. If only he has the sense to listen to his old man, that is.

*"I really think you've had enough, sir. It's time to go home and beat up your loved ones."*

# Mauvais Viveur

## By HUMPHREY LYTTELTON

*"Can I have the toupee tonight, Dad?"*

Sing Ho for the bad things of life (among which singing ho must hold a high place)! Today, thanks to television, free education, colour supplements, cheap travel, handy booklets and advertising, every man is his own connoisseur of the Good Life. The time has come when, to stand out in a crowd, to be acknowledged as a man of distinction, to bring that awed hush to a cultured conversation, a man must be seen to have experienced and *enjoyed* the Bad Life in all its richness.

It's a mistake to think that this is easy. With mediocrity all around, true badness is as hard to find as true goodness. At both extremes, things aren't what they used to be. For instance, I have no doubt that supermarkets today abound in packets of processed, ready-to-mix instant blancmange powder. But you may be sure that no amount of culinary ingenuity will make it taste as majestically gruesome as the classic hand-mixed edifices that used to appear on the table at school dinners, clammy of texture, flavoured with haircream and as thick-skinned as a traffic warden.

A lot of exquisitely bad taste is acquired in childhood. At my private school, first thing in the morning, we were given a glass of milk and a ginger biscuit to sustain us through the pre-breakfast lesson. With that same careful deliberation with which a gourmet lemons an oyster and inhales it from its shell, we used to suspend the biscuit in the milk until it was pliable and then suck it ferociously—an exercise that successfully ruined the taste of the milk and subverted the combined efforts of Messrs. Huntley, Palmer, McVitie, Price, Peak and Frean to produce a biscuit that was firm in texture and crisp to the bite. It's my belief that inside every *bon viveur* who sniffs his wine, crackles his cigar between the finger tips and purses his lips over a *coquille St. Jacques* there is a *mauvais viveur* who still relishes a soggy ginger biscuit when backs are turned.

It's no accident that it was the Americans who actually invented a word—to dunk—for the splendidly barbaric habit of using the liquids to soften up the solids. Classic badness abounds in the New World. My outstanding gastronomic memory of a tour of the States ten years ago is of a Jumbo Butterscotch Sundae experienced within a day or two of my arrival. It came

to the table in a huge glass chimney, and consisted basically of five blobs of vanilla ice-cream submerged in a gallon of molten toffee. I don't know how you react to sweetness, but I tend to loss of vision, throbbing in the ears and a curious itching on the inside of my skull. Halfway through the Jumbo Butterscotch Sundae I lost consciousness altogether. It was the nearest I've ever been to a "trip."

All in all, there's quite an element of luck in being a *mauvais viveur*. Like one's opposite number, one must have that knack of being in the right place at the right time, plus a talent for bringing out the worst in people. I have been lucky in this respect. The life of a touring musician exposes one to fruitful experiences which, if I may say it without snobbism, rarely come the way of the first-class traveller. To be sure, there is casual, inattentive, slipshod service to be found in five-star hotels. But we are not talking about the casual, the inattentive or the slipshod. Genuine badness is a positive thing, involving the kind of genius that inspired a chambermaid in an undistinguished hotel in Staffordshire to hammer on my door at 8.30 in the morning, despite a "Do Not Disturb" notice, with the words "Come on, be a sport—let's 'ave yer sheets!"

This sort of badness is intuitive, often arising out of conscientiousness. There used to be a waitress in a small hotel in Manchester who worked so hard that she seemed to be chasing some imaginary Blue Riband for waiting at table. Every journey with brimming plates was another attempt at the speed record. One night, cornering too fast, she sent a whole plateful of steaming Brown Windsor soup flying into space by centrifugal force. Happily, the knee it landed on was mine, otherwise I should never have experienced that fortuitous follow-up that sets the seal on badness. Gasping apologies, she seized a napkin and pressed boiling soup and sodden trouser-leg to my thigh like a poultice. It was at this point that I revealed one of the qualities essential to a *mauvais viveur*—a total incapacity for righteous indignation. I knew at the time that the correct procedure was to cry "Aaaaaaaaaaaaaargh!!!" and cast her from me. Instead of which, I heard through the agony this voice, strangulated but full of goodwill, saying "Think no more of it—it could happen to anyone."

I don't doubt that this astounding tolerance is one reason why it so often happens to me. It may be, too, that I invite the bad by subconsciously rejecting the good. When I wind down my car window to ask the way, my conscious mind is anxious for clear and concise information. But deep down I dread the Good Giver of Directions, the man who gets himself into a comfortable position with his elbow along my window, takes me in fool-proof language along every inch of the way and then, while I glance desperately at my watch and start to twitch in every limb, goes over the ground again at dictation speed. So I get

the foreigners, the day-trippers, the women who don't know right from left and, on one occasion, an old man whose obscurantist reply amounted to sheer brilliance.

I was heading for Bradford University, rather late for an engagement. On the outskirts of the city, I thought it best to ask rather than follow an unreliable nose. The man I chose was octogenarian, bent, cloth-capped and livid. He looked in fact like a direct descendant of that George Belcher character in *Punch* who replied to the vicar's "Why haven't I seen you in Church lately, George?" with the immortal words "'Cos I ain't bin!" Indeed, my conversation with him can best be set out in the form of one of those old *Punch* captions.

Me: "Which way to the university?"
Old Man (impatiently): "What university?"
Me: "Bradford University."
Old Man (scornfully): "There isn't one."
Me: "There must be—I'm playing there tonight . . ."
Old man (in paroxysms of rage): "Well, where is it, then?"

*"See if you can find a fire-engine—he wants one for his birthday."*

158

*"Do you think they've come to audition?"*

# Unfair to Continental Royalty!

## By PATRICK RYAN

"Right now, ruling monarchs," said King Gustav VI, banging his chairman's mallet. "Let's have best of order, if you please, and we'll proceed with the annual general meeting of the Amalgamated Society of European Crowned Heads and Anointed Ones. Any apologies, Mr. Royal and Honorary Secretary?"

"Only one," said Grand Duke Jean. "From Lizzie, I'm afraid."

"Really!" said Queen Juliana. "With Britain only just crept into the Common Market, you'd have thought she'd have made an effort to get to her first AGM."

"She says in her gracious letter," explained the Secretary, "that she intended to come only she got this red-hot tip for the 3.30 at Kempton Park from the Chairman of the Royal Racehorse Doping Board."

"Very likely needs to pick up a bit of extra money somewhere," said King Olav V, Majestic Treasurer. "She's the only one who hasn't paid her sub yet."

"Thank you for that report, Mr. Treasurer," said King Gustav VI. "Which brings us to the first motion on the agenda . . . 'That this Society is dedicated to the proposition that all monarchs are created equal and are thus entitled to equal quantities of blue-blooded publicity.' "

"I move," said Queen Juliana. "I'm sick and tired of seeing all our Continental papers full of publicity for the House of Windsor, while none of us can ever get more than a column-filler in British mid-day editions."

"I second the motion," said King Baudouin. "Now that we're all Europeans, it should be even-steven on publicity all round. Every time Lizzie gets a front-page spread in *Le Soir* just by lining up her kids and her corgis on King's Cross Station, I want reciprocal coverage for me and mine in *The Times*."

A haughty chuff-chuff of approval echoed among the hammered gold ashtrays and reverberated around the ruby-studded spittoons.

"Every time that young Annie puts on a new sombrero," complained King Frederick IX, "there's barely space left in the *Berlingske Tidende* for the football results."

"It was that Maggie who started it all," said Queen Juliana. "Whetted the insatiable curiosity of the press, with all her goings-on before she finally settled down. And in the end, she took care to marry a professional photographer so that even the family snaps would be glossy enough for *Paris Match*."

"And there's no justice in the male line, either," said King Constantine XIII. "When Philip takes his kids twice round the harbour in his blown-up dinghy, he gets two pages of intimate photogravure in *Oggi*. But when I won the Olympic gold medal for sailing Dragon class, I barely got more than two inches of text in their *Yachtsmen's Own*."

"And don't forget last Christmas," interjected Prince Franz Josef II. "All of we dutiful crowned heads wearing our lungs threadbare broadcasting gracious messages to our beloved subjects and no editor even looks up from his cocoa. While Lizzie gets front-page features all over the world just by deciding *not* to bother herself to broadcast at all!"

"Same as her Phil on television," said Queen Juliana. "Gets all the prime time going on every network by shamelessly admitting that the broker's men are expected at Buck House any minute. And here's me widely acknowledged to be the richest woman in the world and not a cameraman takes a single lensful of notice."

"Where he's concerned, all newspaper reporters are masochists," said King Frederick IX. "He keeps calling them harder names than Aneurin Bevan and telling them to frig off and they just come fawning back for more. And there's us prepared to gin them up to the earlobes for a squib in the gossip column, and you'd reckon we'd all got the dreaded printer's plague."

"Of course, Lizzie does keep all those literary underlings," said Prince Rainier III. "You never get any service at Buck House because all the nannies and second footmen are eternally bashing away at their startling royal revelations below stairs."

"They say she deliberately recruits out-of-work reporters as menials to make sure the publicity pot keeps on the bubble," said King Olav V. "I've given up behaving scandalously myself because none of our staff is literate enough to get us a decent spread in *Spiegel*."

Crowned heads nodded sympathy and a brouhaha about ever-perfidious Albion blimped around the conference hall.

"Thank you, fellow monarchs," said the chairman, gavelling for order. "We seem to have the measure of the injustice involved. So now, what are we going to do about it? Any ideas for making editorial friends and influencing television producers?"

"Could anybody have quins?" asked Prince Rainier III. "Marvellous line for getting yourself in the women's magazines."

"Don't you look at me," said Queen Juliana, "thank you very much. Talk to that young Constantine over there. Or have a quiet, marital word with your Gracie when you get home."

"What about trying that public relations firm that invented Biafra?" suggested King Baudouin.

"I could get us some cut-price time on Radio Luxembourg for a series of royal commercials," offered the Grand Duke Jean.

"Wouldn't really do our image much good," said King Constantine XIII, "sandwiched between the wonder whiteners and the marrowbone jelly. We've got to find a way to show we're more with it than the Windsors. We want to make our impact in the manner of the times . . . What we need is a right royal demonstration."

And a murmur of august approval was followed by a show of majestic hands.

. . . And so it came to pass that on the following Saturday morning, nine flag-fluttering limousines pulled up in Birdcage Walk and the nine paid-up members of the Amalgamated Society of European Crowned Heads and Anointed Ones alighted in full coronation robes, encrusted by historic regalia, and bearing orb and sceptre at the high port. As they processed in single file towards Buckingham Palace, footmen followed behind bearing protest placards demanding NO ANGLO-SAXON DISCRIMINATION IN BLUE-BLOODED PUBLIC RELATIONS and FAIR DOS FOR ALL ROYALS. An army of reporters and cameramen milled about them as the gorgeous panoply stopped at the entrance gates and blocked them with a sit-down demonstration on nine golden thrones produced from a gilded pantechnicon. Vast crowds gathered to watch and traffic was held up from Piccadilly to Victoria, the New Guard couldn't get in to relieve the Old Guard and the mounted band of the Household Cavalry stampeded colourfully around as the nags were frightened half out of their fetlocks by the flashing of the crowns.

"A great idea, son," said King Gustav VI to King Constantine XIII, as TV cameramen hung from trapeze-bearing helicopters. "We'll be all over the papers tomorrow."

"Lovely job," said Queen Juliana. "They'll be cancelling *Coronation Street* for us to over-run in the news."

But they weren't and they didn't. They never got a sniff outside the *World at One* and the mid-day editions. That same afternoon Prince Charles announced his coming appearance on the *Morecambe and Wise Show* with his new curate-in-the-dustbin routine, Princess Margaret proclaimed the publication of her teenage memoirs written up by Marjorie Proops and syndicated to *Playboy*, the Duke of Edinburgh, just for nothing, pushed Hugh Cudlipp, Lord Thomson and Rupert Murdoch into a Japanese-reproduction water lily pool, Princess Anne competed in the Horse of the Year Show in her new outfit by Courrèges featuring see-through jacket and transparent portholes at right buttock and navel, and the Queen advised the agencies that now we were in the Common Market she was giving up horse-racing and graciously accepting the post of Public Relations Adviser to the Amalgamated Society of European Crowned Heads and Anointed Ones.

HARGREAVES

# HOW THEY SEE IT

"*I want you to describe South Africa accurately and objectively—the fantastic nature reserves, our Dr. Barnard, the happiness, sunshine, order, prosperity and culture!*"

SWITZERLAND—Horst (*Nebelspalter*)

THE VIEW FROM HANOI

USA—Corky (*Philippines Herald*)

162

"*They don't exist! They don't EXIST!*"
ITALY—van Wieringen

"*We're not sure, but we've narrowed it down to a side effect of something he bathed in, ate, breathed, drank, handled, looked at or thought of.*"
CANADA—Norris (*Vancouver Sun*)

The triumphal exit of American forces from Vietnam
USSR—Yuri Cherepanov (*Krokodil*)

# You're a Big Girl Now

## By ELLEN GREHAN

Gymnast Jinty's got breasts. The girl's a 36C cup if she's an inch.

Poppy never had breasts. Poppy would Turn Up Trumps, Ride To Win, and occasionally Dance Again. But Poppy wear breasts? Nah, never.

Poppy, I'm going back a good eighteen years now, was a Tokyo Rose of the class war: a composite of all the heroines I remember who used to appear in those weekly girls' comics that were strong on horses, hockey, and midnight feasts in the fourth form dorm. And whose apparent aim was to implant in thousands of eager little working-class hearts an admiration of, and desire for, such middle-class virtues as er . . . well . . . YOU know.

To the children I was brought up among (post-war, Scottish and poor) the strange, all-female, enclosed society of the boarding school as brought to us by courtesy of *Girl's Crystal* and *School Friend* seemed as improbable and exotic as Xanadu. (It took me some time—I was a dim kid—before I grasped the fact that there were girls who were sent away from home to educational institutions even though they hadn't been knocking off gas meters.)

We could scarcely credit a world in which parents only figured as a suggestion of a sensible hat and a well-filled waist-coat come Speech Day. A world in which girls whose names were Monica and Di were

forever winning cups and ribbons and God knows what all on the backs of cuddies they called Rajah and Prince. A world in which an apparently sane child could leap on to a desk and cry: "Remember, girls, the School comes first." And there wasn't a one to throw an ink-well at her.

But ah, lads, times have changed. *Girl's Crystal* has passed away and *School Friend* has merged with the upstart *June*. The half-dozen or so other mags of the ilk that have come into the world since the good old days of The Silent Three—where are they now?—make you realise that you have arthritis where your growing pains used to be. For Poppy and her kind have gone pubescent. They haven't yet got round to giving the Pre-Teen Guide to Orgasm, but the way I see it, give them time.

For where you once had peppy little features on Twelve Ways To Tie A Knot, you now have Personal Freshness for the Under-Tens. Hobby corners that would tell you how to build-your-own-Basilica-out-of-tired-toothpicks now (as in *Diana*) suggest you design a dress. Tasteful snaps of the Royal Family's dogs—aahhh—have given way to pin-ups of pop stars and actors. *Diana* has a gallery of sporting pin-ups chosen by the readers themselves: "Mary Swann of Addington Park thinks Roger Hoy of Crystal Palace is 'the greatest player in the world.' " Picture of "the

164

greatest player in the world" showing teeth and frowning.

And who bumped off Brown Owl? She used to come up with ever such handy hints for happy campers. In her place you have an agony column conducted by Angela (of *June and School Friend*) who dishes the dirt thus: "When girls get around to boyfriend time, parents naturally become anxious so it's time to be specially co-operative and show them you're reliable." Too right, Angela.

But, boy friends! Why, in the old *School Friend* ethos a boy was simply a ripping good sort a girl would meet in the hols, and who was frightfully good at cooking up wizard wheezes to play on his chums. Or some such. The only time they'd touch was when he'd beat her at tennis and thump her on the back with a chirpy: "Hard cheese, old bean."

Take Sally and her gang in *Girl's Crystal* for instance. There were five of them if I remember aright: three boys, two girls. Aged about fifteen. Australian. Kind of pre-permissive Barry McKenzies, all big jaws and bonhomie. Now, they were constantly knocking their pan in swimming, and playing croquet, and thumping hell out of each other at all-in wrestling. But never once was there a suggestion that the twang of knicker elastic might be heard in the land.

Another thing. For all their dedication to the Healthy Way of Life, the girls didn't get much out of it apart from huge teeth and a build like a bouncer's. Certainly they did not possess breasts, just a few discreet tucks in their tennis shirts. But Alona the Wild One who currently stars in *Princess Tina* is something else again. When she wears a swim-suit —two piece of course—I swear there's a definite suggestion of nipple.

In the old days, parents were considered an embarrassing irrelevance, like a wart on the nose, and many a herione thought the clever way to play it was as an orphan with intriguing but safely dead antecedents. But if there were any parents alive off-stage then they were always on the side of right. Unless, that is, they were foster or step. The acknowledged Generation Gap has made it possible for stories ("School for Susan" in *Judy*, "Marge in the Middle" in *Mandy*, and "Her Guardian Angel" in *Bunty*) in which it is taken more or less for granted that parents can be a colossal pain in their children's neck. In fact in "Her Guardian Angel" the parents demonstrate their unpleasantness by packing the poor girl off to boarding school . . . as a punishment. Get it?

Yes, boarding schools do still feature to some extent in the adolescent legend. (As do horses. And stories in which the ballerina heroine has broken glass put in her ballet shoes by a rival on the big night.) But generally heroines are not school children as they were in the old days. They're model girls, Lulu

*"Why is it that everything I like doing causes tumours in mice?"*

type pop singers, nurses, travel couriers, and gym teachers. (Like good old 36C cup Jinty.) And it's changed days since an arch-villain could be defined as someone who'd swipe the Inter-House Sports Cup. Now it's recognised that there is a world outside the bell jar of the school and you have heavies such as corrupt property developers (*Penelope* before it merged recently with *Princess Tina*), sneaky art dealers (*Diana*) and bullying, Rachman-style landlords (*Princess Tina*).

Pupil Power gets featured in *June and School Friend* when the heroine Patsy leads a protest march at her comprehensive because a favourite teacher has been given the boot. No messing about with middle-class old-style remedies such as a massive dose of laxative in the spiteful Head's tea, you'll notice. But straight to the nitty-gritty with the walk-outs, and petitions to the local education chief. That's the spirit.

That's telling them. In another story in *June and School Friend*, dead abrasive stuff, this, there is even—

cripes—a suicide attempt. (There's this girl, see, and she crawls out on to a ledge and she's all set to jump. But Sindy—that's Our Heroine—tells her not to. So she doesn't, Whew.) Apart from all the orphans who used to populate the old *School Friend* stories, and who would tell us in the last balloon that they were princesses of one of the more obscure Royal Houses, the only time death ever got a mention, as I recall, was when Dobbin had to be put down after breaking a leg.

Without a doubt the point where you realise that Poppy's world has changed beyond all recognition is when, in *Princess Tina*, a pop group called *Jackie and the Wild Boys* sing "We're young, we're free, it's wonderful to be we."

Such an attitude would have been totally incomprehensible to the Poppy of eighteen years ago, committed as she was to the view that youth was just a place to hang about in while you waited for Real Life to Begin.

"*He's unorthodox for a managing director, but he gets on well with the workers.*"

# Hanging for Fun

## By B. A. YOUNG

It is good to see that an art, almost forgotten in this country where once it flourished so splendidly, shows signs of a revival. The police want hanging reintroduced for murderers. Not just capital punishment, but real old-fashioned hanging.

Hanging used to be one of our most popular amusements. Hangmen were well known to the public, who called them by friendly nicknames. There were as many slang words for hanging as there are for copulation. All this was lost when, a century ago, execution was driven into obscurity. In 1868 the Irish hero Michael Barrett passed boldly on to, and then through, the scaffold, and among other things his death marked was the end of a once popular public spectacle.

It's not surprising that, condemned to hole-and-corner practice, hanging has so lost the hold it once had on the public that there was little opposition when it was done away with altogether. In this more manly day, when football fans kick each other to death in their enthusiasm and even tennis players indulge in fisticuffs, it is good to see the police taking a lead in the rehabilitation of a traditional art.

One of the saddest things about the present situation is that the artistic side of the business only reached its highest level after it was relegated to privacy. The last British hangman to work in public was the hamhanded Essex shoemaker William Calcraft, who held office for 45 years and never learnt that lightweight subjects need a longer drop than heavy ones, so that many of his patients strangled slowly and inelegantly.

But he was succeeded by the great William Marwood, the father of modern hanging, who worked out a table of falls to ensure that everyone he attended should have his neck stylishly broken; and after him there came among others James Berry, hangman and poet, whose life-story, *My Experiences as an Executioner* (Percy Lund, 1892), is a classic of its genre (an admittedly small one), and who had the courteous habit of sending a verse to the prison chaplain and asking that it should be read to the condemned man at some suitable time.

Executioners like Marwood and Berry, and later experts like Ellis and the Pierrepoints, suffered most unfairly by the enforced secrecy in which they worked. If Sir Laurence Olivier were only allowed the act in private, or Yehudi Menuhin to play the violin, they could never have achieved the fame that rightly belongs to them today. In the circumstances it's pleasant to record that Marwood was at least the subject of a popular music-hall joke:

"If Pa killed Ma, who'd kill Pa?"

"Marwood."

There are no jokes about hangmen today; there are no hangmen. Yet we still feel a thrill of excitement as Macheath is led to the gallows in *The Beggars' Opera* or Dick Dudgeon in *The Devil's Disciple;* and the playwrights of our own day are not unaware of the value of hanging as a spectator activity. At the Mermaid Theatre we may see that sympathetic sneak-thief Jack Sheppard with the noose around his neck; and in John Arden's *Armstrong's Last Goodnight* we actually see a man dangling at the end of a rope, instead of being saved by a last-minute reprieve, the theatrical dodge usually employed to ensure a continuing supply of actors.

But mostly we have to be content with half

*"Look, darling! She's succumbed to her first TV commercial."*

167

measures. In the television soap-operas that offer such a reliable guide to the public taste, there are always ritual interruptions of the action while the performers fight one another. Generally there are two rounds in an hour-long programme; I suppose this is as much as John Steed or Simon Templar can be relied on to undergo without getting a headache or a swollen lip.

That these modest exhibitions of mayhem are to the public taste one can hardly doubt. They are even included in the children's programmes, though the ration of violence allowed in *Dr. Who* would hardly satisfy a decent redblooded teenager.

In the live theatre, as it is curiously called today, things are better. We have a very reasonable allowance of brutality, often presented most entertainingly. The Royal Shakespeare Company lately showed us a hilarious piece about a mass-murderer who liked to asphyxiate his girl friends in a wardrobe; and the Royal Court, earlier this year, gave three plays in a row dealing with the sexual murders of small children, though the priggish laws that restrict the appearance of infants on the stage made it necessary for two of these to take place "off."

It's significant that twenty years ago, when hang-men still flourished, "thrillers" in the theatre usually confined themselves to a single gentlemanly murder in Act One, and of course since the rest of the evening was to be spent worrying about who'd done it, you never saw it done. There wasn't the same need in those days for the sublimation of our violent urges; it was done for us at Wandsworth by a government servant, and we could read all about it the following Sunday in the *News of the World*.

This amenity is no longer available to us, and not unnaturally our urges get out of control. Despite all the film producers and the television pundits do, young people still feel the need to work off their high spirits, and we have all this unnecessary aggression towards Negroes and university professors, football crowds and the residents of Grosvenor Square.

This kind of mindless violence cannot be healthy. Far better to offer properly conducted exhibitions of public homicide, decently presented at a reasonable charge for the spectators, perhaps televised with a respectful commentary by Eamonn Andrews or David Dimbleby. Besides being truly in the spirit of the times, this would also help with the problem of our over-crowded prisons.

# A PERMANENT LONDON THEATRE GUIDE

**Maim!** (*Aldvic*)—the new Vietnam musical. The plot, characters and dialogue aren't up to much, but who cares when Esme Elena makes such a glorious comeback. Remember her fabulous duets in the thirties with Bertholt Brecht? And those breathtaking escapades along the Party line? Thirty years later she seems as young and idealistic as ever—each of her twenty-two changes of costume is more peasant-like and tatty than the last. The audiences may have panned the show, but the critics are going to be flocking for months to come. ("I laughed till I cried"—D.T.)

**Puss In Boots** (*Eros*)—the newest in Christmas pantomimes. A marvellous showcase for shoe fetishist Agatha Fielding, it gives him or her the chance to delight the general public with the same act that has long been attracting show-biz people to a flat in Bayswater. The Army boots scene is a scream.

**Hey, What's All This About You And The Chauffeur, Not To Mention Ex-King Zog of Albania?** (*New Free Wide Theatre Club*)—a searching examination of a group of actors who determine to take off their clothes in public, but find themselves enmeshed in an orthodox production of Macbeth. David Tremblow is a great discovery as a naked Banquo. ("I ate till I burst"—E.N.)

**Smell** (*St. Giles*)—the hippy musical to end all hippy musicals.

**The Trombone Section** (*Marlborough*)—too much attention been paid to the theory of playwright Wolf Rothschneider Harold Macmillan arranged for Glenn Miller's plane to cras that his collection of Miller records would rocket in value. V Rothschneider is trying to say is that unless we take a much gr interest in the lessons to be learnt from the incident, his play never be turned into a film.

**My Shameful Story** (*Coventry*)—the spectacular based on Augustine's Confessions. It has already done six weeks of p previews, followed by seasons of press views, Royal premi charity showings and low price performances; the promoters that after this six-month run it will at last officially open on Mon if attendances pick up. ("I ran till I dropped"—S.T.)

**At A Pinch** (*Duke of Gloucester's*)—dreary British comedy a two husbands who exchange wives by accident.

**The Deep End** (*National Theatre*)—Feydeau's brilliant, spark razor-sharp farce about two husbands who exchange wives accident.

**Vital Clue** (*Majestic*)—a tense, gripping thriller. Sir Ro Chichester receives an anonymous note warning him that his licence is due for renewal and is later found prostrate on his draw room floor, trying to disconnect his aerial. Gradually his ex-advertisement wife pieces together his past as a major share-ho in a Rhodesian firm of transistor manufacturers and face agonising decision; should she phone William Hickey or the 7 *Diary?*

168

# Give Prejudice a Chance

## By FRANK MUIR

I wrote my autobiography the other Saturday afternoon. In between weeding the gravel and *Please, Sir!*

To be fair I had put in a deal of spadework before that. Choosing the title took me nine years. In the early sixties I was all for calling my life-story by one of those elusive, meaningful quotations like *Such Charm That It Is A Temptation* (Elizabeth Goudge. "St. Francis of Assisi." p. 109), or *Isolated By Dams* (Lewis A. Edwards. "Inland Waterways of Great Britain and Northern Ireland." p. 161), or, a hot contender round about 1966/7, *A Mist Of Insufficiency* (Helen Y. Campbell. "Practical Motherhood." p. 375).

The later sixties produced a drift towards the more jaunty phrase: *Muir The Merrier*, *Private I*, *Ego All Over My Face*, and so on. By last Christmas I had vaguely settled for *Myself—A Modest Excursion into Self-Revelation*. A title, I felt, dignified and yet toney.

So it was with a light heart that I sat at the type-writer and thundered out the hardest bit, the title.

Twenty minutes later, appalled, I found myself typing "The End."

Forty-nine years of eager living had yielded literary fruit to the sum of two and three-quarter foolscap pages. And one and a half of those was a description of Broadstairs bay seen from the groin.

At first I thought it was just memory being a fickle jade. A few write-aboutable occurrences must have occurred between the cracks. I belted back down Memory Lane and finally emerged with the three most colourful episodes of my life:

*At Home With The Great Americans Of Our Time.* I was in Hollywood about three years ago in the house of a man whose name I have forgotten. Miss Lillian Hellman was upstairs but she had had a tooth out and might or might not come downstairs. Miss Hellman stayed up. Mr. Moss Hart was due to call in at any moment. I delayed my departure to the limit of human insensibility. Mr. Hart did not call. My host then asked me whether I would like to meet Mr. Frank Sinatra who was next door at a party given by Miss Rosemary Clooney. Rather than give offence to my host I signalled my willingness to meet the man. After dialling and waiting for about ten minutes my host replaced the telephone. "Sure is a swinging party!" he chuckled. "They can't hear the goddam phone ringing!" I left and went to the pictures.

*A Hell-Raising Escapade Involving The Law.* I was once nearly arrested in London's Chiswick High Road for driving a vehicle whilst under the influence of Meltis New Berry Fruits. The police officer involved thought I was drunk and couldn't understand why my breath smelt of tangerine. I was driving home rather late, having missed both meals of the day, and I incautiously ate nearly half a pound of warm Meltis

*"Of course I'm happy—I have my own little country to play with."*

New Berry Fruits which I found in the glove compartment. Overcome, presumably by a sudden rush of sugar to wherever sugar rushes to under these circumstances, I went wobbly and had to stop the car. The constable was very civil about the whole affair and refused even to report me for being in possession of an unsigned driving licence. Which would at least have been *something*. He finished off the Meltis New Berry Fruits.

*A Forbidden Glimpse Behind The Scenes of Famed Paris Nude Niterie.* When I was with BBC TV, I went to Paris with the producer Michael Mills to inspect the Lido Cabaret, a noted display of colourful costumes, ear-splitting music, Dutch conjurors and extremely effeminate nude show-girls. The thought was that we might film the lot for BBC-2. Warts, as it were, and all. Unhappily I had managed to get a small splinter of metal in my right eye on the previous day whilst demolishing my children's garden caravan. Skilled doctors removed the mote but the right eye was covered with a dressing and the left one wept copiously in sympathy. Mr. Mills had to lead me by my tie round the show-girls' dressing-rooms. It could have been the Battersea Dogs Home.

Stimulating little happenings, yes. But not, I venture, the kind of Memoirs for the possession of which the editors of the *News of the World* and the

*People* would outbid each other to the point of financial ruin.

I had to face up to the unpalatable truth that my life had been a succession of tiny, shapeless non-happenings. But why? Where did I differ from, say, the Rev. Ian Paisley? Nobody would suggest that he would have to pad out his piece with a description of Gweebarra Bay seen from Crohy Head. Or Richard Harris, the actor? A volume of his recountable anecdotes would need to be lifted by crane. Mr. Enoch Powell? Where to start would be his problem.

The answer came to me late that same traumatic Saturday. It was way past *Please, Sir!* and a chap, or a girl, was on in colour singing rather drearily to a guitar. I was about to switch it off when I hesitated. After all, I thought, he's doing his best. The penny dropped. My trouble is that I'm a Sweetly Reasonable Man.

I represent a generation or more of souls who were brought up to be Sweetly Reasonable. The Rev. Ian, Mr. Harris, Mr. Powell missed the training I underwent. They are Grittys. When they are about things happen and colourful incidents descend upon them as surely as burning tobacco upon a new carpet.

We Sweetly Reasonables were trained to avoid all contention. We are "eager always to see the other fellow's point of view." We never dream of judging until we know all the facts. We freely bestow "the benefit of the doubt." We feel deeply for those unfortunate people who are less fortunate than the fortunate people who more fortunate than the unfortunates who are less fortunate than ourselves.

A fully realised Sweetly Reasonable is so liberal that he doesn't vote Liberal because there's a lot in what the other two chaps say. So he doesn't vote at all. And he doesn't do anything to anybody and nobody does anything to him.

Tolerance is our pride:

"Don't complain to the waitress over a mere boiled egg, she's awfully busy. Just leave the beak and feathers on the side of your plate."

"I collected my new Mini yesterday and the engine fell out on the way home. The poor old Motor Industry is having its full share of troubles."

"That chap who hit the old lady over the head with a pick-axe handle and stole her handbag—he's mentally ill, poor fellow."

"You know that oriental lodger Mrs. Weeks has got. Well, last Tuesday he sacrificed an ox on her spare-bedroom carpet. Its nice to feel the old customs aren't entirely dying out."

Tolerance means the ability of the human body to withstand poison and Grittys will have none of it. They prefer having prejudices. These are things you have made up your mind about before being befuddled by facts. Grittys have great knobs of prejudice sticking up all over them which catch in other people and cause things to happen and get done. For good or evil. Everybody knows the knobs are there so there is nothing crafty about it.

"Switch that damned television off—it's awful!" I roared at my wife that Saturday evening, my voice ringing with a new authority. The impact of this was a little mitigated by the fact that the television was already off and my wife had gone to bed. But it was a beginning.

The main task then was to make a list of all the personal prejudices I could muster and hew to them. I append the list herewith:

*Don't like short people.* This is partly due to my difficulty in hearing what they are saying. I am a bent six foot six and the human ear is designed to receive sound-waves from the side, not upwards.

*Don't like ill people.* This is a nicely nasty one. But ill people make me feel apologetic for not being ill too, and the smell of hospitals gives me hiccoughs.

*Don't like the "Sunday Telegraph."* Irrational, undeserved. *Real* prejudice.

*Don't like Switzerland.* All that hygiene and money.

*Don't like bread-and-butter pudding.* Really a question of taste but my dislike is so profound that it must rate as a prejudice.

*Don't like having my hair cut.* Very strong one, this.

*Prefer white people to coloured people.* A bit of a cheat. It's like saying I prefer people I know to people I don't know.

*Prefer attractive people to ugly people.* They are more attractive.

*Don't like people who don't like me.*

A feeble list, you would be excused for thinking, compared to such as might be presented by The Train Robbers, or Moses. Perhaps. But it can be added to. And already my life has started to change because of it. The knobs are beginning to catch on to things and an occurrence has already occurred to me worthy of note.

A scant few days after that Saturday I became, quite surprisingly, unemployed.

"*I used to be a tramp, but now I'm more of a retired hippie.*"

# SAM HINCHCLIFFE LOOKS BACK

**Chapter headings from the memoirs of a Northerner as disclosed by BILL TIDY**

*"You won't understand, lad. Being on t'dole for years does summat to a man."*

*"Another link wi' past gone. I were conceived behind that chimney."*

*"Mother and me lived on nowt but tripe for ten years. Then the Depression came . . ."*

"Every lad in t'works were after her, but you couldn't marry boss's daughter in them days."

"Aye lad, many's the bath I've 'ad in front of that fire!"

". . . and we didn't have to crack black puddings wi' a hammer, either!"

"Ah well, can't live in past, lad. The Yacht, Barrington."

# Country Life

Not everything that happens in Britain gets into the national press. This feature presents some of the news which never made it:

"Hey, Sarge, I've just defected."

Mrs Mitchell then took Her Majesty upstairs and showed her the bathroom and the three bedrooms. The Queen Mother admired the views from the upstairs windows and asked what it was like at night.

(Fife Free Press)

The relevant chapter for electrical machinery and equipment is number 85, and for all other types of machinery and mechanical appliances it is number 84. In general, chapter 84 covers machinery and mechanical appliances and chapter 85 electrical machinery and equipment. However, certain machines are specified in headings of chapter 85 (eg electro-mechanical hand tools) while chapter 84 on the other hand covers certain non-mechanical apparatus (eg steam generating boilers). If there are doubts as to which is the appropriate chapter, please tick both boxes 84 and 85.

(Export Intelligence from the Board of Trade)

"We sat and watched a rat chew through the floor one night until I poured bleach on its head," said Mrs Moore.

(Kingston Borough News)

Keys to the wrought-iron gates sealing off the consecrated burial ground have been lost. "I have no idea how many there are," said Canon Gethyn Jones, who lives in the vicarage with his wife and three children. "We see a lot of them in summer when they play, but this time of the year they hardly appear. We don't feed them, they find their own food. They are certainly no nuisance," he said.

(Western Daily Press)

A man was jailed for 60 days at Edinburgh, for assaulting a policeman by throwing a collie dog at him.

(West Lothian Courier)

The explanation given by Patrick Steven Ryan to police for a dead but still warn pheasant found in the lining of his jacket was that he had seen the bird walking down the road looking poorly and he felt sorry for it.

(Leicester Mercury)

He said the car came out of the car-park at about 10 mph, straight at him. "It was very close and I was frightened," he told the jury. "I thought it was going to hit me. Then it turned to the right. I said 'You silly bastard' to the driver." He said an elderly man got out of the front passenger seat, took him by the shoulders and told him not to swear. This caused three tins of dog food which he had inside his shirt to start falling out. He took the tins out and put them on the bridge parapet behind him. As he did so the driver came up and hit him in the eye.

(Western Gazette)

Scots-born Roy Downie, of Vyner Grove, Sale, seems to be taking a leaf out of the book of his famous fellow countryman, Robert Bruce. Three times Mr Downie has tried to form a flying club for Manchester civil servants and three times he has failed.

(Sale Post)

"Great news! Your Majesty—the attempted revolution has been crushed!"

Zoo keepers at Paignton took turns to row round a lake last night to stop it freezing over. In the middle is an island where uncaged wild apes live. The zoo's general manager said: "Once ice forms the apes can walk off the island at will."
(*Wolverhampton Express and Star*)

Roy Fielding of Selkirk Road was on his way to shoot rabbits when he accidentally shot a slug from his air gun into his hand. He was taken to Bolton Royal Infirmary but allowed home after treatment. "He quite often goes out shooting very early in the morning but he doesn't often hit anything," said his mother, Mrs Annie Fielding.
(*Bolton Evening News*)

Earlier today the Royal Family watched a stage show by eight trained sheep on the west coast of New Zealand's South Island, where they flew this morning from Christchurch. A Buckingham Palace spokesman said the Royal Family had been delighted by the "absolutely brilliant" performance.
(*Evening Standard*)

Because of her skill with the euphonium, Miss Ceneta Miller was allowed to join the Women's Royal Air Force on a direct entry with the elevated rank of Senior Aircraftwoman.
(*Darlington and Stockton Times*)

*"Just watch it, buddy. You're speaking to a delicacy."*

On one occasion Mr Lister had pursued a man who failed to stand for the national anthem. "That is something I have often felt the urge to do, but never had the guts," observed the judge. That should not have brought the marriage to a tottering state, he added.
(*Oxford Times*)

Mr Day knows something about coins. He claims his own collection is worth more than £380. If he had a certain penny and a certain half-crown he reckons it would be worth £25,000.
(*Sevenoaks Chronicle*)

Hampshire police have called off their digging in a field at Farleigh Wallop near Basingstoke. They said: "We did not say in the first place that bodies were there. We were just digging for objects." (*Manchester Evening News*)

A sheep yesterday jumped through the window of a house at Tonyrefail, missed a baby by inches and landed on the head of a woman. Mrs Elsie Griffiths was sitting on a settee in the home of her neighbour. She said: "I was shaking for hours after the sheep landed on my head. I had a headache. We hardly ever see a sheep around here."
(*South Wales Echo*)

The new Rhyl lifeboat "Har-Lil" was launched in early June and later in the month the world was enthralled with pictures of the first moon landing.
(*Rhyl Gazette*)

**INTERNATIONAL SECTION**

Fire has partially destroyed a small side altar in the cathedral at Toledo. Firemen quickly snuffed out the flames. The blaze was blamed on an electric blanket which apparently short-circuited in a confessional box.
(*Iberian Daily*)

ROME—Maria Marcon, 24, told police Tuesday she accepted a ride from a dark-haired stranger and was robbed by a three-foot dwarf who popped out of a cardboard box on the back seat.
(*Regina Leader-Post*)

*"I think the pet shop's remembered our Silver Wedding."*

# Country Life

Plaster has been falling on patients at Rowley Bristow Hospital because squirrels have been gnawing through ward ceilings.

*(Surrey Herald)*

Bibles from Folkestone are on their way to Ghana after Roman Catholic schoolboy Emmanuel Akomesh, who lives in Kumasi, wrote to the town council asking for a Bible. He said in his letter: "Jesus said 'ask and it shall be given'." The council decided that it could not send a Bible so it sent young Emmanuel a copy of the town guide.

*(Kent Messenger)*

Miss Annetta Gavioli (34) of 16 East Avenue pleaded guilty at an earlier hearing to stealing goods worth £25 0s 2½d from Tesco supermarket, to assaulting a policewoman and to dishonestly handling a garden gnome.

*(Oxford Mall)*

Mr Maley said he and Mr Reilly were sitting on the parapet when he saw a hand pushing Mr Reilly into the water. He alleged he saw Munro running at him as he sat on the bridge. Mr Maley said he got off the bridge and on to the pavement and struggled with Munro. He stopped a taxi and both got into it. In the taxi they struggled all the way to the Central Police station. Later, with the police, they followed footprints in the mud from the embankment to a bus stop and found Mr Reilly on a bus.

*(Scottish Express)*

The printers apologise for the spelling of **JANUARY** on page one; this mistake was largely due to dislocation as the result of an influenza epidemic.

*(Organists Review)*

"Being born again" was the subject of the talk given at the last meeting of the Norcross branch of the Civil Service Christian Union. He referred to John's Gospel where Jesus explains regeneration to Nicodemus. There were quite a few new faces at the meeting.

*(Thornton Clevelys Times)*

# The Optimists

## by Graham

"Well?"

"Give us Tchaikovsky's Sonata in G Major, Opus 37."

176

"Oh, stop fussing . . . there's bound to be a space in the car-park behind the Town Hall."

"You advertised for a personal assistant."

"I say, it won't be an expensive job, will it?"

"Anything interesting on television?"

177

# Looking for an Orgy

## By KEITH WATERHOUSE

I, Charles Septimus Parkin of 23A Jubilee Mansions, Norwood, make this statement voluntarily in the presence of Detective-Sergeant William Cooney and PC Throstle of "E" Division. I am forty-three years old and a clerk in the employ of British Fat Products Ltd. I am married in name only. I do not wish to add to that.

I first became aware of the permissive society on or about September 5 1969. I remember the date because it is the birthday of my niece Avril, and I had bought her a Kooky-doll as a present. I do not know why the Kooky-doll is still in my possession, or why she was in the cistern cupboard. I cannot explain why she is wearing fish-net tights, see-through bra and a PVC mackintosh instead of the après-ski outfit depicted on her box. The Action Man produced by Det.-Sgt. Cooney from the cistern cupboard in my presence does not belong to me. I do not know why Action Man is wearing only his boots. The Polaroid camera is for the purpose of taking holiday snaps. The photograph which I ate before being cautioned by Det.-Sgt. Cooney was a holiday snap.

On or about September 5 1969 I read in a Sunday newspaper about a wife-swapping ring in Mauncey Road, Birmingham, together with an exposé of certain magazines "for swingers only," also photographs allegedly taken at a drag party in Leeds before the reporter made an excuse and left. It is not true that from that day on I became obsessed by the permissive society, although what I read was certainly an eye-opener. I did not suggest to my wife Noreen that we should engage in similar activities. The phrase, "Let's get some fun out of life while we're still young, or are you too frigid?" is not one that I would normally use. I did not place an advertisement in the *Swapper's Digest*. I have never heard of the *Swapper's Digest*.

I now recall that I did place an advertisement in the *Swapper's Digest*. The fifteen back numbers of this publication under the towels in the airing cupboard are for my own use. The advertisement was a joke. It has been put to me that "Virile husband-and-wife duo wish to meet AC-DC couples, no prudes" does not sound like a joke, but I do not agree. It was an exercise in parody. I know nothing about an accommodation address in Soho. I received no replies to my advertisement.

I have never been in Mauncey Road, Birmingham.

I now recollect that I went to Mauncey Road, Birmingham, on September 9 and spoke to a woman now known to me as WPC Hawkins. My purpose in journeying to Birmingham was to visit an old army friend, 586 Cadger McNally, whose address I cannot at present remember. I asked WPC Hawkins to direct me to New Street Station. I did not employ any words such as "Are you a swinger?" I recall employing the phrase, "Where is the action?" This is an idiomatic expression indicating that I was looking for New Street Station.

I did not deposit a suitcase in the left-luggage office at New Street Station. I identify a suitcase produced by Det.-Sgt. Cooney as my property. I confirm that it did not fly to Birmingham of its own volition. The mask, riding-crop and length of rope are all my property. I purchased the mask at a novelty shop in Paddington in case my friend 586 Cadger McNally was giving his annual fancy-dress party. The riding-crop was a present for my married niece June, who is a keen horse-woman. I have no recollection whatsoever of proposing to my married niece June

*"It makes me feel adequate."*

178

*"I don't know that they've any right to expect a Royal Tour from a Bicycle Monarchy."*

that I should be her gee-gee and that she should ride me around her living room, The length of rope was in case of fire. I have always carried a length of rope in case of fire ever since reading that Hans Christian Andersen did likewise. It has been put to me that Hans Christian Andersen is the same "Fancy-pants" Andersen who is now doing bird at the Scrubs for thieving lingerie off of clothes lines. To the best of my knowledge Hans Christian Andersen was a writer of fairy tales. I have been informed what the expression "fairy" means in common parlance. I have never been that way inclined. I have never been to Hampstead Heath.

It is not true that I was wandering about Leeds in a polka-dot dress and steel-blue nylon stockings on the night of September 9-10. The polka-dot dress produced by Det.-Sgt. Cooney was purchased at Selfridge's for my friend 586 Cadger McNally's fancy-dress party. I regard flushing clothes down the lavatory as a normal method of disposing of unwanted property.

Having been shown certain photographs, I now wish to correct any suggestion I may have made that I was not wandering about Leeds on the night of September 9-10, but I deny that I was looking for a so-called drag party. I was in Leeds for the simple reason that I got on the wrong train at Birmingham New Street Station. I was suffering from flu and had taken some tablets shortly before drinking a glass of beer. This must have made me light-headed. I was definitely not wearing the polka-dot dress, except for a short period.

I admit to having knocked at a door in Victoria Hospital Avenue, Leeds, between 12.30 and 12.45 am. I deny asking the lady now known to me as Mrs. Jeanette Henderson if there was room for one more. I deny suggesting to Mrs. Henderson that nobody would take her for a sailor. My purpose in knocking at the door was to ask for a glass of water. I was not wearing the polka-dot dress. I had recently drunk a carton of milk which must have splashed over my overcoat, giving it a polka-dot effect. I did not raise my overcoat to thigh level while in conversation with Mrs. Henderson.

Having been given an opportunity to reconsider that portion of my statement relating to the *Swapper's Digest*, I now believe that there may have been one or two replies to my advertisement. There may have been 1,753 replies. Certain parcels which Det.-Sgt. Cooney removed from under the floorboards in my presence may contain replies to my advertisement. I have not read any of them. I do not recognise a typewritten manuscript entitled *Kitty's Awakening*. I do not know of any invitation to attend a party in Tulse Hill for sex fun.

I am familiar with Tulse Hill. I may have been there on the evening of December 18. An important invoice had blown out of my office window on that day and I thought it might have landed in Tulse Hill. I may have been wearing a shortie

*"If I've got to teach it, headmaster. I'll teach it in my own way and nobody else's."*

*"My God, they're here already, and just look at the place!"*

you need friends. Like now. And you have to set about making them as calculatingly as the man who tips when he *arrives* at an hotel. Of course, if Rene or Jimmy or any of the usual bunch are already there, they'll give you a steer—provided you didn't bribe the cable clerk to send your stuff before theirs in Dacca. Or was it Jerusalem? But if you are first on the scene you find yourself evincing passionate concern for the health, emoluments and family illnesses of a Levantine immigration officer, a Bengali terrorist or even, on one ludicrous occasion, an Idaho hog-caller.

When really sticky stories are at last over, it can take several days to remove the fixed smile from your face. But that's no excuse for forgetting Indian Joe's name. We were practically blood brothers. Dammit, he even gave me his card. What happened was that the Navaho, who live in the top right-hand corner of Arizona, wanted a Scout Commissioner. Having what they like to think of as a British sense of humour, the tribe decided to hire an Indian. So they hired a Sioux, and dubbed him Indian Joe. In fact he's a Harvard man who wears Brooks Brothers' suits, but he's still Indian Joe to the Navaho. When Navaho kids play cowboys and Indians, they make the white American kids on the reservation play Indians. And the cowboys always win.

Indian Joe flew me all over the tiny nation. So many Westerns are made there that the tribe has a regular scale of charges, ranging from wholesale massacres down to sitting still on a pony on an outcrop and just looking at John Wayne. My friend showed me the lot, with a generosity that extended to putting the little plane down in the desert just for a pee. Fine friend I turned out to be. I can't even remember his name.

Then there was Hymie. Or was it Schloime? Something like that. You'd think you'd remember the name of a chap who gives you his bed. He was a stonemason who lived in the shadow of the wall in divided Jerusalem. His army boots sat beneath his bedside chair, the rolled-back socks inside them. His denim trousers, flies agape, rested on the seat. Over the chair back, his battledress jacket, the webbing held on by the shoulder straps. He changed the water in the bottle once a day. I remember him asking me not to leave my change and cigarettes on the trousers. When the sirens went, he had five minutes to climb into that lot and get to the bus stop at the top of the street which was his section's assembly point. I said I'd write. I didn't, of course. He must have had other things on his mind since then. But I haven't. Nothing to compare, anyway. Now all I can remember is his chair.

And the chap who saved my sanity, if not my life, in Algiers—all I can remember about him are his bloody cockroaches. Big as tortoises, they were. Step on one, and it would just snarl at you. They used to invade the kitchen of the hotel he kept, rattling like a Zulu impi. I swear the chef fed them just to make them go away. I'd been thrown out of my own hotel for reasons I'd rather forget. It wouldn't have mattered except that this was two am, Algiers was under curfew, and the guardians of the peace were the Legion, mainly Germans, who, when they weren't singing the *Horst Wessel*, would spray a few rounds into the shadows. I had two bags, a typewriter, a hangover, and one of these patrols baying after me when Pierre, or was it Armand, opened the door of his cockroach farm and pulled me in. It was the world's worst hotel. He was the world's nicest man. I'll never forget old—oh, never mind.

There was the Indian in Mussoorie, high above Dehra Dun. We became good friends after he refused to give me curry on a Sunday because, though the Raj had long departed, Sunday was forever roast beef and Yorkshire. Memorable character. I'll think of it in a minute.

And the girl who gave me eggs Benedict and Bloody Marys for breakfast on a Sausalite balcony overlooking the Golden Gate. You know. Whassername. She said she'd be in touch. Never did, though.

Just before he left England I was talking to one of her countrymen, Joe Harsch, for many years the chief correspondent of NBC here, and a considerable Anglophile. I asked him to switch off the Anglophilia for a moment and tell me what he most disliked about us. Reluctantly, he reminded me of American generosity to visiting Britons. Over there "Come home for the weekend and meet the wife and kids" means just that. Dazed with hospitality, the Englishman says "If you're ever in London . . ." He will be. He'll ring his British buddy from the airport. "Hi, Charley, it's Hank. Just got in . . ." And what does Charles reply? "Oh, er, hello Hank. We must meet. How about a drink, say a week on Thursday . . . ?"

Come to think of it, none of my foreign friends has ever been in touch. Hang on. You don't suppose they could have forgotten *me*?

*"Aw c'mon, Genghis—we need one more to make up a horde!"*

# Cartoons by Readers

Autumn at *Punch* was complicated by a thick fall of amateur drawings, in answer to our Can You Draw Cartoons contest. After days of sweeping up, William Hewison, David Langdon and Chic Jacob picked out these six as the best and most original. They also reported that many of the situations chosen by the amateur cartoonists had a familiar ring, but in all fairness the same can be true of submissions from professional cartoonists.

F. Heingartner, Brighton

"It's Bing Crosby **again!**"

**K.** Pyne, London

"It should be a fine summer."

**M. Handley**, Saffron Walden

GO AWAY

**B. Stringer, Manchester**

**L. Hellman, Ealing**

185

# All You Need to Know About the North

*An authoritative selection by MILES KINGTON*

## From "Talk Lancashire or Belt Up", the BBC language handbook

It's reet starving outside.
*"Our relations are at the door, expecting dinner."*
He's not so much green as cabbage-looking.
*"We thought he was mad at first—then we found he came from North Wales."*
It's only them as knows their own as knows.
*"If you haven't missed the last train to Formby on a freezing night in Liverpool and then run foul of the police, you haven't lived."*
Once every Preston Guild.
*"About five times a week." Preston Guild is a mythical trades union which brought the art of frequent striking to such a pitch that its members never actually worked and most of them never even held a job.*
He favours his mother.
*Not an implication of incest but of being queer.*
A penk in a colander.
*A man who talks too much. A Southerner with bad breath. A salesman who has been too long on the same round. A budgerigar with bad breath. A nudie calendar. Harold Wilson. Cold pork fat garnished with cold potatoes. A man from Newton-le-Willows. A referee with bad breath.*
Bootle, where the bugs wear clogs.
*A reference to the famous though long defunct Knowsley's Bug Circus of Bootle. Sid Knowsley trained his clog-shod, chain-smoking troupe of performing bugs until they could re-enact any given dock strike, Liverpool-Everton match or Saturday night function. He was forced to retire in 1933 after a disastrous Catholic/Protestant punch-up among the bugs.*
He's just popped his clogs.
*"I hope he takes his socks off more quietly."*
Hickey the fire bobby.
*A legendary figure used to frighten Lancashire children. The threat was that if they didn't behave they'd have to join the Fire Brigade which meant, of course, that they'd always miss the match on Saturday.*
Ey oop, t'whistle's went!
*Nothing to do with football, trains or police raids. Nor is it anything to do with drinking-up time. In fact, nobody knows what it means.*

## From the "Concise Northern Dictionary"

**Ilkley:** descriptive of the feeling of omnipotence, tinged with nausea, that is induced by the tenth pint of beer. As in "I'm feeling somewhat ilkley, by Crikey. Let me pass, lad."
**Bawtry:** "That were right bawtry of thee, lad." Decent or despicable, depending on the intonation.
**Pudsey:** approaching middle age, putting on a bit of flab.
**Todmorden:** a traditional pie made from sheep's knees and old potato skins.
**Goole:** the ghostly sigh of a football crowd.
**Cleethorpes:** "A touch of the cleethorpes." A mysterious disease which strikes most often on Monday mornings.
**Giggleswick:** an impromptu party held to celebrate the humiliation of a local dignitary.
**Bacup:** a stew made from the leftovers of a todmorden.
**Batley:** odd, but not enough so to attract any attention.
**Shap:** an affectionate punch. "Get back on feet, lad. T'were only a shap on shoulders."
**Rawtenstall:** a seat in the theatre behind a pillar, hence, being beaten up by opposing supporters at Anfield. "He's daft enough to get into a rawtenstall before kick-off."

## From the "Oxford Book of Northern Quotations"

"Wogs begin at Chesterfield." (Traditional.)
"Happen it looked like a yorker to you, but to me it were just resting for the next bouncer." (F. Trueman to numerous departing batsmen.)
"Where there's muck there's bras." (Dan Hinchcliffe, of Hinchcliffe Striporama Ltd, branches throughout parts of Lancashire.)
"I only ever met one man who said he liked Birkenhead and he also claimed to be the rightful King of France." (Hilaire Belloc.)
"Some people say they can't see any use for the South of England. I reckon they're barmy. If it weren't for the South of England, we'd have two hundred bloody miles of rough water between Manchester and France." (Big Wilf. Second name unknown.)
"Hell, Hull and Halifax." (Old Third Division North saying.)
"I have talked with men who fought throughout both world wars and I once met a fellow who'd walked across most of the Sahara, but none of them believed me when I told them about Saturday night in Liverpool." (Anon.)
"The man who invented tripe and onions could have made a fortune if he'd thought of a good name for it." (Rochdale Chamber of Commerce.)
"I bitterly regret the insulting things I said about Manchester. I had not seen Leeds at the time." (Disraeli.)
"Stuff Disraeli." (G. Dickinson.)

## Common fallacies about the North from the Home Office Diplomatic Guide

Yorkshiremen are mean.
*False. They are thrifty, hard-headed, inscrutable, incomprehensible, often implacable, but never mean.*

Northerners keep their coal in their baths.
*False. They keep it in their second family car.*

Lancashiremen hate Yorkshiremen.
*Not really true. At least, it would be much worse if the Pennines weren't there.*

All northern towns are dirty and undistinguished.
*By no means. Kendal has its own charm and Penrith has its admirers.*

It always rains in the north.
*False. It only seems to be raining.*

Tyneside is the true North and the Geordie is the true Northerner.
*And Allah is the true prophet.*

The inhabitants of Lancashire are the lost tribe of Israel who wandered for centuries through Eastern Europe and Heligoland before setting up camp in the promised land north of Warrington.
*Untrue. They are all descended from Frank the Smith, an Eleventh Century boarding house owner and part-time scrap wood dealer.*

On an evening out a Northerner goes to a working man's club and eats scampi and chips.
*False. That is an evening in. For an evening out, he switches on the telly.*

Beyond the North of England is the fabled country of Scotland, land of mists, princes and whisky.
*Well, the Royal Scot must be on its way to somewhere up there, but who cares?*

The North of England is the rubbish dump of the South.
*I'll smash your bloody face in!*

# The Uniform 'e Wore Was Nothin' Much Before an' Rather Less Than 'arf o' that Be'ind

## By ALAN COREN

"Norman!"

"What?"

"It's that loathsome Mr. Coren again."

"What is?"

"In this paper. He's going to write about underwear. I can feel it."

"It'll make a change from sex."

"Not with him it won't. He's obsessed. You can tell from his eyes."

"That's why they print his picture. To show that the opinions expressed in this article are not those held by the editor. To show it's all the work of a loonie."

"They probably can't help themselves. They probably have to print his stuff or he'll have a go at them with a chopper, like Clapham Common."

"They ought to lock him in his room and send for a sexologist. What's on the telly?"

Well, who could blame them? Except for failing to appreciate that journalists are mere aeolian things, responsible not for the world's moods and preoccupations but only for passing them on to a public slavering to discover what they ought to be thinking about.

And this week they ought to be thinking about vests and pants.

Because I have before me an embittered pamphlet of ululation turned out by the clothing industry's Economic Development Council; and the gist of this sad

*"What's he doing anyway, building a rockery or something?"*

"*Incredible, Sergeant!*

*Fantastic! Every man dead at his po...*

tract is that the bottom is dropping out of British underwear, quite literally: the British body, male and female, bears the oldest, tattiest underwear in the civilised world, as a result of which selfishness the industry commited to our nether garments is plummeting downhill into unemployment, bankruptcy and shame.

And taking the rest of us with it, what's more. Because, once the world's newspapers get hold of this savoury gobbet and blow it up with that lip-smacking anglophobia which has characterised every foreign journalist ever since Johann Gutenberg's first bed of type began slowly to creak back and forth, how shall we ever lift our heads, not to mention lower our trousers, on the international stage again? England is, has always been, façade; and great façade. Indeed, we gave the world the word (the French still think it means a row of shop-fronts). What are the stiff upper lip and the empire eye, the apparent coolness of our behaviour and the matchless conservatism of our dress, our sense of protocol and our knack of understatement, what are these items but elements in the great impassive mask which England has always shown to lesser breeds without the law, and behind which she has worked those subtle subversions which put her where she is today? Or, at any rate, where she was yesterday, before the collapse of the three-piece suit and the fall of the bowler-hat started that downward slide which will never be arrested, now that the truth about our underwear is out.

Façade and uniform, the public presentation of calm and control, where should we have been without them? What of the British soldier, a legend of immaculacy and hence of discipline, going over the top and across the salient, boots buffed to sunshine and webbing blancoed to snow, as if to some regimental dinner with the Hun, brass shining like a thousand shooting-stars in the twilight of the battle-smoke? What if the enemy had known that beneath the knife-edged khaki creases, the British were no more than running rags? What if the world had realised that under the spotless pinstripe and the luminescent dickie, our Ambassadors stood like aertex ruins, nipples poking through elderly cotton holes, underpants sagging and inept? And how, today, can we maintain our necessary façades, of nuclear strength, economic stability, moral rectitude and political credibility, when our statesmen walk into the conference chambers of the world to a burst of foreign tittering and off-colour jokes in a dozen upstart languages?

But if it's too late now to stop the rot, can we not perhaps take that rot and make of it a virtue? Point out, in short, the great qualities that go to build a nation unpreoccupied with bras and Y-fronts; ridicule the races mincing along boulevard and strada, their tiny minds awash with dreams of Swedish string and Sea Island cotton. Explain, for example, why the honest British road-accident

*What are we going to do with the girls, sir?*

*Filthy scum! I thought that would do the trick!"*

figure is so much better than its French, or German, or American counterpart—what can the reason be, if not a salutary caution bred from the age-old fear of being ambulanced away to a place where men will reel and snigger at your tatty underwear? The French, who go in for bikini briefs, step self-confidently across their rues with their privates clutched in these tiny, fashionable, cellular fists, clean, neat, and, no doubt, pressed into appropriate mini-creases; the Americans face the freeways in Furmgripp Staybrite Nonwarp jockey shorts on which highly paid artists have signed their names to realistic representations of grapes, cocktail glasses, and small, technicolor birds—is it any wonder that decimation of the mobile foreigner is the popular thing it is, with such exposure as the incentive? Many of our less fortunate brothers overseas, in fact, are undoubtedly knocked down by doctors and nurses panting for a glimpse of the latest thing in mono-grammed briefs, and the casualty wards from Athens, Georgia, to Paris, France, must echo day and night with the ooohs and aaahs of theatre sisters goggling at each new detrousered masterpiece?

And is American hypochondria, perhaps, no more than a pitiful desire to have your vest applauded? God preserve the NHS from crazed exhibitionists in hand-embroidered winceyette!

And, worse, if tatty underwear goes, what checks to promiscuity remain? The divorce rate in the States, the unbridled randiness of Gaul and Latin—need one probe further for the root cause of this moral disarray than just beneath their outer garments? More marriages have been saved, more lives stabilised by British underwear than by any other factor: what lust could survive that terrible unveiling, on some drizzled Weybridge evening, when two would-be English adulterers stare at one another's drooping ex-WD (As Worn By Genuine World War I Naval Officers) knee-baggy combinations, at the vast black sateen drawers, the grey bra with its erratic bones and sad, uneven cups, the slip and vest, both shot through with holes like an honoured battle-flag borne home from Waterloo and not laundered since 1815? Take these away, replace them with Lo-Line Reeveel-All Push-U-Up Mini-bras, and Mister Snugg V-Kutt Jock-straps by Charles and Brian Modes (Greek Street), and what will this island race be reduced to but a rutting camp of pulsing madmen, prowling the streets in unadjusted dress and selling their birthrights for a mess of how's-your-father?

No. Leave us instead march proudly down the remaining eons, in flawless measured ranks, pacing the steps of Milton, Clive, the Venerable Bede and Drake, jaws set, lips stiff, eyes bright, heedless alike of foreign furbelow and our own decrepit undies working their ragged way into our private grooves. Expelled from Paradise in nudity, man shall not thence return by underwear alone.

# THE CHAINS OF OFFICE

**by LARRY**

# Index of Artists

# Index of Writers